HUMAN TRAFFICKING, HUMAN SECURITY, AND THE BALKANS

edited by

H. RICHARD FRIMAN and SIMON REICH

University of Pittsburgh Press

Published by the University of Pittsburgh Press, Pittsburgh PA 15260
Copyright © 2007, University of Pittsburgh Press
All rights reserved
Manufactured in the United States of America
Printed on acid-free paper
10 9 8 7 6 5 4 3 2 1

Library of Congress Cataloging-in-Publication Data

Friman, H. Richard.
 Human trafficking, human security, and the Balkans / edited by H. Richard
Friman and Simon Reich.
   p.   cm. —   (The security continuum : global politics in the modern age)
   Includes bibliographical references and index.
   ISBN-13: 978-0-8229-4338-9 (cloth : alk. paper)
   ISBN-13: 978-0-8229-5974-8 (pbk. : alk. paper)
   ISBN-10: 0-8229-4338-7 (cloth : alk. paper)
   ISBN-10: 0-8229-5974-7 (pbk. : alk. paper)
   1. Human trafficking—Balkan Peninsula.   2. Human trafficking—
Government policy.   3. Human trafficking—Prevention—International
cooperation.   I. Reich, Simon, 1959–   II. Title.
   HQ281.F75 2007
   364.15—dc22   2007025330

HUMAN TRAFFICKING,
HUMAN SECURITY,
AND THE BALKANS

THE SECURITY CONTINUUM:
GLOBAL POLITICS IN THE MODERN AGE

Series Editors:
William W. Keller and Simon Reich

A series published in association with
the Matthew B. Ridgway Center for
International Security Studies and
the Ford Institute for Human Security

Contents

Acknowledgments

In May 2005, the Ford Institute for Human Security at the University of Pittsburgh and the Institute for Transnational Justice at Marquette University assembled a small group of leading scholars from an array of disciplines, past and present representatives from nongovernmental organizations, and government officials to explore human trafficking in and through the Western Balkans. This volume expands on the human security themes raised by that workshop.

The victims of human trafficking in the Balkans and elsewhere clearly lack the protection of human rights engendered by the rule of law, are preyed upon by traffickers as well as corrupt governments, and live in extreme conditions of fear and socioeconomic injustice. Though acknowledging these dimensions, the governments of powerful states and leading international organizations have placed greater emphasis on the criminalization of trafficking and enhanced border control. The experience of the Western Balkans reveals in stark detail the ineffectiveness and unintended negative consequences of such an approach.

This volume would not have been possible without the insights and support of many individuals. We wish to thank the workshop participants, those whose work is included here and others whose questions and comments played an important role in facilitating the rethinking of individual chapters and the volume as a whole. Special thanks go to Peter Andreas, William Keller, and Kay Warren. The workshop participants came highly recommended by leading scholars and policy practitioners in the United States and Europe and more than exceeded our expectations. The products of a workshop benefit greatly from the insights of a wider audience and we would like to especially thank the two anonymous reviewers for the volume for their insights and suggestions. We greatly appreciate the assistance of graduate students at both universities, including Evan Bambakidis and Milena Deric at the University of Pittsburgh and Manohar Thyagaraj and Alex McShiras at Marquette University. The conference and project would not have been possible without the extensive financial support of the Ford Institute assisted by the Matthew B. Ridgway Center for International Security Studies at the University of Pittsburgh, the Helen Way Klinger College of Arts and Sciences, and the Eliot Fitch Endowment at Marquette University. Special thanks go to Patricia Hermenault and Sandra Monteverde for their editorial assistance and logistical support on the project. At the University of Pittsburgh Press, we express our thanks to Peter Kracht and Deborah Meade for bringing the manuscript to publication. Finally, we thank Ariane, Julie, Amanda, Melissa, and Jamie for their support during this project.

HUMAN TRAFFICKING,
HUMAN SECURITY,
AND THE BALKANS

HUMAN TRAFFICKING AND THE BALKANS

H. RICHARD FRIMAN and SIMON REICH

In the aftermath of four Yugoslav wars during the course of the 1990s, South Eastern Europe is "now a vast political laboratory on top of a mass grave."[1] Ongoing efforts at reconstruction have focused on rebuilding the security of governments, states, and the region as a whole. These efforts, however, have devoted less attention to dimensions of human security—securing freedom from want and freedom from fear and establishing and strengthening the rule of law—that enhance protections for the region's most vulnerable populations in their daily lives.[2] It is in this context that South Eastern Europe, and especially the Western Balkan region,[3] has emerged as a nexus point in the trafficking of persons into the European Union, especially women both from within the region and from other areas of Eastern Europe and the former Soviet Union.[4] The contributors to this volume explore the trafficking in human beings and its ramifications for human security in the region.

According to the 2006 U.S. *Trafficking in Persons (TIP) Report*, each year an estimated six hundred thousand to eight hundred thousand men, women, and children are victims of international human trafficking worldwide, with women and girls constituting up to 80 percent of those trafficked. Internal trafficking—trafficking that does not cross national borders—claims an estimated additional four to twenty-seven million persons.[5] In an effort to gain insights into these patterns, scholars and analysts since the late 1990s have turned to the exploration of trafficking patterns especially in Europe and Asia, particularly those involving the former Soviet Union and Thailand.[6] With the fragmentation of Yugoslavia and the expansion of the EU's borders through the process of enlargement, however, the Western Balkans also emerged as an area of concern.

By 2001 the International Organization for Migration (IOM) was reporting that the Balkans had emerged as a significant region in the trafficking of women and children to Western Europe.[7] Estimates of the scale of human trafficking varied. IOM discussion of estimates reported by the European Commission in 2001 became recast in media and United Nations reports as IOM claims of 120,000 women and children trafficked annually into Western Europe, mostly through the Balkans.[8] By 2003, the European Security Strategy, adopted by European Council meeting in Brussels, proclaimed that "Balkan criminal networks" were responsible for the trafficking of 200,000 women victimized in the worldwide sex trade.[9] The role of the Western Balkans in human trafficking, however, was and is not as simple as a transit point into the EU or as a base for Balkan criminals. Reports released by Human Rights Watch in 2002 and Amnesty International in 2004 also revealed extensive trafficking into and within the region beginning in the 1990s to meet demand generated by an expanding pool of United Nations and NATO international peacekeepers, private subcontractors, and relief workers.[10]

The *TIP Report* process initially designated Bosnia and Herzegovina, Croatia, and the Former Yugoslav Republic of Macedonia as primarily countries of transit and destination; Albania and Serbia and Montenegro (and Kosovo) were characterized as primarily countries of source and transit. Over time, the annual reports have become more nuanced in recognizing that multiple dynamics are at play within and between the individual countries that compose the Western Balkan region. However, this volume reveals an even greater complexity in trafficking patterns in the region. These patterns vary extensively by the country of origin and ethnicity of the women being trafficked; by economic conditions within different areas of individual countries and relative to other countries in and outside of the region; and by shifting patterns of local and foreign demand. In Bosnia and Herzegovina, for example, local women were trafficked out of the country while women from elsewhere in the region were trafficked into the country for prostitution networks that focused on the growing international community as clientele. In Albania, women and girls from Moldova, Romania, Russia, and other countries were trafficked through the country on the way to the EU, as well as into the country as a final destination. Albanian women were also trafficked into Europe, while Albanian girls were trafficked into Kosovo. The traffickers also reveal considerable diversity, ranging from family members of victims, to local and foreign organized criminal networks, to corrupt government officials and members of international stabilization and police forces charged with helping to rebuild order in the region.[11] This diversity, and especially the participation of the latter groups in human trafficking, represents a profound challenge to the establishment of the rule of law.

Global and Regional Contexts

Human trafficking since the 1990s has taken place in the context of broader processes of globalization and regionalization. Globalization processes, linking economic liberalization and technological innovation in transportation and communication, have increased the incentives for labor movement as the distribution of wealth becomes increasingly attenuated and differentiated. Expanding global flows of goods and services have facilitated development while threatening less competitive manufacturing and agricultural sectors and marginalized populations in developed, transitional, and developing countries alike. Formal and informal social safety nets have become overwhelmed by this process, leading to the displacement of marginalized populations and, in turn, increased incentives for migration and the rise of transnational criminal networks.

Some migrants have sought assistance from smugglers for transport across borders into the labor markets of advanced industrial countries. Others, especially women and children, have been recruited into trafficking networks with deceptive promises of employment abroad.[12]

Parallel to these globalization processes, regionalization processes (particularly in Europe) have contributed to the increasingly porous nature of national borders. Within the EU, states have become less able to regulate transnational flows as external borders have pushed deeper into geographic areas where the institutional apparatus and physical capacity to guard borders have not, historically, been as well developed. The rapid expansion of the EU, for example, has pushed its geographical eastward borders to the point where new member states have less capacity to regulate, or interest in regulating, transnational flows.[13] Although EU policymakers have emphasized enhanced border security measures as well as intensified steps against transnational organized crime, human trafficking continues.[14] Intergovernmental organizations and nongovernmental organizations active in Europe have attempted to offset economic deprivation through alternative development programs; they have also tried to counter deceptive recruiting practices through educational and support programs targeted at likely trafficking victims. Both initiatives have met with varying degrees of success.[15]

For the Western Balkans, the fragmentation of Yugoslavia intensified the impact of processes of globalization and regionalization. Unbridled ethnic conflict on a scale not witnessed in Europe since 1945, several episodes of external intervention (often involving the overwhelming use of force), and the unabated use of violence by criminal elements provided waves of challenges to civil society in the region. Even as the more explicit challenges to law and order—genocidal activities and open civil war—were quelled through external intervention, transnational crime surged. Transnational crime networks have a long history of presence in the Balkans, and include cigarette, heroin, and arms trafficking that predate the collapse of Yugoslavia. Nonetheless, the Yugoslav wars and their aftermath intensified the scale of transnational crime and the levels at which criminal networks preyed on the population.[16]

Human Trafficking Contested

Human trafficking is neither a new nor an uncontested phenomenon. Despite successes against the trans-Atlantic slave trade in the mid-nineteenth century, and the curtailing of *"legal* ownership of human beings," new challenges of exploitation soon emerged.[17] The end of the nineteenth century saw an expansion of "migratory, multinational prostitution" internationally and regionally, especially into the Americas and Asia. This expansion was pulled and pushed by a combination of economic displacement, colonialism-induced flows of indentured and non-indentured male labor, and, by the early twentieth century, the effects of war.[18] State-regulated prostitution, and proposals to improve these regulations during the 1800s, had already attracted the concern of groups in the United States and Europe. Drawing on the successes of the earlier campaign against the slave trade, these groups posited the intersection of prostitution and the state as the threat of white slavery. By the end of the nineteenth century, the concept of white slavery had broadened to include all forms of prostitution, with special emphasis on white European and American women recruited into prostitution "by force or fraud."[19] The rise of what Peter Andreas and Ethan Nadelmann term "transnational moral entrepreneurs" during this period, such as the National Vigilance Association of London, Josephine Butler, and the American Purity Alliance, sparked a "moral crusade" to prohibit white slavery, either broadly or narrowly defined.[20] Moral entrepreneurs claimed that the widespread risk to unsuspecting white women and children from organized trafficking networks necessitated international conferences and agreements to criminalize human trafficking and prostitution, despite the fact that "99 percent" of those trafficked were "women of color" and trafficking was taking place primarily "in colonial areas."[21]

Although international conferences were held and agreements on trafficking were reached, these efforts failed to create a successful global prohibition regime against human trafficking, and they did not generate widespread national "legislation prohibiting prostitution."[22] The 1904 International Agreement for the Suppression of the White Slave Traffic and the 1910 Convention for the Suppression of the White Slave Traffic, for example, focused on detecting and preventing the "procuring of women or girls for immoral purposes abroad." Yet the agreement was primarily limited to calls for broad measures, including the identification and eventual repatriation of prostitutes and the need for governmental oversight of employment agencies and transportation facilities.[23] As Andreas and Nadelmann observe, World War I and national restrictions on migration flows had a greater effect on migration and human trafficking than those early steps toward a prohibition regime.[24]

As concern over the trafficking of women and children reemerged in the aftermath of World War I and the "reopening of commerce and frontiers," the League of Nations (LON) held international conferences and conventions on the issue.[25] Steps such as the 1921 Convention for the Suppression of Traffic in Women and Children and the 1933 International Convention for the Suppression of Traffic in Women of Full Age rejected the narrow focus on white slavery and included calls for wider criminalization and greater punishment of trafficking offenses. But as Eileen Scully observes, with the LON "organically unequipped to force compliance," steps toward implementation of the conventions relied primarily on "self-reporting by signatories."[26] As concern over trafficking in Asia and Europe reemerged after World War II, the United Nations drew on previous LON efforts and earlier agreements and conventions to introduce the Convention for the Suppression of the Traffic in Persons and the Exploitation of the Prostitution of Others in 1949. This convention broadly called on member states to punish those engaged in the trafficking of persons for purposes of prostitution, but again gave governments "primary responsibility for reporting their own compliance."[27] Only fourteen signatories initially endorsed the convention, and seventy-two parties had signed by the year 2000.[28]

From the 1950s through the 1980s, the trafficking of women and children from developing areas of Asia, Africa, and Latin America into Europe, Japan, and the United States, coupled with a thriving international sex tourism trade involving nationals from developed countries traveling to developing countries, continued to raise concerns among reformers. Transnational moral entrepreneurs again worked assiduously toward the goal of instituting global prohibitions with limited results. Steps such as the passage of Article 6 of the 1979 Convention on the Elimination of All Forms of Discrimination against Women (CEDAW), for example, consisted of only a broad provision requiring the suppression of trafficking and exploitation of prostitution of women.[29]

The political and economic collapse of the Soviet Union created new challenges as trafficking of white women and children surged from Russia, the Ukraine, and other former Soviet Republics into Western Europe.[30] By the mid-1990s, the Global Survival Network estimated that upward of five hundred thousand women were being trafficked from Eastern Europe and the former Soviet Union into Western Europe each year.[31]

The convergence of the interests and influences of transnational moral entrepreneurs on trafficking with the interests and influences of the governments of powerful states (especially the United States) on the broader issue of transnational organized crime prompted significant steps toward a global prohibition regime in 2000. The UN Convention against Transnational Organized Crime and especially the Protocol to Prevent, Suppress and Punish Trafficking in Persons, Especially Women and Children (Trafficking Protocol) consisted of several components. It included a legal definition of human trafficking; it extended beyond the issue of exploitative prostitution and the focus of prior initiatives on women and children; and it contained detailed requirements for signatories in areas of criminalization and prosecution, prevention of trafficking, and protection of trafficking victims.[32] This protocol entered into force on 25 December 2003, and by 2006 had 117 signatories and 110 parties.[33] Unlike earlier steps against human trafficking, the United States also supported the Trafficking Protocol through funding for foreign anti-trafficking programs and personnel training, and, more importantly, threats of shame and sanction linked to assessments of the activities of foreign governments as published in the annual *TIP Report*.[34]

Nevertheless, the Trafficking Protocol has not resolved disputes over how best to conceptualize human trafficking. For example, Article 3 defines trafficking in persons as:

> the recruitment, transportation, transfer, harboring or receipt of persons, by means of the threat or use of force or other forms of coercion, of abduction, of fraud, of deception, of the abuse of power or of a position of vulnerability or of the giving or receiving of payments or benefits to achieve the consent of a person having control over another person, for the purpose of exploitation. Exploitation shall include, at a minimum, the exploitation of the prostitution of others or other forms of sexual exploitation, forced labor or services, slavery or practices similar to slavery, servitude or the removal of organs.[35]

In practice, governments and nongovernmental actors continue to define trafficking in terms of two broad categories—forced labor and sexual exploitation. The latter has attracted much greater attention in the campaigns against human trafficking for diverse reasons, including: the interests of political conservatives, religious leaders, feminists, and other moral entrepreneurs advocating trafficking controls; and the media sensationalism of, and public fascination with, incidents of female sexual exploitation. Even as official trafficking definitions have become more broadly interpreted as "involuntary servitude" and "modern-day slavery," sex trafficking remains a high-profile issue of concern.[36]

A challenge for the introduction of effective measures against trafficking, however, is that the definition of sex trafficking itself remains contested. The glaring absence in the definition adopted in the Trafficking Protocol is an explicit link between prostitution and trafficking. The definition adopted reflects a divide between those contending that all prostitution is a form of exploitation and involuntary servitude on the one hand, and those contending that persons can choose freely to work in the commercial sex industry and migrate to work as prostitutes, but that they become trafficked when they lose the power of choice and are forced to work in "slave-like conditions" through threat of violence, force, or deceit by another.[37] The *travaux preparatoires* (interpretive notes) for the Trafficking Protocol reveal that the terms "exploitation of the prostitution of others" and "other forms of sexual exploitation" in Article 3 remain consciously undefined in the protocol in order to allow states flexibility in how they "address prostitution in their respective domestic laws."[38]

Differences in policy and practice among the member states of the EU regarding sex work have led to pressure for alternative frameworks—some that define trafficking in terms of labor and sexual exploitation, including exploitation in prostitution, but stop short of equating prostitution with trafficking.[39] The U.S. government backed the compromise in the Trafficking Protocol, over domestic opposition for stronger language, in order to obtain European and other international support for enforcement provisions in the Transnational Organized Crime Convention. However, the primary U.S. legislation on human trafficking, the Trafficking Victims Protection Act of 2000 (TVPA), reauthorized in 2003 and 2005, defines trafficking more broadly to include prostitution and other commercial sex acts. In practice, nonetheless, U.S. operative regulations on trafficking have focused on its "severe" forms—those entailing the use of "fraud, force or coercion."[40] Under the George W. Bush administration, and especially since 2003, the line between the operative and broader definitions in the TVPA has blurred with the U.S. government's posited linkage between trafficking and prostitution, regardless of its legality, and push for criminalization abroad.[41]

Andreas and Nadelmann observe that, as in earlier efforts against human trafficking, the contested issue of prostitution appears likely to continue to derail the global prohibition regime against human trafficking.[42] As played out in the Western Balkan region, the absence of a consensus on the definition of trafficking or on how best to address the trafficking problem has resulted in institutional steps by governments geared more toward the goal of EU accession than actual problem solving and in policy practices mired in contradictions.

Trafficking Responses in the Balkans

The challenge of human trafficking for the Western Balkans has been raised in numerous multilateral and regional forums, reflecting, in part, the concerns of the United States, the EU, North Atlantic Treaty Organization (NATO), and the Organization for Security and Cooperation in Europe (OSCE) with the spillover effects of instability and organized crime. Hosted by the United States, a February 2003 conference called Pathbreaking Strategies in the Global Fight against Sex Trafficking, for example, included workshops exploring strategies to combat trafficking from Eastern to Western Europe.[43] Human trafficking also emerged as a central theme in the summit held in Ohrid, Macedonia, cosponsored by the EU, the OSCE, NATO, and the Stability Pact for South Eastern Europe on 22–23 May 2003, and the 2 June 2003 follow-up declaration by five Western Balkan presidents.[44] These and subsequent forums have consistently highlighted the need for: national legislation criminalizing trafficking; greater regional and subregional cooperation; and anti-trafficking measures that conform to EU standards, especially for those countries seeking eventual membership in the EU.

Regional steps incorporating these themes have taken place through the Stability Pact Task Force on Trafficking in Human Beings (SPTF), and the South Eastern European Cooperative Initiative (SECI) Task Force on Human Trafficking and Migrant Smuggling. International organizations—ranging from the United Nations Office of the High Commissioner for Human Rights (OHCHR) to IOM—and nongovernmental organizations, such as the La Strada Foundation and the Save the Children Alliance, also have prioritized steps against trafficking. The result has been the introduction of National Action Plans by Western Balkan governments that incorporate, to varying degrees, new laws and institution building measures, targeted education efforts, victim assistance and protection programs, and broader public relations campaigns against trafficking.

Yet throughout the Western Balkans, distinctions between contending views of trafficking remain blurred in policy and practice. At times regional and individual governmental law enforcement efforts have treated all prostitutes as trafficking victims, arrested trafficking victims as prostitutes, drawn distinctions that equate only foreign prostitutes or prostitutes under eighteen years of age as those having been trafficked, or simply treated foreign prostitutes as illegal migrants.[45] According to the extensive UN overviews of the trafficking situation in South Eastern Europe, most Western Balkan governments entered the new millennium with criminal codes that criminalized prostitution and the mediation of prostitution. Enforcement of these measures, however, was limited at best. Furthermore, anti-trafficking legislation and consideration of the treatment of prostitution in such legislation were still in varying stages of introduction.[46] National Action Plans have increased the institutional infrastructure against trafficking, but the blurred intersection of sex trafficking and the treatment of prostitution remains.

The conceptualization of the nature of the trafficking problem remains even more contested. At a basic level, data problems concerning the extent of human trafficking plague the Western Balkans. Clearly this is not a problem unique to the region. Issues of underreporting and corruption, and the blurring of irregular migration, immigrant smuggling, and trafficking have challenged anti-trafficking efforts around the world.[47] Additional data issues in the region, however, include arguments that the figures are alternatively classified or not suitable for publication as well as arguments by governments that estimates of trafficking are being fabricated by nongovernmental and intergovernmental organizations with a stake in overstating the trafficking problem. Data collection in the region has improved with the establishment of the Regional Clearing Point under the auspices of the SPTF in 2003 and the Nexus Institute to Combat Human Trafficking in 2005.[48] Yet insights into the magnitude of trafficking remain woefully incomplete.

Nicole Lindstrom observes an even greater source of tension between and among governments, intergovernmental organizations, and transnational and local nongovernmental organizations active in the Western Balkans.[49] The tension stems from four major conceptual approaches commonly used to address human trafficking as: a migration problem, a law enforcement problem, a human rights challenge, or a broader economic issue. Each of these approaches advocates a different solution, including border control, repatriation, and suppressing traffickers; expanding the legal and socioeconomic rights of those at risk of trafficking; and addressing the broader challenge of poverty that places especially women and children at risk.

Elements of all four approaches appear in regional initiatives as well as in the National Action Plans adopted by individual Western Balkan governments. However, the prioritization of trafficking as a migration/criminal problem has held sway.[50] This pattern has reflected the influence of the United States, IOM, the OSCE, and especially the EU through its accession requirements. Though acknowledging the broader socioeconomic conditions that lead women and children into the arms of traffickers and the need for extensive victim protections, the United States and the EU have placed greater emphasis on rule of law approaches by calling on Balkan countries to both criminalize human trafficking and enhance border control, especially on those borders shared with EU member states. Yet this prioritization has led to unintended results that erode, rather than enhance, human security.

Important steps against human trafficking have been taken in the Western Balkans. As shown in table 1.1, the rankings of countries in the region by the U.S. *TIP Reports* from 2001 to 2006 suggest an improvement. However, despite such steps and efforts at greater exploration and dialogue between governments, nongovernmental organizations, and international organizations, the region continues to reveal deep-seated challenges to resolving human trafficking.

Human trafficking is a complex problem that requires a nuanced exploration of its sources and ways in which to develop and implement a coordinated, multifaceted response. This volume seeks to facilitate such exploration for the Western Balkans. The following chapters explore the economic dynamics of human trafficking, the impact of international and transnational policies and practices framing the issue of trafficking in the region, the impact of peacekeeping forces, the emergence of national and regional action plans in the Western Balkans and more broadly in

Table 1.1. Annual *Trafficking in Persons Report* Tier Rankings for the Western Balkans

	2001	2002	2003	2004	2005	2006
Albania	Tier 3	Tier 2	Tier 2	Tier 2	Tier 2	Tier 2
Bosnia and Herzegovina	Tier 3	Tier 3	Tier 3 but updated to Tier 2 (9/03)	Tier 2	Tier 2	Tier 2
Croatia	Not reviewed	Not reviewed	Tier 2	Tier 2 watch list	Tier 2	Tier 2
Macedonia	Tier 2	Tier 1	Tier 1	Tier 1	Tier 2	Tier 2
Serbia and Montenegro	Tier 3	Tier 2	Tier 2	Tier 2 watch list	Tier 2	Tier 2

Notes: The tier rankings in table 1.1 are drawn from the 2001–2006 annual *TIP Reports*. As discussed in the reports, a Tier 1 ranking reflects full compliance with the U.S. Trafficking Victims Protection Act of 2000's "minimum standards for the elimination of trafficking"; a Tier 2 ranking is for countries that have not met the minimum standards but are making "significant efforts to bring themselves into compliance"; a Tier 3 ranking is applied to countries who are not making "significant efforts to bring themselves into compliance." In 2004, the Department of State added a Tier 2 watch list category.

Although discussed separately, Serbia, Montenegro, and Kosovo are given one combined tier ranking as the Federal Republic of Yugoslavia in the 2001 and 2002 *TIP Report* and as Serbia-Montenegro in subsequent reports. Montenegro's independence in mid-2006 came too late for a separate tier ranking in the 2006 *TIP Report*.

South Eastern Europe, and the nature and ramifications of the gap between human security rhetoric and institutional and policy steps against human trafficking.

Lynellyn Long argues that the trafficking of women for sexual services is best understood in the context of cultural practices and economic incentives. Long posits trafficking as an exchange transaction involving an array of different parties and women as the objects/providers of services being exchanged. She identifies and analyzes the motivations of such actors and the conditions and organizational patterns that facilitate the trafficking exchange. Different forms of exchange transactions can exist. Long focuses on "the gift, the service and the commodified exchange" and, drawing on examples from Serbia and Bosnia and Herzegovina, traces the ways in which these dimensions have changed over time. For example, gift transactions involving women have a long history in the Balkans. However, the violent Yugoslav fragmentation and economic downturns altered traditional social relations in ways that led to more exploitative trafficking exchanges of women and young girls and the proliferation of new networks of suppliers, distributors, and clients. Exploring trafficking as an exchange transaction, Long reveals, can help to explain the unintended negative effects of counter-trafficking programs based on "moral regimes" that often clash with "economic incentives and deeply-rooted cultural practices." She argues for developing effective anti-trafficking measures that address the transnational vertical integration of human trafficking. Moreover, she contends, strengthening economic rights approaches would address underlying incentives that can place women at risk. Such steps include altering the incentives that shape gift, service, and commodity exchanges. Long advocates empowering women through measures ranging from education and skill training to allowances for legal circular migration, as well as addressing the demand side of the exchange through education and holding past perpetrators of war crimes to task for their actions.

Julie Mertus and Andrea Bertone focus on international efforts against human trafficking and their implications for the Western Balkans. These authors argue that international approaches have addressed human trafficking as more of a "social and criminal phenomenon" isolated from broader structural challenges of "poverty, unemployment, discrimination, violence in the family, and [sources of] demand." Narrowly focused law enforcement approaches have overshadowed broader human rights approaches in international efforts and, in turn, the National Action Plans adopted by West Balkan governments, with unintended results. Mertus and Bertone note the persistence of human trafficking despite the proliferation of enforcement strategies as traffickers move operations underground and shift to new routes. They also reveal how enforcement and preventative measures that are informed by the conceptual framing of those trafficked as victims and that conflate human trafficking and human smuggling can fall short. For example, treating women as victims of trafficking fails to capture the broader structural economic forces and migration regimes that lead women seeking economic opportunity to risk being trafficked. Mertus and Bertone also address operational factors that have inhibited the effective implementation of anti-trafficking measures. These include resource tensions between international organizations and local nongovernmental organizations, disputes over information sharing and the "blending and burying" of counter-trafficking initiatives into broader enforcement, and migration and development programs. The authors reveal that despite these problems, progress has taken place. Governments in the region have taken important legislative steps. The capacity of NGOs and governments to address trafficking and to identify and assist trafficked persons has increased, as have regional cooperative efforts. "Transnational advocacy networks" active in the region have been especially instrumental in facilitating the shift toward expanding human rights approaches to trafficking with positive results. Nonetheless, the authors conclude that further efforts, including more research on trafficking and its socioeconomic sources and impacts, are necessary.

Nicole Lindstrom focuses on transnational responses to human trafficking, with a particular emphasis on politics and practice in Serbia and Montenegro. She argues that "transnational policy actors" have played a critical role in the development, diffusion, and implementation of anti-trafficking programs in the Balkans. Transnational networks have linked external actors, such as representatives from the United States, EU, United Nations, IOM, and the OSCE, with local nongovernmental organizations and governments. Lindstrom reveals that the policy process has been largely top-down in framing the problem of human trafficking as well as solutions to the problem. Transnational actors, however, have differed in their approaches. As noted above, Lindstrom explores contending and in some cases overlapping approaches emphasizing law enforcement, the control of irregular migration, the protection of human rights, and the socioeconomic conditions that facilitate human trafficking. She argues that differences in the approaches and influences of transnational policy actors help to explain patterns of variation in the National Action Plans adopted by Western Balkan countries. Focusing on the cases of Serbia and Montenegro, Lindstrom reveals top-down dynamics in both countries, though leading to "slightly different" anti-trafficking mechanisms and institutionalized roles for transnational actors. She also notes the unintended consequences of such steps, including: the reliance on flawed indicators of success, shortcomings in victim assistance and protection as trafficking moves underground in the face of enforcement, and the rise of re-trafficking of women who have been repatriated to their home countries. The path to resolving these problems, she argues, lies in opening the policymaking process by giving greater voice to relevant actors, including trafficked persons. Immediate and broader policy steps also are necessary to address the underlying socioeconomic factors shaping trafficking. Lindstrom concludes with recommendations for modifying visa regimes to reduce the risk of re-trafficking, and linking EU development assistance and trade liberalization policies to steps by Western Balkan governments to combat corruption and crime.

Martina Vandenberg focuses on Bosnia and Herzegovina and the evolution and failure of United Nations anti-trafficking policies. Drawing on fieldwork conducted for Human Rights Watch from 1998 to 2001, additional field work in 2006, and documents obtained through the Freedom of Information Act, she argues that international peacekeeping operations in the region created the context within which human trafficking thrived. The chapter details the expansion of a diverse community of peacekeeping personnel in Bosnia and Herzegovina during the 1990s, including thousands of military troops, contractors, UN civilian personnel, and international civilian police officers. Vandenberg explores how this community infused millions of dollars into the local economy, expanding demand for licit as well as illicit goods and services. She argues that in this context, the trafficking of women for prostitution boomed. Vandenberg traces the growing patterns of corruption surrounding human trafficking, the gradual rise of ad hoc UN and Bosnian responses, and the impact of patterns of immunity accorded to members of the international community in eroding anti-trafficking efforts. She reveals how as negative publicity in the local media made the trafficking issue too difficult to ignore, new anti-trafficking initiatives turned to aggressive policing steps, including the Special Trafficking Operations Program (STOP).

These measures, however, were poorly integrated into local civil society, spurred more corruption, undermined the human rights and protections for victims of trafficking, and often drove the practice of human trafficking underground. Although statistics from 2005 suggested that trafficking of women into Bosnia and Herzegovina had declined, Vandenberg concludes by cautioning that such shifts may have less to do with the successes of local and international anti-trafficking strategies in curtailing trafficking or in driving trafficking underground and more with the shrinking international military and civilian forces in the country. Thus, a key step against human trafficking lies in addressing the ability of internationals to "act with impunity." Vandenberg notes in closing that while extensive reform in this area has yet to take place, there is "room for some optimism" with steps in mid-2006 to address the criminal accountability of UN personnel.

Vasilika Hysi focuses on the rise and persistence of human trafficking in Albania, beginning with the country's democratic transition of the 1990s. She argues that Albania's emergence as a source, transit, and destination country for trafficked Albanian and foreign women and children stems from a convergence of factors, including: poor socioeconomic conditions, fragile state and societal institutions, and the country's location between the former Federal Republic of Yugoslavia and the European Union. Hysi traces the rise of human trafficking during the 1990s and the subsequent shifts in transit routes and methods used by Albanian and foreign traffickers. Though slow to recognize and acknowledge the problem, Albania's government has amended the criminal code and criminal procedure to explicitly address trafficking, ratified and begun to implement international conventions on organized crime and trafficking, and engaged in international police and judicial cooperation. Yet Hysi reveals that institutional reforms of the police and judiciary have fallen short, especially in the identification and protection of trafficking victims. In addition to further work in this area, Hysi suggests that the region must address socioeconomic factors that increase the risk of victimization for women and children, especially those from rural areas. Hysi calls for greater cooperation between the Albanian government and civil society groups, nongovernmental organizations, and regional partners to meet the challenge of human trafficking and, in turn, to enhance regional stability and security.

Gabriela Konevska places the issue of human trafficking in the Western Balkans in the broader context of challenges and responses in South Eastern Europe. She argues that a "comprehensive legislative framework" is essential to combat the multidimensional and multinational aspects of human trafficking. Such a framework, drawing on European and international standards, must incorporate common patterns of criminalization; procedural tools for investigation, prosecution, and trial; and especially provisions for victim and witness protection. Moreover, legislation incorporating prevention, protection, and prosecution measures and the implementation of such legislation must be embraced not only by governments but also by the private sector and civil society. Regional integration efforts that link governmental and nongovernmental actors have played an important role against human trafficking. Konevska offers insights into the role of the SECI Regional Center for Combating Trans-Border Crime as a positive example on how to facilitate cooperation. She concludes the chapter by offering a series of recommendations for addressing the challenges of human trafficking in the Western Balkans and paths for their implementation.

In our concluding chapter, we focus on human trafficking as an issue of human security and the lessons that the Western Balkans hold for how to bridge the gap between human security in principle and practice. We argue that the issue of human trafficking requires a multifaceted, integrated response, which a human security approach is, in principle, capable of offering. We review the development of human security as a concept, which is contested not only by advocates of state security but also by proponents of human security arguments who seek to privilege the need to address the proximate causes of fear and violence over underlying issues of economic development and need, or over rights protections and the rule of law. We explore the extent to which elements of human security appear, in principle, in the prevention, protection, and prosecution measures in the UN Trafficking Protocol, the U.S. TVPA and *TIP Report* process, the EU Council Framework Decision on Combating Trafficking in Human Beings, and the proposed EU Plan of Action. Drawing on the Western Balkans and the insights of the volume's contributors, we reveal ways in which considerations of state security have overshadowed human security in practice and the impact of uneven prioritization and implementation of prevention, protection, and prosecution that has left human security as well as state security unrealized. The experience of the Western Balkans reveals that the problem is not "the absence of ideas" for a multifaceted, integrated approach to human trafficking, "but the failure of these ideas to attract the requisite support for integrated implementation." We conclude by exploring the sources of resistance to this implementation and the potential for governments and nongovernmental moral entrepreneurs to realize a human security approach to human trafficking.

2

TRAFFICKING EXCHANGES AND ECONOMIC RESPONSES

Reflections from Bosnia and Herzegovina and Serbia

LYNELLYN D. LONG

Trafficking for sexual exploitation involves an exchange transaction of gifts, services, and/or objects. The elements and terms of the exchange reflect the relations and forms of organization of the particular economic system in which the transaction occurs. In traditional cultures and local economies, women may be exchanged as gifts to create alliances, to make peace, and to ensure the continuity of lineages.[1] In market economies, women supply services for the financial benefit of sellers (others) who try to maximize their own profits by controlling the exchange relationship. In a global market system, commodified bodies are exchanged across large distances to the locales that offer the highest prices. While these forms of exchange may be analyzed discretely, in practice, there is often vertical integration between the different markets, and a woman may be initially exchanged as a gift between patriarchal lineages and eventually sold as a commodity in a London market.

The contemporary political economy of trafficking in women, in particular, for sexual services reflects both historical and contemporary

cultural practices. Strong economic incentives and rewards further reinforce the current forms of trafficking. In contrast, counter-trafficking
programs represent moral regimes that often conflict directly with the
economic incentives and deep-rooted cultural practices. These programs
also employ forms of regulation and control that may deny a woman's
agency without assuring her security or well-being. Because contemporary counter-trafficking regimes do not address the underlying reasons
for sexual trafficking in women, they have, at best, a short-term, palliative
impact for a few individuals; they may instead have little impact or even
cause harm to many others.

Examples from my own work in Serbia and Bosnia and Herzegovina
reveal three different forms of trafficking exchanges—the gift, the service, and the commodified exchange. Given these forms of exchange,
interventions to address trafficking from an economic rights and human
security perspective may be more successful.

Current international legislation treats trafficking as an international human rights violation and the trafficked person as a victim of
crime. For over two centuries, states have sanctioned and criminalized
forms of trafficking, forced labor, child labor, prostitution, and slavery.[2]
In 2000, heads of state from eighty countries convened in Palermo to
sign the UN Convention against Transnational Organized Crime and to
promulgate two protocols, the Protocol to Prevent, Suppress and Punish
Trafficking in Persons, Especially Women and Children (Trafficking Protocol), and the Protocol against the Smuggling of Migrants.[3] At Palermo,
the South Eastern European countries also established the Stability Pact
Task Force on Trafficking in Human Beings as part of the Stability Pact
for South Eastern Europe. The Stability Pact was organized to move its
members toward eventual accession into the European Community and,
thus, provided incentives for member states to implement the protocols.
Subsequent implementation of the Palermo protocols has focused on
developing National Action Plans against trafficking, harmonizing anti-
trafficking legislation across the region, indicting and prosecuting traffickers, and tightening migration regimes and controls.[4]

At both national and international levels, funding for anti-trafficking

interventions reinforces the priorities of migration controls, crime prevention, and victims' assistance. Most of the U.S. and Western European
funding goes for: returning women to their countries of origin (e.g., the
United States supported the Global Return Program Fund); training for
police and judges; conducting journalists' workshops; supporting local
NGO shelters; information and awareness-raising campaigns; and assisting institutions and organizations working with trafficking victims.[5] As
these interventions suggest, most of the assistance to prevent trafficking
is used to create a counter-trafficking framework and set of institutions.
Very few actions directly address the underlying economic incentives or
are aimed at preventing actual trafficking exchanges. Even in cases of information sharing, women are often well aware of the dangers of trafficking but they and/or their families may still believe that the potential
advantages outweigh the risks.

Currently, most Western European states counter trafficking through
the control of irregular migration: readmission agreements, forcible de-
portations, and "voluntary" returns.[6] However, increased regulation of
migration may further endanger those whom policies and programs are
ostensibly designed to protect. Migration barriers may have the unintended effect of forcing women to seek out smugglers and traffickers to
achieve their migration objectives. All too often, return programs send
women who wanted to migrate to a major Western economy back to
the same miserable economic conditions and/or the abusive family situations that forced them to leave originally.[7] Border and customs controls
to stop traffickers may lead to the development of more complex and
decentralized forms of organization at local levels, smaller business operations, and more diffuse networks.[8] Regionally, such barriers may encourage increased flexibility and globalization of operations and, thus,
larger profits for the primary organizers. Such sophisticated operations,
in turn, make it more difficult for women to negotiate a better situation,
leave, or escape their traffickers.

National regimes that legalize prostitution, such as that of the Netherlands, are not universalized throughout Europe and do not apply to
migrant women. Within Europe, legalization within one country creates

incentives for traffickers to locate there rather than in other countries where there is no tolerance for sex work. Trafficked women in the Netherlands, however, are treated as illegal migrants: they cannot avail themselves of services, their work is illegal, and they are subject to deportation. Traffickers will often hold their passport, which increases their vulnerability to arrest and deportation, and will use the women's "irregular" status to pay below market rates. In turn, they are resented by national sex workers, who see them as unfair competition. Thus, partial legalization has created a two-tiered market that distinguishes legal nationals from migrant sex workers. Such segmentation provides an incentive for traffickers and clients to undercut the regulated market.

Bureaucratic regulation may also affect both the market demand and increase women's vulnerability. The U.S. State Department's *Trafficking in Persons (TIP) Report* seeks to abolish "trafficking for sexual exploitation." That definition, which includes a disparate set of practices and conditions, effectively demarcates regimes of individual moral worthiness.[9] A woman's degree of volition is set up as the determining factor that distinguishes good, "trafficked" women worthy of support as opposed to "voluntary" sex workers, who are excluded.

The *TIP Report* also distinguishes between origin/source, transit, and destination countries. Yet a woman may voluntarily leave her origin/source country, be trafficked as she journeys from one place to the next, and eventually join a trafficking operation in a destination country. Categorizing countries as origin, transit, and destination usually quickly breaks down from the perspective of vertically integrated markets. Within a given country, if trafficking of any kind occurs, there are generally motivations to organize other stages of the business.

Each country's moral regime is also defined by the *TIP Report*. The reports annually catalog trafficking situations and categorize countries into one of three (plus) tiers. Tier 1 countries are those applying the strongest sanctions; Tier 3 countries are those not applying or showing little to no progress in applying sanctions. The U.S. government then uses foreign aid and the threat of its withdrawal to encourage countries to develop and implement counter-trafficking programs. Definitions of worthiness or progress, however, have little to do with economic activity and market participation but create new regulatory agencies and institutions. If economic activity were measured along with the number of trafficking incidents per capita within a given country, it is doubtful that the same rankings would prevail. The United States, unranked in the *TIP Report*, and the United Kingdom, for example, would probably not be seen so positively. The *TIP Report* framework may also encourage countries to regulate trafficking activities in ways that lead to more decentralized local operations coupling with highly organized international ones. This approach has also led to a few well-publicized cases and show trials of traffickers without fundamentally changing the incentives.[10]

Different approaches between countries may also provide incentives to traffickers to seek out the most advantageous economic zones. Abolitionist approaches, as promoted by Sweden, have in practice led to regulating prostitution and sex workers. Such approaches may increase the price of the sexual transaction without controlling the traffickers and their profits (which are inherently more elusive). At best, different regulatory practices establish moral regimes of rights and at worst, they engender new moral panics.[11] Not surprisingly, such efforts have been as effective in stopping contemporary trafficking as those of the nineteenth-century abolitionists and regulators who decried the "white slave trade."[12]

Beyond the rhetoric and debates are compelling stories and a reality that trafficking is widespread, and there is little evidence that counter-trafficking efforts to date are addressing the incentives that drive the overall trade.[13] There has also been little to no evaluation of the effectiveness of these programs. As those working on counter-trafficking regularly attest, there is little evidence that sexual trafficking of women has decreased, and in some regions it appears to be increasing. NGOs also observe that trafficking in some locales is becoming more decentralized, and that women are being held in more isolated bars and apartments and often subjected to greater risks. Such decentralization may also be a response to market regulation and counter-trafficking measures.

Trafficking exchanges presuppose various kinds of relationships between patriarchs, sellers (pimps and bar owners) and/or commodity traders, clients, and the gift (provider of services and/or objects). Trafficking has different functions, incentives, and meanings in local, regional, and global economies. Over time, a particular trafficking event or situation often covers several different kinds of transactions and relationships. For example, a young woman may be initially abducted (or captured), then negotiate with her trafficker to gain some financial recompense from her services, and eventually become one of the organizers of a global business. From an international humanitarian or human rights perspective, she becomes part of the network and problematic of trafficking. Viewed from an entrepreneurial perspective, the woman has adapted to her environment and negotiated to enter into the exchange as an active player.

In economic and anthropological terms, trafficking for sexual exploitation may be conceptualized as an exchange relationship. Viewed from this perspective, one analyzes the different parties and their motivations in the exchange, what is transacted, and how the exchange is organized (under what conditions certain forms of exchange become possible and desirable). One may then consider at what point in the exchange relationship particular transactions occur and/or change over time and appropriate points of intervention.

Trafficking encompasses several different kinds of exchanges: those that are embedded in household and local economies, and those that involve large profits, are well organized within a larger trade tourism and entertainment industry, and are increasingly global. In contrast, the counter-trafficking financial resources are quite limited, bound by national boundaries, and constrained by bureaucratic rules and procedures.

Theories and Practices of Trafficking as Exchange

In Marcel Mauss's terms, many traditional marriage practices—such as "marriage by capture," giving away a woman in marriage in Christian ceremonies, and the handing over of a bride to the groom's family—both symbolically and de facto embody gift-giving relationships.[14] Women are gifts to be given to solidify clan and kinship networks, to make peace between warring factions, and to ensure familial, ethnic, and/or religious continuity. Sexual trafficking may reflect long-established beliefs and practices regarding a woman's role and position in these exchanges. In rural areas, particularly, marriages still may be arranged and gifts exchanged to assure the welfare of both households (not just bride wealth or dowries). Thus, many initial trafficking exchanges resemble an abbreviated marriage exchange between families and/or clans, and may involve less exchange of common economic and social resources.

Gayle Rubin argues that all marriage exchanges involve a form of trafficking.[15] From the young woman's perspective, she may expect to benefit her family members and may be less concerned about issues of autonomy and rights than about the fulfillment of mutual obligations. The receivers of the gift are other village men, who have the means to provide gifts in return. Although such gift-giving negotiations are usually between two patriarchs, both fathers and mothers may be involved in these discussions. In rural Serbia, these negotiations traditionally took place between two families and/or clans, which often led to the formation of stem households of two brothers and their wives.

The rupture of certain beliefs and practices during periods of conflict transforms traditional relationships in ways that lead to service exchanges and commodity forms of trafficking and exploitation. During the recent conflicts in the former Yugoslavia, for example, raping one's neighbor was a clear denial of the traditional exchange relationship and a very powerful tool for ensuring ethnic purity and the denial of the other.[16] Denying or destroying the gift itself became a way of breaking down traditional ties and trust. The raping of women in war may have also created the conditions that rationalized trafficking a neighbor's daughter for sexual prostitution—of course, provided the woman exchanged was from another ethnic or religious group (e.g., Roma vis-à-vis Serb or Christian versus Muslim). Thus, rather than ensuring continuity, such exchanges were designed and motivated by the desire to create discontinuity and conflict. Contemporary trafficking exchanges—particularly those that are the outcomes of vendettas between one family, mafia, or clan and the next village—reflect similar processes. For example, a young girl of twelve, abducted on her way to school, was sold to traffickers because her father's business associate was seeking some form of revenge.

Economic hardship further rationalized the growth of a cottage and familial industry of trafficking. Contemporary internal trafficking in Serbia is often organized as a family business. An uncle or parent provides his niece or daughter to a neighbor who runs a local café or bar. The bar or café owner rapes the young woman to prepare her for customers and his wife is charged with providing the young woman basic necessities and for controlling her behavior. A recently celebrated court case revealed that the bar owner used the proceeds in turn to send his own daughter to university abroad.[17] Rather than considering how the young woman could have been his own daughter, ethnic, religious and/or socioeconomic differences allowed the bar owner to objectify the gift as the other and to derive a surplus from her labor to benefit his own daughter.

The clients in this system are reportedly local young men who belonged to an irregular militia during the recent conflict. Many were initially attracted into service when they could not find employment and/or were released from military service. The notorious gangs and militia (such as Arkan's Tigers or the bodyguards around Milosevic and his son) used rape as a tactic of ethnic cleansing. During the war, women of any age could be raped. Such rapes often occurred en masse as a part of identity formation of the militia itself.

Such practices continue as part of a rite of initiation into a local mafia or gang. In certain gangs, contemporary norms of masculinity may include having one or more beautiful women as trophies to be discarded when they no longer impress. Raping other groups' women (not necessarily another ethnic group but simply those associated with a rival group) is used to develop group cohesion and identity. Alcohol and/or drugs are used to enhance and play a role in these initiations. Once implicated in acts of sexual violence, the young men have to be ever more loyal to their own while necessarily denying the humanity of others.

The unwillingness to hold many different perpetrators responsible and redress the war crimes of the recent conflicts has exacerbated the effects of post-traumatic stress.[18] The guilt and denial of perpetrators may have increased the levels of domestic and local sexual violence.[19] Regardless of men's roles in the recent conflicts, many households have experienced the effects of post-traumatic stress in familial relationships. In such circumstances, trafficked women observe that they do not necessarily suffer any greater abuse than many other women currently suffering ongoing domestic violence. Consequently, for some young women, seeking immigration through trafficking does not represent a terrible risk.

Another important group of clients domestically has been the international community. Although women provided estimates that suggested members of this group made up from 5 to 25 percent of the clients, their ability to pay higher prices created tiers of local services.[20] The "peacekeepers" and international community generally created a new demand and source of financing after the war.[21] Even though they may not have constituted a large part of the initial demand, they provided the contacts, networks, and financing that may have moved trafficking exchanges from local to regional markets. At the same time, many trafficking routes also followed some of the same trade routes organized for gun and drug smuggling and earlier irregular migration during and before the war. Because of proscriptions on fraternizing with local women, the international community also enhanced the demand and market for foreign women (thereby regionalizing and internationalizing the market).[22]

To move trafficking from local prostitution rings to a trade across international boundaries requires explicit collusion or at least acquiescence of police and customs officials. Such officials often become the most ruthless customers and organizers of the business. They may still organize disappearances when someone comes too close to their operations. Traffickers also buy off law enforcement officials and/or blackmail them by providing them with free services.

As these examples suggest, trafficking for sexual exploitation involves exchange relationships that go beyond gifts and become transactions in which money or favors are exchanged for sexual services. An infrastructure of suppliers and distributors also develops. In such exchange relationships, sellers are interested in maximizing their profits and buyers in minimizing their costs. Thus, if a bar owner can decrease his costs by exploiting a trafficked woman rather than employing a prostitute, he will have an incentive to organize his business along these lines, particularly if the risks and protection money required are reasonable. In Serbia and Bosnia and Herzegovina, some law enforcement officials observe that the financial and physical risks of being involved in trafficking are lower than trading drugs or weapons, and that trafficking operations are used as a cover for the former, riskier trades.[23] At the same time, drugs may be used to bind women: by becoming addicts, the women become dependent on and indebted to their traffickers and/or bar owners for their fix and are easier to control.

The sale of sexual services also explains the increase of trafficking in a period of economic transition with high rates of unemployment. Throughout the poorest countries of Central and Eastern Europe, for example, many women admit risking being trafficked since they see no other way out of long-term unemployment, poverty, and/or abuse. In a transitional economy with a limited supply of jobs and employment opportunities on one side and limited skills and knowledge to compete in larger regional economies on the other, there are many incentives for women to sell their sexual services and for others to organize the industry. Selling their bodies may be the only way for some young women to access regional and international markets. Opportunities are also highly gendered with segmented labor markets—young men are more likely to access irregular migration routes to sell their labor while women access trafficking routes to sell sexual services. Access to different markets and kinds of trade reflects patterns of demand—the demand for young boys, for example, is a more limited market than that for young women.

A characteristic profile of a young woman who returns or is returned from trafficking situations is emerging. A large number of women in shelters report coming from families with an absent father and/or with divorced parents, from impoverished families, and/or from situations of domestic sexual abuse and violence.[24] However, it would be difficult to establish valid control and experiment groups to determine vulnerability to trafficking and/or to access the profiles of trafficked women who do not come into direct contact with social service agencies. It may be, for example, that trafficked women who end up in shelters are more likely to come from such backgrounds, whereas trafficked women who negotiate their own release and/or are able to derive some benefits from the trafficking experience are more likely to be well educated, come from stable families, and/or have relatively well-off socioeconomic backgrounds. The only common defining characteristic of trafficked women may be their willingness to assume a higher level of risk.

Ironically, by ignoring supply and demand factors in trafficking exchanges (and the incentives structuring the kinds of services exchanged), many social programs designed to prevent trafficking often end up facilitating its economic organization. Shelters and return programs may facilitate offloading those women who no longer bring a high price and may further the circular migration of labor. Efforts to crack down on bars selling trafficked women's services lead bar owners to move women around regularly and to diffuse their operations to one or two women in each bar (thus making it more difficult for the woman to negotiate a release or more favorable terms). Involving the women in such exchanges (particularly in local and regional economies where she can more easily leave) is usually the most effective means of operation because then she has a stake in its outcome. Thus, there are incentives for traffickers to implicate the women in the operation to improve the quality of the services offered and to avoid some of the costs of holding her captive, such as paying off local law enforcement officials. Enforced slavery may be an earlier and less well-organized form of increasingly sophisticated and efficient sexual exchanges.

The forcible exploitation of a woman's services is the one most analyzed in the trafficking literature because a local bar's financial transactions can often be tracked and because the presumed incentives for trafficking are the potentially enormous profits (estimated in the millions of dollars). Monopolization of a particular market, though, often makes bar owners and traffickers more visible and puts them at greater risk of being raided. The scale of operations in local and national economies is difficult to hide, and it is more difficult to move and launder vast sums of money without being noticed. Several major trafficking rings in Romania, Serbia, and Bosnia and Herzegovina have been recently busted, in part, according to some law officials, because they were so large and visible. Similarly, if traffickers create conglomerates involving trafficking, drugs, and arms trade simultaneously, they may be more vulnerable to arrest as their operations diversify and expand. In Serbia, for example, a few major traffickers were rounded up in the recent arrests following the assassination of Prime Minister Zoran Djindjic (even though they were not cited for trafficking). With this kind of market visibility and intervention, there may be a greater incentive for trafficking operations to decentralize and to be smaller, more hidden, and more diffuse with many different suppliers. This tendency is reportedly happening in Serbia. Anti Sex Trafficking Action (ASTRA) also reports that, increasingly, trafficking is moving out of Belgrade to smaller cities and towns, from particular bars to small apartments and from organized, large-scale mafia operations to family businesses.[25]

There are, likewise, economic incentives for successful trafficking ventures to scale up by becoming transnational and globalizing their operations. An international trafficking business may franchise its operations so that there are many small suppliers (family businesses) but trade and transport networks are organized on a global scale—allowing traffickers to move commodities (certain categories of women) quickly across large distances and to the most desirable and profitable markets. Women who are moved globally may be recruited and tested first in regional markets. In a kind of beauty contest, the most resilient and attractive are chosen for Paris, Amsterdam, or London. In addition, as one young woman (who was trafficked to Sweden at fifteen) reported, traffickers recruit and groom young women who can be properly formed for the business.

Although the global operations are quite hidden, key destination countries offer a glimpse of the scale and sophistication of trafficking operations. For example, in 2003 in London, a major destination point, women working in 730 flats, parlors, and saunas represented some ninety-three different ethnic groups (with only 19 percent of the women coming from the United Kingdom), and women in 164 escort agencies came from some seventy-nine different ethnic groups (only 20 percent came from

the United Kingdom). Although these figures do not necessarily represent women working in exploitative, abusive, or dangerous situations,
they depict London's global sex trade and services. That a large number
are migrants also suggests that many may be trafficked (especially given
increased migration barriers). Eastern Europeans, whose models are currently in vogue, represent the largest regional group (with some 25 percent of those working in the industry from Eastern Europe). The British
tabloid press publishes stories of an impoverished Russian woman marrying a British Royal, thus contributing to an illusion many woman have
of marrying up or being spotted for a modeling assignment. Over time,
however, different waves of migrants come according to changing routes
and market demands. At the destination, there are again many small distributors—for example, 140 sites in the borough of Westminster alone.[26]
Sites for trafficking include small hotels, apartments, and escort services,
which are advertised quite openly in the local media, telephone booths,
hotels, and tourist sites.

The women destined for the major capitals, depending on their
working conditions, do not necessarily see themselves as trafficked and/
or may feel they have succeeded in attaining their migration and professional objectives. They sign up with escort services and may have the
opportunity to take English language classes. When they can no longer
work in the sex industry, or to supplement their income, they may find
jobs cleaning houses and providing other services in the underground,
non-formal economy. Some are married off to traffickers, distributors,
or clients. They may face continuing sexual violence and have little to
no recourse. In certain capitals and locales, the less fortunate are sold
for pornographic productions. While providing sexual services, trafficked
women are kept in bondage largely because of their illegal migrant status and they—rather than their traffickers—are subject to legal sanctions.
The fear of possible arrest, detention, and deportation gives traffickers
and their distributors continuing power over these women's lives.

In the global economy, women are traded as commodities—perhaps
less precious than gems, guns, or drugs—but as objects to be transported,

auctioned, and sold in different markets according to the particular demands. Autonomy and self-preservation for the particular woman at this point comes from her ability to market her own body effectively, to fit contemporary styles, trends, and tastes. Even though only some women are trafficked and commodified, the sale of women—as objects—is embedded within larger global markets of tourism, entertainment, advertising, media, and the beauty industry, all of which create the infrastructure, values, and conditions that allow women to be transported, packaged, bought, and sold.

Clients in international markets are predominantly men of all nationalities. As a recent MTV campaign against trafficking suggests, many are well aware that the women are being held forcibly and mistreated—of the actual labor conditions—but are probably afraid to confront the situation. Trafficked women are usually cheaper than local prostitutes, although not necessarily, since the costs of their movements and upkeep in more expensive locales have to be recuperated. Where prostitution is legalized, as in Amsterdam, trafficked women may be even more marginalized since they are promoted as less expensive commodities.

Economic hardship, global market penetration, and transitional economic conditions along with conflict and postwar trauma have transformed many traditional relationships and gift exchanges into service exchanges. Interactions with international communities and markets, the incentive to scale up successful ventures, and the need for greater flexibility and protection in response to police raids have created incentives to globalize service exchanges into major commodity exchanges. Although the gift of a village girl and the sale of a top model in a London market seem far apart, such transformations and distances are covered quite rapidly. Household economies and local, regional, and international markets are increasingly vertically integrated and thus the distance from the village bar to an escort service in South Kensington becomes only a matter of determining the best market for one's product and having the means to trade in more than one market.

Addressing Economic Incentives of Trafficking

Given the organization, complexity, and infrastructure of trafficking exchanges, it would be naïve to suggest that a particular intervention or
even set of interventions will have a serious impact on countering the
sale of women as commodities in a globalized market economy. Understanding some of the sources of trafficking as a gift exchange in basic
familial alliances and relationships also points to the deep cultural roots
and traditions underlying these particular exchanges. Most responses to
trafficking, as shown earlier, address the provision of services and tend
to regulate and control women's movements more than those of traffickers, suppliers, and distributors. Some of the regulation of traffickers
through arrests may only temporarily increase the costs as long as there
is a market and demand for trafficked women's services. However, addressing some of the underlying economic incentives in the different exchange relationships suggests some alternatives to business as usual and
the current exploitation of women's sexual labor. An expanded definition of human rights also argues for interventions to protect women's
economic rights rather than treating them ex post facto as victims and
further victimizing and/or disempowering them. From this perspective,
alternative responses are possible for each of the three kinds of exchange
and on both the demand and supply sides of the equation.

In the gift exchange, patriarchs (and sometimes their wives) seek to
maximize their future household welfare. This may include ensuring care
in their old age, creating peaceful relationships, and improving the overall
social and economic status of the household. The young woman has attributes (gifts) that can be used to enhance overall household welfare and
she is part of a larger corporate identity. Thus, alternative incentives are
required to keep her from being exchanged.

One of the most powerful interventions in transforming some of
these traditional arrangements and structures is through educating girls.
Although there are numerous educational opportunities in Serbia and
Bosnia and Herzegovina, the hidden and opportunity costs of schooling are causing many young women to drop out at earlier ages and/or

for their parents to pull them out for financial reasons. Many trafficked women, particularly from rural areas, reported that they were never encouraged to remain in high school and obtain their diploma. Parents often do not see or derive the benefits of girls' education because many educated girls migrate to the major cities and do not necessarily look after their parents, particularly if they cannot find work.

Parental perceptions about the value of and returns to education could be changed through more scholarships and/or financial incentives for girls to complete their high school degrees (even paying young women and men to stay in school). Program evaluations in Brazil and Mexico have been shown that well-targeted, conditional cash transfers can mitigate shocks during periods of economic stress and provide an important social safety net for households.[27] Serbia and Bosnia and Herzegovina both have high rates of unemployment and many poor families can no longer afford either the direct or opportunity costs for their children's schooling. Although parents are likely to require children's labor, such programs improve attendance.[28] The argument for such investments, particularly if well targeted, would be that the training and skills gained would likely be more beneficial over time to the household and local economy than losing that labor. At the same time, more attention may need to be paid in the curriculum to ensure that at the gymnasium level, young women, in particular, learn computing, driving, typing, foreign language, and business skills that will benefit them professionally.[29]

In the service exchange, many women are trafficked while seeking to immigrate to find jobs in Western Europe or the United States. They would be less in harm's way if legal migration regimes facilitated temporary and circular legal migration for employment in areas where there are shortages of qualified personnel, such as nursing, housekeeping, child and elder care, information technology, and the like. In-country training programs could then be established for young women and men to obtain necessary skills prior to leaving for two- to three-year employment contracts in the West. At the end of their contracts, they could be eligible for loans to establish similar operations back home and/or receive priority for employment.[30] Such legal migration regimes would lessen the demand for irregular migration and allow benefits to accrue to both send-ing and receiving countries.[31]

In the commodified exchange, women are treated as objects to be moved around at will. They, rather than the traffickers, are more likely to risk arrest, detention, and deportation. Their skills and labor need to be revalued; however, the migration system treats them as irregular mi-grants and/or criminals. Instead, they should be encouraged to evalu-ate their skills and expertise and to make their own investments in their migration decisions. Women trafficked across international borders are often forced to learn new languages and vocational skills. For example, among a group of recently trafficked young women in Serbia, several had learned foreign languages (English, Italian, and Swedish), one had gained computer skills, and another had taken a course in furniture restoration while held in Italy.[32] These women could be provided with job prepara-tion and entrepreneurial training either to return to their country of ori-gin or to find employment in the destination country depending on their civil and legal status. Those who have had to survive by selling themselves could parlay those skills into entrepreneurial activities.

Protecting trafficked women's human rights should not inherently lead to treating them as victims or further disempowering their economic intentions. The enlarged definition of human rights, outlined in Article 4 of the Universal Declaration of Human Rights, includes the protection of economic rights and obligations relating to the prohibition of slavery. Economic rights include core minimum obligations with respect to the right to work and core labor standards.[33] Protecting the right to work leads to assessing women's particular economic interests and motivations as well as their migration intentions in terms of seeking employment through trafficking exchanges. Protecting core labor standards, specifi-cally with regard to slave labor and work not freely chosen, argues for considering all aspects of the exchange relationship to determine the na-ture and kinds of exploitative practices involved in various markets and locales.

Interventions also need to address traffickers and clients—not only the supply but also the demand side of the exchange. Demand side interventions are inherently more difficult to assess because the demand is difficult to identify and measure. However, these interventions are equally as important if not more so. At the household level of the gift and in local economies, assumptions about gender roles and definitions of masculinity are at stake in some of these transactions. Challenging traditional assumptions, however, may only endanger women further by invoking a backlash. Instead, concrete interventions such as encouraging sports teams and events (for both men and women) as a means of building group cohesion and support may be less threatening and, ultimately, more effective.[34] Having girls' teams alongside those of boys is empowering and challenges traditional assumptions about male/female roles but through positive interactions and experiences.

In the case of Serbia and Bosnia and Herzegovina, perpetrators of war crimes also need to be held responsible—not just to heal the past but also to send important messages about current norms of political and civil behavior. The licensing of such past activities, particularly when war criminals continue to benefit economically and politically, sends the wrong messages for young people about how to succeed and what constitutes success. Schools, civil society, and religious organizations also need to reward and promote new concepts of masculinity based on mutual respect, courage, hard work, and honesty versus images based on bullying, conspicuous wealth, and violence.

In service exchanges, clients, particularly the military, need to be made aware that they should not be buying the services of trafficked women. The current abolitionist campaign is likely to be as ineffective as curtailing cigarette industry profits by banning smoking, and regulation has already been shown to create a two-tiered market of more affluent, legal nationals versus less affluent, illegal migrant sex workers. The current MTV approach along the lines of promoting "fair trade practices" stands a greater chance of having some impact on tastes and preferences.[35] The message is: "if you are going to frequent a sex worker, make sure she is not trafficked." Concurrently with such campaigns there could be serious

fines and sanctions for abusive labor practices of and tax evasion by traffickers and clients, rather than arresting sex workers (who may or may
not be trafficked but whose economic survival depends on selling sex).

Commodified exchanges need to be addressed by challenging the
assumption that it is natural to sell women's bodies.[36] However, moral
regimes may be equally destructive by denying, hyper-eroticizing, or pol-
luting bodies. Instead, a recent Swedish information campaign tries to
achieve some gender equality in sexual image making by providing similar images of men's bodies for sale. Such campaigns encourage people to
reevaluate gendered assumptions about what is natural. A male modeling
an erotic pose similar to one found in many fashion magazines, for example, may appear ridiculous or sublime—according to the viewer's tastes
and values. Such images though force a reassessment of how women's
bodies are routinely portrayed. Women activists and artists themselves
are also challenging and changing traditional gendered assumptions
about what is beautiful, erotic, and/or desirable. Rather than ignoring
or banning "pornographic or erotic" material from media and popular
culture, educational systems could encourage youth to develop critical
perspectives, to distinguish violence from sexuality, and to question those
images that glorify violence and domination of others.[37]

In a globalized market exchange in which women are merely the
commodities, it also makes more sense to regulate buyers and sellers
than the commodity itself. Put crudely, one does not imprison or fine the
good being exchanged (although authorities may seize the supply) but
the commodity trader. Likewise, counter-trafficking efforts should focus
more on regulating and/or putting traffickers out of business rather than
in controlling trafficked women. Underlying trafficking is also an infrastructure that needs to be engaged in preventing the sale, transport, and
exploitation of women's bodies—thus, the tourist, media, and transport
industries need to be engaged or, if necessary, sanctioned to stop trafficking internationally.

Addressing some of the economic incentives underlying different
forms of exchange leads to a different focus on what interventions are
needed for the prevention of trafficking for sexual exploitation. As the lit-

erature attests, trafficking exchanges range from small family enterprises to multimillion dollar operations, all with significant economic incentives and rewards. The gift of women for a larger social benefit also has deep historical and cultural roots. Continuing to address family franchises, a vast network of suppliers and distributors, and globalized trade with nineteenth-century morality and institutions is bound to have limited success. However, an analysis of the exchange relations would also suggest that there are powerful economic incentives not to do otherwise.

3

COMBATING TRAFFICKING
International Efforts and Their Ramifications

JULIE MERTUS and ANDREA BERTONE

Over the last five to eight years, a large and growing number of state, quasi-state, and non-state actors have been actively involved in combating trafficking in the Western Balkans.[1] Many of these actors respond to human trafficking as if it were a social and criminal phenomenon that can be isolated for moral condemnation and addressed separately from other problems. Such efforts are destined to fail because the connection between trafficking and poverty, unemployment, discrimination, violence in the family, and the demand in countries of destination is undeniable. The more effective responses to trafficking are those that address these structural problems head-on, and those that look to the future by strengthening the nascent human rights-based system for counter-trafficking, with a focus on prevention, protection, and prosecution.

Our goal is to provide a constructive critique of international efforts that will take into account the larger implications of their actions. The particular configuration of the international efforts to fight trafficking—how the efforts began, who has been involved, what issues have constituted the political agenda—all have definite social, political, economic, and legal implications for actors and issues: for the people who have been trafficked as well as those who traffic them; for human rights in general and for women's human rights in particular; and, finally, for civil society and the process of democratization in fragile countries. Improving the track record of international anti-trafficking programs will require both structural changes in the manner in which the problem is conceptualized and operational changes in the manner in which programs are implemented.

Trafficking and the Western Balkans

The dramatic rise in trafficking of persons in the Western Balkans during the mid-1990s was prompted by two major factors: the collapse of the Soviet Union and the subsequent economic and social turmoil that spread into the region, as well as the presence of thousands of international peacekeepers and other international workers in conflict areas. War-torn areas are acutely at risk of becoming sources or destinations for trafficking in persons. The disintegration of legal and political systems in the Balkans, combined with the region's porous borders, lack of visa requirements, high rates of corruption, and a surge of foreign capital fueled trafficking.[2]

All of the countries in the region have been implicated in the trafficking of women and girls into the sex industry. According to the 2006 U.S. *Trafficking in Persons (TIP) Report*, Albania is a source country; Bosnia and Herzegovina is a source, transit, and destination country; Croatia is a source, transit, and destination country; Former Yugoslav Republic of Macedonia is a source and transit country; Serbia and Montenegro is a source, transit, and destination country; and the UN Administered Province of Kosovo is a source area.[3] Yet Kosovo illustrates the limits of such categorizations. By late 1999, over forty thousand NATO-led Kosovo Force (KFOR) and UN personnel troops had arrived. Soon afterwards, United Nations Development Fund for Women (UNIFEM) reported a significant rise in organized prostitution in four locations near significant concentrations of United Nations Mission in Kosovo (UNMIK) and

KFOR troops. By January 2001, UNMIK and KFOR listed seventy-five restaurants, bars, and clubs as off-limits to their personnel as it was believed that trafficked women were being forced to work in these locations. By January 2004, the list had grown to over two hundred premises. While the arrival of an international community catalyzed the growth of the sex industry, the clientele has become increasingly local. Both the International Organization for Migration (IOM) and the Center for Protection of Women and Children estimated in 2004 that 80 percent of men who patronize these premises are native residents.[4]

The vast majority of victims of trafficking in the Western Balkans are women and girls who have been coerced into prostitution or forced marriage by recruiters, pimps, boyfriends, or relatives. Many women know that they may very well become prostitutes, but are willing to take a risk given the very poor economic and/or family conditions they are currently experiencing. The profile of most trafficked women in the region indicates that, in addition to being poor or unemployed, the vast majority are between eighteen and twenty-four years in age, are unmarried, and live with their families at the time of their recruitment. These women are lured or coerced into prostitution via promises of a high-paying job or of marriage to a Western European or national abroad; by comparison, only a small minority are kidnapped.[5] Between December 2000 and December 2003, IOM interviewed 105 trafficked women in Kosovo. Of those, 22 percent had been physically or psychologically abused within their family, 15 percent reported having experienced either physical or sexual abuse, and 7 percent testified to having been physically or psychologically abused by a spouse.[6] In 2002, Human Rights Watch (HRW) surveyed 36 trafficked women in Bosnia and Herzegovina and all but one of them admitted to having voluntarily migrated for employment, desperate to escape appalling socioeconomic conditions. Over half of the trafficked women in Bosnia and Herzegovina who were interviewed by HRW were recruited by someone they knew, being promised jobs as waitresses, dancers, and housekeepers.[7] In Kosovo, IOM found that over 80 percent of the women interviewed had been recruited by a friend or relative, while 22 percent professed to have been "at least partially aware that they might work in some sector of the sex industry" in addition to being legitimately employed. Trafficked women commonly reported that their documents, including passports, were confiscated in transit and many indicated having been subjected to a "breaking process" that often included violent threats and abuse. Even before they arrived at their destinations, these women were deprived of their liberty and forced to endure cruel or inhumane treatment. For example, 40 percent of trafficked women entering shelters bore signs of physical abuse.[8] In Bosnia and Herzegovina, all the trafficked women interviewed by HRW reported not being given enough to eat, while one-third of them maintained that they were "psychologically tortured" by their "owners," including, but not limited to, intimidation, threats, lies and deception, emotional manipulation, and blackmail. All those interviewed reported losing their earnings through travel debts, fines, forced purchases, and outright theft.[9] Trafficked women in Kosovo reported similar difficulties as well as confinement to "unhygienic, overcrowded, and stressful conditions."[10]

The data on how many women are trafficked into and within the Western Balkans are extremely unreliable. Most information is derived from women who have been rescued or who have sought help from international and national organizations. Therefore, it is impossible to extrapolate from that population a reliable estimate of the total number of women who are in a situation of exploitation from which they cannot escape. Furthermore, government data collection generally does not distinguish between women who are irregular migrants, smuggled, or trafficked, resulting in an undercounting of the latter. Some Balkan government agencies also are reluctant to publicize or share data on trafficked women as they consider that data "classified" or simply too "poor" to publish.[11] Finally, it is sometimes the case that police and other authorities are in connivance with trafficking and organized crime rings, and their best interests are served when data on trafficked persons are not collected or publicized.[12]

International Responses

International organizations, governments, and nongovernmental organizations have compiled extensive reports on trafficking in the Western Balkans and the broader area of South Eastern Europe.[13] These reports reveal international responses to trafficking as falling into two major categories—law enforcement and human rights approaches.

The law enforcement approach to combating human trafficking refers to activities relating to writing and implementing anti-trafficking measures, capturing and prosecuting traffickers, and the training of police and other defenders of the law such as lawyers and judges. Whereas these activities are obviously necessary to combat trafficking, many have argued that the state and international organizations undertake these activities to the detriment of the human rights of trafficked persons. The law enforcement approach is viewed as encompassing "repressive" strategies that focus on the suppression of negative phenomena related to trafficking, including illegal migration, labor migration, illegal and forced labor, prostitution, child labor, and organized crime. These strategies implemented by law enforcement agencies are designed to stop illegal or undesirable activities and to punish those who are found guilty of trafficking and related crimes.[14]

A human rights approach refers to activities that emphasize prevention of trafficking, protection of trafficked persons after they have been removed or escaped from the trafficking situation, and psychosocial rehabilitative services. Strategies within a human rights framework are "empowering" to victims of trafficking through their focus on enabling people to protect themselves by addressing the root causes of the crime. Such strategies might include measures to overcome poverty, procedures to address discrimination, and mass education and public-awareness programs to publicize the risks and dangers involved in trafficking.[15]

In the past, the majority of programs implemented by international organizations and funded by foreign donors have focused on narrow approaches to combating trafficking, including training police or carrying out an information campaign on the dangers of trafficking. For funding

purposes, law enforcement and human rights approaches have been segmented into limited length projects. Many of the current criticisms of
international organizations are that anti-trafficking programs are rarely
coordinated among the multiple governmental, nongovernmental, international, and local actors in a country. Ideally, rights-based strategies
should be subsumed under prevention of trafficking, prosecution of
traffickers, and protection of trafficked persons.[16] Illustrating an integration of approaches, the European Union, in its Strategy on Trafficking,
suggests two interrelated solutions: strengthening law enforcement capabilities (a "repressive" strategy) and improving economic conditions
(an "empowering" strategy). In essence, the EU has applied its accession
guidelines toward the issue of trafficking.[17]

While empowering strategies have been adopted by many values-
based NGOs, some governments, and some intergovernmental organizations, Western Balkan countries and their international counterparts have
tended to follow another route. The law enforcement approach has been
their dominant method in combating human trafficking, as reflected in
the countries' National Action Plans. These plans address the interests of
the state—prevention of migration and prevention of organized crime—
as opposed to protecting the interests of victims of human rights violations.[18] As Barbara Limanowska reports: "The strategies used were, in
the first place, of a legislative and prosecutorial nature, while long-term
prevention and protection of the rights of the victims were seen as second, or distant, priorities."[19]

The Organization for Security and Cooperation in Europe (OSCE)
has also taken a law enforcement approach to combating trafficking.
With a focus on creating legal remedies and strengthening the capacity of
local police, the OSCE has worked with governments to write and implement anti-trafficking laws and has supported the training of judges and
lawyers. Moreover, the OSCE has primarily undertaken the responsibility
to encourage the development and implementation of National Action
Plans of the Balkan countries, although recently it has also concentrated
a great deal on the prevention of trafficking and the protection of trafficked persons.

Most organizations and governments have seen legislative and prosecutorial activities as effective long-term strategies but have viewed the
prevention of trafficking and protection of trafficked persons as secondary.[20] Even as the law enforcement approach has remained dominant,
however, some organizations are developing an improved human rights
approach. International organizations have for many years recognized
the need for treating trafficking as a violation of human rights. Yet putting human rights norms into practice has taken time. Such steps entail
rewriting laws, providing legal and social protection for victims who are
witnesses in criminal investigations, training police to be sensitive to victims of trafficking, creating a national referral mechanism (which does
not exist even in the United States), and providing training and technical
assistance to officials in the judicial system.

The actions taken in response to trafficking in Kosovo illustrate the
difficulty of such a shift. In 2000, a Trafficking and Prostitution Investigation Unit (TPIU) was formed as a subunit of the UNMIK police, and
the Trafficking Regulation was passed in January 2001. The aims of the
TPIU are to "gather intelligence and construct a database of information
on premises and suspects involved in trafficking," to identify trafficked
women, and to prosecute traffickers.[21] The latter criminalizes involvement in trafficking. However, it appears that neither UNMIK, the Kosovo
Police Service, nor the Kosovo judiciary have been fully informed of the
regulations' provisions and measures; hence, enforcement, prosecution,
and successful convictions have been minimal. Because the focus of TPIU
seems to be to register and monitor women suspected of prostitution,
women are often left in dangerous circumstances while the investigation
proceeds. Furthermore, these women are saddled with the nearly impossible responsibility of "proving" that they are victims of trafficking. Unable to do so, most women are often detained ("soft arrest") and labeled
by the police as "prostitutes," a status that entails a criminal offense.[22]

While the Kosovo police carried out close to four hundred raids on
premises involved in trafficking in 2002, only sixty-one locations were
closed, ninety-two indictments filed, and less than thirty convictions were
obtained. Of those convicted, the great majority received sentences of

less than the two- to five-year requirement under the Trafficking Regulation. Trafficked women in Kosovo are entitled to legal assistance and witness protection under Kosovo law, but victims are rarely informed of these rights by judges, courts, or the police. In addition, women who are recognized as "trafficked" often face intimidation, coercion, threats, or further violence to themselves or their families by traffickers and local authorities and, if they return home, by their native communities.[23]

Government responses to the rise in trafficking in Bosnia and Herzegovina have been characterized as "ineffective at best."[24] Failure to prosecute suspected traffickers, the prosecution and deportation of trafficking victims as guilty of prostitution, a lack of a witness protection program and long-term shelters, and the refusal to provide temporary or permanent immigration status to trafficking victims all point toward a general sluggishness on the part of the government to tackle the serious problem of trafficking. Many judges, prosecutors, and police officers in Bosnia and Herzegovina openly blame the low conviction rate of traffickers on most victims' refusals to testify in court or their choice to return to their homeland.[25] This is also the case in Kosovo, where members of the provisional government were directly involved in trafficking.

Further hindering a systematic attack on trafficking is the fact that members of the international community are afforded immunity from prosecution for engaging in trafficking. Perhaps the most well-publicized instances of human rights abuses committed by members of UNMIK are those involving the trafficking of women and girls in Kosovo. As noted earlier, the arrival of international military personnel and civilians in Kosovo in 1999 created a market for prostitution, and Kosovo soon became a major destination for trafficked women. Amnesty International documented the role of the international community as clientele for women forced into prostitution, representing an estimated 80 percent of clientele in 1999 and 2000. By 2002, international clients had fallen to 30 percent though generating "80 percent of the industry's income." Although by 2003, the figure had fallen further to 20 percent, Amnesty International observed the gap between this percentage and the international population: "the international community (both male and female), probably make up around two per cent of the population of Kosovo." In some cases, UNMIK police were involved in the trafficking itself, and in 2003 at least one UNMIK police commander was sent home and an international police officer was arrested for suspected involvement in forced prostitution. Civilians and military working with UNMIK can be prosecuted only if the UN secretary general or the KFOR national battalion head, respectively, waive immunity.[26]

Procedural and legal mechanisms undoubtedly have the capacity to respond to the phenomenon of trafficking, but the process of incorporating anti-trafficking norms into the governmental, legal, and judicial systems is slow. After all, it was only in January of 2000 that UNMIK acknowledged trafficking as "a problem."[27] Moreover, there are more macro-level problems that, as of yet, have not been addressed. Profound poverty, lack of jobs in the home country, lack of legal migration routes, lower social status for women and girls, and domestic violence against women, girls, and boys are all widespread in the Balkan region. In general, there is a great deal of insecurity, daily violence in certain regions, and high levels of organized crime within and outside of the political system—all of which can be related to socioeconomic uncertainty and high unemployment.[28] These conditions greatly increase women's and children's vulnerability to being trafficked. In Kosovo, as elsewhere, the objective of prevention is not well integrated into anti-trafficking programs, and it is not coordinated with other action plans.

Analyzing the Impact of International Intervention

International efforts, spearheaded by large international nongovernmental and governmental organizations headquartered in Western countries, have been both praised and criticized by researchers and practitioners. Over the last five years, international organizations, including the OSCE and various UN agencies, have worked diligently with the governments in the Western Balkans to build their capacities and therefore strengthen their responses to trafficking. As a result, the institutional response in the region is well developed; however, there are varying levels of effectiveness in this institutionalization. Despite concentrated international and local efforts over the last six years, trafficking in persons continues.

There is evidence that traffickers in the Western Balkans have simply changed tactics to dodge increased international enforcement. For example, in 2003 and 2004, traffickers employed new strategies to regularize foreign victims' status in Bosnia and Herzegovina. IOM and others report that raids conducted by local law enforcement are causing trafficking to go underground.[29] One consequence is that girls and women now are exploited in private apartments and houses, where they are connected with clients through escort services, mobile phones, or the Internet.[30] Some traffickers now rely upon more subtle forms of exploitation, such as providing small payments to the women to avoid their denunciation and allowing participation of women as traffickers and pimps. This development has entailed an increase in trafficking in children, reliance on legal travel documents, and an increase in government corruption.[31] Forced prostitution is now more exploitative and dangerous because it has become less conspicuous. Traffickers no longer want to take the risk of the bar or brothel being raided; therefore, they transport the women and girls from apartment to apartment, catering to wealthier clients.

Traffickers also have responded to new enforcement strategies by changing their routes of movement. For example, in an unprecedented example of cross-border police cooperation, Albanian and Italian law enforcement agents have effectively shut down speedboat traffic from Albania to Italy across the Adriatic. However, the traffickers have found other routes to Western Europe.[32]

Activity in Albania and Kosovo illustrates the persistence of trafficking in the region. In Albania, women have suffered varying levels and types of abuse while being trafficked. In 2004, though, fewer victims of sexual exploitation suffered abuse and much of the abuse exerted was psychological. Rebecca Surtees found that traffickers modified the forms of abuse in order to prevent victims from seeking escape. Moreover, since late 2003–early 2004, some trafficked women have been paid "just enough money"—approximately two hundred to three hundred euros per month—for what was originally forced sex work in Kosovo "to make it less likely that victims would accept assistance." Some of these women now have valid documents and are registered as working in bars as wait-resses or dancers. Even if they were initially trafficked, they are now claiming that they reside in Kosovo voluntarily.[33]

To the extent that local reporting indicates a decline in trafficking, the change is likely temporary. The statistics from Bosnia and Herzegovina are illustrative here. While there is clearly a decrease in the number of identified and assisted foreign trafficked women, most counter-trafficking actors maintain that the number of victims trafficked to and increasingly from Bosnia and Herzegovina remains high. The numbers presented in these reports, of course, refer only to victims identified and assisted by service providers in Bosnia and Herzegovina. There was a "dramatic in-crease in the identification and assistance of national victims" in 2003 and 2004. However, it is not clear whether the rise in victims found is due to Bosnia and Herzegovina increasingly becoming a country of origin or to the increase in the visibility of service providers. This is also the case for Serbia, Montenegro, Croatia, and FYR Macedonia.[34]

Throughout the region, awareness-raising programs are not work-ing as preventative measures as intended. Girls and women are generally aware of the risks involved in traveling abroad or entering the sex trade; nevertheless, they engage in these activities anyway. One IOM report in-dicated: "vulnerable girls are very informed about migration risks . . . [although] they are more aware of the risks in the period preceding the departure and upon arrival in the destination country than they are re-garding the problems that might arise during the journey . . . including being lied to by intermediaries; being kidnapped and taken to a different destination than one chosen initially; being sold and forced to become prostitutes; . . . having one's passports taken by the employers; getting paid below expectations or below initial agreement; and being deceived by the very acquaintances one had trusted."[35] While hundreds of thou-sands of dollars have been spent on prevention and awareness programs in the Western Balkans,[36] research shows that simply telling someone that something is wrong or dangerous does not change behavior, especially when the economic incentives pull in the other direction. More and more women in the Western Balkans choose to migrate in hopes of becoming the principal wage earners of their families. Changing the incentive structure means the creation of economic activities in their home countries and the opening of channels for legal migration.[37] Yet very few international efforts address these systemic issues.

The primary responses to human trafficking in the Western Balkans have been limited in their ability to address the problem. Insights into these limitations lie in the conceptual models underlying the primary responses. The law enforcement model sees women as victims and focuses on the criminal elements of perpetrators' behavior. The illegal migration model equates trafficked women with illegal aliens. Both models have failed to capture the fundamental nature of the trafficking phenomenon.

The law enforcement model emphasizes the identification of discrete cases of trafficking involving specific victims and the prosecution of alleged perpetrators. The narrative of individuals labeled as victims in this process, however, often reflects a far more complicated self-understanding of their own status, one that is not static and devoid of agency. These individuals stress that they were not always victims. At some early stage, their involvement was completely willing, albeit tremendously ill-informed. Seeking better economic opportunities and unable to migrate legally, they enlisted the help of agents who would facilitate their movement across borders to obtain work. Whether traveling for a position as a domestic servant, agricultural laborer, or sex worker, many individuals intentionally and willfully set out to obtain a new position in a new locale. At some point in time, however, the transaction became more exploitative and thus could no longer be said to have been chosen freely. In one common scenario, a woman is told by a relative or a friend/boyfriend about an opportunity to work as a waitress in Western Europe; she is transferred across the border by the relative or friend and then handed over to an agent, who then extorts a high fee for having just *purchased* the woman; the working conditions of the new job prove to be incredibly inhumane; the agent refuses to permit her to leave her job unless she pays an astronomically high fee. At some point along the way, the individual did become a victim, although she did not begin this journey as a victim, wholly devoid of agency, as envisioned by the law enforcement model.[38]

One negative effect of the conceptualization of trafficked woman solely as victim has been the denial of these women's humanity and agency in governmental and NGO programming. A major report of the Geneva-based International Council on Human Rights Policy found that, in contrast to other recipients of international assistance, sex workers are very often treated differently. The study concluded, "Though they too are the subject of NGO actions, NGOs do not always feel obliged to consult them and are sometimes even prepared to take initiatives of which sex workers disapprove."[39] Consequently, much of the resulting programming is inappropriate.

Enforcement of anti-discrimination laws is needed to address the "underlying economic disadvantages" for women that lead to trafficking. The governments and publics of countries of destination participate in the conditions that encourage trafficking and they should "develop compassionate approaches to victim identification" and victim protection.[40] The criminalization approach contributes to worsening conditions for women in the trade because it strengthens the position of authorities without empowering the women. This puts sex workers at greater risk. Strengthening the powers of police to raid sex-work establishments pushes the industry further underground and into less and less safe areas. It also often means that women are either jailed or put into protective state programs where they are frequently ill-treated and denied opportunities for reintegration into society in a manner respectful of their free agency.

The conflation of human trafficking, illegal migration, and alien exploitation is also problematic. The act of trafficking in women for sex differs greatly from smuggling aliens for other forms of exploitative labor. Not only is the intrusion into women's bodies of a different nature, but also the dynamics of the economic transaction are radically different. As Amy O'Neill Richard has explained, "Whereas alien smuggling usually involves short-term monetary profit, trafficking usually involves long term exploitation for economic gain."[41] Jennifer Murray further explains, "According to the International Labour Organization: smuggling occurs because borders have become barriers between jobseekers and job offers. Trafficking occurs not only when borders are barriers to labour supplies meeting demands, but when no knowledge is available about proper migration channels, when employment is itself illegal and/or underground, and where conditions of work much worse than legal minimums are tolerated or ignored."[42] Despite the differences between alien smuggling and trafficking in women, the association remains pervasive in the media and by governments all over the world, thus leading to the adoption of inappropriate programming. The conflation of trafficking and smuggling is most acutely a problem when it comes to gathering accurate data on trafficking.[43] The U.S. government requests that governments annually provide data on how many people were trafficked, but these governments present aggregate data that do not always distinguish between illegal migration, smuggling, and trafficking victims.

For many researchers, the most disturbing trend in the responses to trafficking is the lack of reliable information sharing between institutions responsible for addressing trafficking, especially information concerning patterns and the changing scope of the problem. For example, the OSCE recently coordinated with UNMIK in Kosovo to pool resources and plan an awareness project that would set long-term goals to combat trafficking. The OSCE asked IOM to participate in this campaign because of their extensive knowledge of trafficking and their significant resources. However, IOM insisted that it did not want to cooperate and has planned its own awareness campaign with Save the Children and USAID.[44]

Researchers are realizing that despite the creation of structures at the governmental level to address trafficking, effective implementation of programs and goals is just beginning. Limanowska observes: "the cooperation between governmental agencies, as well as between government and non-governmental partners, is insufficient. Also, the programmes implemented by international agencies are not always adequately coordinated with local partners and often do not provide opportunities for local ownership. While [Western Balkans] governments have recognised their responsibility, have taken ownership of the issue and made huge progress in the area of legal reform and establishment of anti-trafficking structures, the process of effective implementation of appropriate activities has only just started."[45] Ultimately, the system of assistance for trafficked persons, which should be the crux of the anti-trafficking response, does not meet the victims' needs, and many women refuse assistance.

Even as many international organizations seek to build local capacity, their operational relationship with locals often works to undermine capacity. Local NGOs in the Western Balkans were the first to recognize trafficking in persons in the late 1990s, but international governmental organizations such as IOM and the OSCE took the lead in tackling the problem of trafficking at the institutional level and providing protection and shelter to women who had been trafficked. Some IOM offices initially struggled to find the funding to run safe shelters, and IOM Missions became very ambitious in their pursuit of international money in order to continue doing so.[46] Local NGOs have had greater difficulties accessing external funding, both because their capacity has been lower than that of the international organizations and because of the nature of donor/organization relationships inherent to international development in general. This dynamic works to stunt the development of civil society in already fragile and burgeoning democracies.

There have been few successful efforts to discern the actual effectiveness of the current anti-trafficking projects in the Balkans. Currently, these activities are supported regardless of effectiveness and costs of program. Donors are willing to finance them even without some, if any, concrete results. The contributors, predominantly European countries and the United States, are satisfied to fund many narrowly focused anti-trafficking programs for short periods of time. However, these programs lack a long-term vision for truly reducing trafficking in the Western Balkans. In addition, activities are not properly monitored and evaluated. No one checks whether these programs are necessary or appropriate, if they fit into a broader country or regional strategy, or if they duplicate already existing projects.

The blending and burying of anti-trafficking efforts in larger law enforcement or anti-migration programs also interferes with program effectiveness. Often anti-trafficking funding is directed to law enforcement agencies to build capacity, such as creating a database of migrants and technical capacity building, all under the rubric of anti-trafficking programs. Donors continue to provide the majority of grant money directly to large international organizations that are then responsible for subcontracting to local NGOs. This leads to a "negative selection" of NGOs that view anti-trafficking work as an income-generating activity rather than part of a larger human rights mission.[47]

Projects by international organizations aimed at the economic empowerment of women also have tended to be components of broader economic development programs rather than anti-trafficking strategies. Until 2003, there was little exchange of information or cooperation between institutions working in trafficking and development agencies, and little research or information available on the "impact of economic reform and development programs on trafficking in the region" or on how these programs might benefit potential or actual victims of trafficking.[48]

The well-intentioned National Action Plans strategy also has been beset by operational difficulties. Each of the countries in the Western Balkans has been encouraged by the international organizations and donors to create plans, in which national actors were to take the lead and international organizations were to play a supportive role. However, National Action Plans have opted for solutions that lack creativity, and government agencies have lagged behind in anti-trafficking assistance. Therefore, international organizations have filled the gap by directly implementing anti-trafficking projects with the cooperation of local NGOs.[49] Most of the assistance for trafficking victims is provided through shelters where adult females only receive "short-term services." The services are usually "provided by NGOs or international organizations and funded by foreign donors."[50]

The international donor community also has caused competition between NGOs and governments for foreign funds earmarked for anti-trafficking projects. Government representatives are "distrustful of NGOs relying on foreign donations and accuse them" of exaggerating the country's social problems "to obtain more funding." However, NGOs have little recourse, as the governments do not provide their own funding to support the work of the organizations.[51] "Cooperation and exchange of information with and among the donors" is seriously lacking in the region and meetings to encourage information-sharing among stakeholders have not continued. The Stability Pact Task Force on Trafficking in Human Beings (SPTF) has played a crucial role "in supporting anti-trafficking work"; however, with the dissolving of the SPTF in late 2004, the difficulty of communication between "local institutions and the donor organizations" is likely to increase.[52]

Despite the challenges created by the involvement of international organizations in combating trafficking, there have been many positive consequences. The focus on increasing the capacity of NGOs and governments in the Western Balkans often has been successful. The creation of, and support for, the shelters for trafficked women in Bosnia and Herzegovina is one example. When IOM set up its first shelter for trafficked women in 1999, the experience was akin to trial by fire. They simply tried to fill a dearth in services as quickly as possible but had no user's manual on how to run a shelter specifically for trafficked women. Because IOM had immediate access to funding, it was able to start up the shelter more quickly than local agencies. In the case of IOM in Sarajevo, however, local staff played an integral role in setting up the shelter, therefore, local capacity strengthening was being imparted indirectly. According to a former IOM Chief of Mission in Bosnia and Herzegovina, IOM would have preferred to allow local NGOs to manage the shelters for trafficked women, although the NGOs did not yet have the capacity to run them. It was also an extremely dangerous undertaking, as traffickers routinely threatened the lives of IOM staff.[53] In this manner, the local staff's ability to look to internationals for support was crucial.

Additional progress has been made on the legislative front. All six countries in the Western Balkans have passed some form of anti-trafficking legislation, and all countries have created National Action Plans and are receiving assistance in implementation by the OSCE. At least some police in each country have been trained in order to raise awareness and foster better identification of trafficked people. Albania, Bosnia and Herzegovina, Croatia, FYR Macedonia, and Serbia all have some form of anti-trafficking legislation with varying levels of implementation. Finally, UNMIK is aware of the problem of trafficking and has provisions in the legal statute to prosecute traffickers.

According to IOM, there were a number of positive developments in the area of victim assistance and protection in 2003 and 2004.[54] For example, some countries have referral mechanisms in place, and others are in the process of developing and/or implementing such structures. Although some observers argue that the relationship between governments and NGOs has been problematic, various ministries within the governments of the Western Balkans have played significant roles in supporting prevention, protection, and prosecution activities. A diverse group of anti-trafficking actors—including "law enforcement, NGOs, international organizations, embassies, help lines, medical staff, social workers, families of victims, trafficked persons themselves and private citizens"—have been instrumental in helping to increase the identification of trafficked persons. In addition, international organizations have provided extensive training to help law enforcement authorities identify victims, sensitize personnel, train help line operators, and offer assistance to service providers.[55]

Without support from the international donor community, very few initiatives to combat trafficking at so many institutional levels would have been undertaken. For example, in FYR Macedonia in 2004, there were approximately thirty-five local NGOs "implementing anti-trafficking prevention projects, with support from the international community." One of the international funders, the OSCE, provided support for a dozen local NGOs to conduct training workshops and public awareness campaigns. The challenge for donors is to encourage and support governments in the region to assume the responsibility of funding their own national NGOs.[56]

Another way to conceptualize the unprecedented national and regional efforts to combat trafficking during the last several years is to define them in terms of the development of transnational advocacy networks (TANs). Margaret Keck and Katherine Sikkink define transnational advocacy networks as "sets of actors linked across country boundaries, bound together by shared values."[57] TANs comprised of local NGOs, international governmental and nongovernmental organizations, governments, and donors have developed in order to combat trafficking in the Western Balkans. Regional cooperation was a means to guarantee political stability in the Balkans, "by leading to better coordinated efforts of combating organized crime, illegal migration and human trafficking." The EU has supported initiatives derived from civil society, such as the South East European Cooperation Process (SEECP). When the SPTF was launched in September 2000, it raised expectations of greater regional cooperation. Although the SPTF during its existence played a role in coordination of anti-trafficking efforts, its goals were unclear and funding limited.[58] The OSCE, one of the SPTF members, is generally viewed as extremely instrumental in creating and maintaining a network of organizations within the region.[59]

One of the most interesting outcomes of the development of TANs to combat trafficking in the Western Balkans has been in facilitating the normative shift from a law enforcement approach to a human rights approach. Though both approaches still coexist, local NGOs and international organizations have learned simultaneously the necessity of providing services and building institutions that are victim-centered rather than law enforcement–centered. Numerous conferences throughout the Balkan region are being held on this issue, and "high-level delegations reaffirm that fighting trafficking in human beings remains a top priority."[60] In September 2004, a conference entitled "Ensuring Human Rights Protection in Countries of Destination: Breaking the Cycle of Trafficking" was held in Helsinki as a follow-up to the 2001 Berlin conference "Europe against Trafficking in Persons." The discussions at the Helsinki conference focused on finding new strategies to address the protection of the human rights of trafficked persons. The conference also provided a forum to exchange good practices with the aim of identifying practical measures that should be taken to implement the OSCE Action Plan in countries of destination.[61]

To increase networking in the region, the NGO Vital Voices Global Partnership helped to arrange and fund a seminar in Warsaw in March 2002 for women political activists from the Balkans to discuss trafficking. The Regional Initiative for Central and Eastern Europe at the National Democratic Institute for International Affairs (NDI) hosted twenty-two women leaders from Bosnia and Herzegovina, Bulgaria, Croatia, FYR Macedonia, and Montenegro. At the seminar, participants received training to enhance political leadership skills to fight trafficking, developed ideas for regional cooperation, and built a network of colleagues across the region for future collaboration on anti-trafficking programs.[62]

The organization Geneva Global Inc. has provided grants for several victim-focused initiatives in the Balkans since 2000. Focusing on integrated and local community efforts to curb trafficking, Geneva Global has networked local and national groups that would otherwise be operating in isolation. These initiatives have been used in public information campaigns and education programs; training of peer advisors, teachers, police, and community leaders; income generation alternatives to trafficking; rescues; counseling; legal assistance for victims; literacy and skills training for victims; and family counseling.[63] Between 2002 and 2004, the Zonta International Foundation provided over $300,000 in funds and technical assistance in Bosnia and Herzegovina to bolster the effectiveness of local anti-trafficking coalitions. The foundation targeted funds to augment communications and public relations in order to increase media and public awareness of trafficking prevention and to aid in collaboration and coalition building to create public policies to stop trafficking, support prevention activity, and provide assistance to victims and those at risk.[64] These and other creative projects illustrate the many ways in which international anti-trafficking efforts have made welcome contributions in the region.

Looking Ahead

The international approach to combating trafficking in the Western Balkans has had both a positive and negative impact on the region. Because socioeconomic factors are strongly connected to trafficking, effective policies and strategies will address these linkages. We hope that this chapter prods other researchers to gather more information on the changing nature of trafficking and its socioeconomic impacts.[65] Data collection on trafficking still remains insufficient. As Frank Laczko of IOM warns, "Despite the growing literature on trafficking, relatively few studies are based on extensive research, and information on the actual numbers of people trafficked remains very sketchy."[66] Significant steps are being taken to eliminate this problem. Future efforts must center on an increase in government and multilateral efforts to combat trafficking and more deliberate institutional strategies to systematically deal with trafficking data. Traffickers have proved incredibly adept at transforming themselves in order to continue their work; anti-trafficking programs must prove even more proactive at adapting to new challenges as they arise.

4

TRANSNATIONAL RESPONSES TO HUMAN TRAFFICKING

The Politics of Anti-Trafficking in the Balkans

NICOLE LINDSTROM

Human trafficking has become a top priority of the international community in the past decade and the Balkans a key target in anti-trafficking efforts. Anti-trafficking policy exemplifies a transnational policy by Mitchell Orenstein's definition, one that is "developed, diffused, and implemented with the direct involvement of global policy actors and coalitions at or across the international, national, or local levels of governance."[1] In the case of anti-trafficking in the Balkans, transnational policy actors have not only been involved directly in all stages of the policy process but one might argue that anti-trafficking policy would not exist without the participation of transnational actors. That is, transnational actors have placed trafficking high on the agenda and produced policies to combat it. These are often top-down policies, whereby external actors rely on a combination of incentives and sanctions to pressure governments to conform to a common set of legal standards and procedures. An expanding network of transnational and local nongovernmental actors works directly with states throughout every stage of the policy process, from development to diffusion to implementation. While global and regional anti-trafficking policies interact with different domestic conditions, to date, anti-trafficking policy in the Balkans appears to follow a one-size-fits-all pattern.

However, if we view anti-trafficking policy in the Balkans as a strictly top-down process, backed by a consensus among international actors, we neglect other interesting questions. How do transnational and domestic actors conceptualize the problem of trafficking? How is the diffusion of transnational anti-trafficking policy mediated within different domestic contexts? What can we learn from the implementation of anti-trafficking policies in the Balkans to date, namely some of the unintended consequences? This chapter investigates these three sets of questions by tracing the process through which anti-trafficking policy has been developed, diffused, and implemented in the Balkans, with a particular focus on Serbia and Montenegro. While anti-trafficking policy in the Balkans has largely followed top-down logic, whereby a common set of laws and procedures are developed and diffused by transnational actors, important differences exist in how actors conceptualize the problem of trafficking. These differences, in turn, shape the way that states adopt and implement anti-trafficking policies, leading to a degree of divergence in domestic anti-trafficking strategies. Contradictions among different approaches, however, can result in a number of unintended consequences, leading, in turn, to a reconceptualization of the problem and its solutions.

Four Approaches to Developing Anti-Trafficking Policy

A critical juncture in the development of transnational policies to combat human trafficking was the United Nations Assembly's adoption of the Convention against Transnational Organized Crime in November 2000, and the accompanying Protocol to Prevent, Suppress and Punish Trafficking in Persons, Especially Women and Children (Trafficking Protocol), which entered into force in December 2003. The UN protocol's definition of trafficking aimed to provide a general baseline from which transnational actors could develop and implement a common set of standards to prevent trafficking, protect victims, and prosecute offenders. The protocol provides the single most authoritative collective statement on the goals of policies to combat trafficking and the kind of instruments that should be used to achieve them. These standards have also spurred coordination of anti-trafficking efforts in regions like the Balkans, where the problem is considered most acute.

One might assume that extensive transnational and regional coordination in this policy area is based on a consensus on the nature of the trafficking problem. Yet in practice, we can observe significant differences among actors in their conceptualization of the trafficking problem and how it should be tackled. These can be categorized into four interrelated approaches: the migration approach, the law enforcement approach, the human rights approach, and the economic approach.[2] In the context of the Balkans, these four approaches are intertwined with which transnational and local actors have framed the issue of human trafficking, how these frames have engendered different strategies to combat trafficking, and the potential overlaps and conflicts between each strategy.

Migration Approach

The migration approach is based on the understanding of the trafficking problem as one of unregulated or irregular migration. The International Organization for Migration (IOM) is a primary proponent of this approach to trafficking in the Balkans, although it works in cooperation with other transnational and local actors. Two main activities of IOM in the Balkans are providing direct assistance to trafficked persons through funding and operating a network of emergency or temporary shelters throughout the region and collecting, consolidating, and analyzing information on human trafficking in the area. Trafficked persons are either brought to the shelters by law enforcement agents when they are apprehended on borders or in brothel raids or they seek assistance voluntarily. They are given emergency shelter, and in some cases temporary residence permits, before they are repatriated to their countries of origin.

IOM also leads regional data collection efforts in the Balkans, often in tandem with its direct assistance programs. Measuring the volume, scope, and patterns of trafficking is a notoriously difficult process.[3] National authorities are generally considered unreliable sources for data on trafficking, partially because border control authorities generally do not distinguish between trafficking, smuggling, and irregular migration. Moreover, governments might be inclined to underestimate or overestimate the scope of the trade depending on financial sanctions or incentives, or be reluctant to open their policing activities to international oversight. In order to collect more systematic data on trafficking in the region, in 2003 IOM founded the Regional Clearing Point (RCP), which operates under the umbrella of the Stability Pact Task Force on Trafficking in Human Beings (SPTF). International anti-trafficking experts herald the RCP as a positive example of what can be achieved through better data management. By creating a sound mechanism for the collection, consolidation, and analysis of information for the region, drawn from a wide range of sources, the RCP helps to foster a "comprehensive understanding of human trafficking throughout the Balkans."[4] The RCP's primary data source is IOM shelters, which provide numbers of trafficked persons assisted, their countries of origin, and more qualitative data collected from victims concerning recruitment strategies and trafficking routes. The RCP supplements IOM data with information collected from national and international law enforcement agencies and other local and transnational nongovernmental organizations.

Law Enforcement Approach

The law enforcement approach operates according to the definition of trafficking in persons as a crime under international law that must be prevented, prosecuted, and punished. Within this approach there are different emphases on various dimensions of trafficking. Understanding human trafficking as a crime equivalent to trading in drugs and arms can justify many of the same strategies used to suppress dealings in other illegal commodities. Indeed, many of the same routes and actors involved in the illegal trade of arms during the 1990s embargoes in former Yugoslavia now traffic women, which can be more profitable and less risky. Thus, many of the same global and regional anti–organized crime tactics are considered transferable to anti-trafficking initiatives. Framing trafficking as a problem primarily of illegal migration can lead to strategies more oriented to tightening borders or implementing stricter visa regimes. Linking trafficking more closely to prostitution or sex work has led to the targeting of local sex industries, including brothel and nightclub raids. All three kinds of law enforcement strategies work concurrently in the region, yet with different focuses by different actors. Agencies within the national governments, such as customs and border control, pursue the issue as one of organized crime or illegal migration while local law enforcement agencies often police the sex industry. International or regional law enforcement agencies and initiatives, such as the U.S.-led South Eastern European Cooperative Initiative (SECI), Europol, and Interpol, tend to promote more comprehensive transnational strategies that incorporate all three aspects.

In September 2002, SECI organized the largest regional anti-trafficking action to date, coined Operation Mirage. With the cooperation of local law enforcement agencies, the international Stabilisation Force (SFOR) mission in Bosnia and Herzegovina and the UN Mission in Kosovo, Operation Mirage resulted in over 20,000 police raids throughout the region in bars, hotels, nightclubs, and border points. After conducting 13,000 interviews with women and children, 237 were identified as victims of trafficking, only 4 percent of whom were provided assistance in shelters. Another 2,700 women and children were classified as voluntary migrants and arrested, deported, and in several cases prosecuted. The operation resulted in the identification of 293 traffickers, several of whom were tried in Bosnia and Herzegovina, Kosovo, and Serbia and Montenegro.[5] SECI continues to coordinate regional law enforcement activities in antitrafficking. In recent years, SECI's mandate has expanded to include the transborder policing of organized crime, terrorist groups, and other illegal trade networks.

Human Rights Approach

The human rights approach "frames trafficking in persons as a violation of individual human rights."[6] The violent and coercive nature of human trafficking is emphasized in such accounts. This approach thus seeks to ensure that every individual is protected from future human rights violations. This understanding of trafficking underlies the approaches of international organizations such as the UN Office of the High Commissioner for Human Rights and the Organization for Security and Cooperation in Europe/Office for Democratic Institutions and Human Rights (OSCE/ODIHR). The SPTF asserts that trafficking is "first and foremost a violation of human rights," but "advocates that this approach works best in tandem with the law enforcement approach."[7]

Such a definition distinguishes the approach of "most transnational and local human rights groups" who "organize their efforts around such a definition, although with notable differences" among them. For example, the Coalition against Trafficking in Women (CATW) and the Movement for the Abolition of Pornography and Prostitution (MAPP) place "trafficking in the context of sexual exploitation, resist attempts to separate trafficking from prostitution, and often frame trafficking in women as 'slavery' or a 'slave trade' in their public awareness campaigns."[8] The Global Alliance against Traffic in Women (GAATW), on the other hand, has introduced broader definitions of trafficking into public debate, framing trafficking in women as primarily an issue of social justice and economic human rights. "By defining prostitution as 'sex work' or an income generating form of labor GAATW seeks to counter the efforts of organizations such as CATW to portray trafficking as solely sexual exploitation or slavery."[9] Recently, groups such as GAATW have argued that the focus of anti-trafficking efforts must expand beyond "sex-trafficking" to address other forms of human trafficking such as forced labor for manufacturing and assembly work or child begging.[10]

Differences in definitions and approaches are also visible among local anti-trafficking groups. Some local NGOs in the Balkans, such as the network of La Strada chapters, organize media campaigns to raise awareness of trafficking as modern "slavery" and work with IOM and other agencies to assist and repatriate victims of trafficking to their countries of origin. Other local NGOs, such as the Belgrade-based Anti-Trafficking Center, come closer to GAATW's approach to trafficking. These NGOs lobby governments to decriminalize migration and prostitution. "They also advocate the creation of reintegration centers, which offer educational and vocational services to integrate women into the local economy, as an alternative to IOM's repatriation-oriented assistance model."[11] Empowerment strategies developed with the aim of enabling people, especially potential victims of trafficking, to protect themselves, are at the forefront of this approach.

Economic Approach

An economic approach to anti-trafficking shares much in common with the human rights approach advocated by transnational groups like GAATW. It shifts the emphasis away from strict law enforcement or migration approaches in favor of policies that not only protect victims of trafficking but address the broader socioeconomic conditions that lead to the problem. This approach also contests the rigid binaries of trafficking versus smuggling, legal and illegal migration, and voluntary versus involuntary prostitution. One underlying assumption of this approach is that women are trafficked for work in the sex industry for a variety of reasons. Many women are coerced to leave their homes under false promises of legal work in the West, and some are forced into prostitution through threats, bondage, and even torture. While such egregious violations of human rights attract the sensationalist headlines and place anti-trafficking efforts high on the policy agenda, advocates of this approach suggest that in reality most women migrate more or less voluntarily.[12] Indeed, few people would opt for prostitution if not for economic hardship or lack of access to legal labor markets. Seeking work in illegal markets abroad is viewed as one of the few available means for people to escape poverty in their home countries and secure legal employment in the West.[13]

Transnational and local groups adopting this view, such as the No Borders activist network or the Anti-Trafficking Center, promote the interrelated aims of easing restrictive migration policies in the EU that make trafficking more profitable for the traffickers and more exploitative for the women and shifting the international community's funding priorities away from law enforcement and border control to direct assistance and economic and political development. Proponents of an economic approach draw attention to the limitations of migration and law enforcement approaches by citing the inadequacies of international law. For instance, while states are forbidden to expel persons who face possible torture or degrading treatment in their home countries, in most cases trafficked women face a high probability of deportation to their countries of origin. Limited economic opportunities in their home countries increase the risk that women will reenter the cycle of trafficking. In broader terms, an economic approach draws attention to the emerging patterns of exclusion and inclusion in Europe, where the new boundaries of the EU divide the prosperous zones of stability from the impoverished zones of instability. The borders "between law enforcement exporting states of the new EU are increasingly fortified against the crime-exporting states of the Balkans"[14] and regions to the east through heightened policing of external borders, stricter immigration policies, and more vigorous policing of sex work—all at great cost to the EU and its new member states. Meanwhile, traffickers profit from the steady supply of unemployed and displaced persons who are forced to take more desperate measures to penetrate fortress Europe.

Diffusing Anti-Trafficking Policy in Serbia and Montenegro

If the development of anti-trafficking policies exhibits four overlapping, and sometimes contradictory, approaches, how might these different conceptualizations of the trafficking problem shape the diffusion of policy strategies within different national contexts? In 2001, the SPTF set out guidelines for the development of National Action Plans, designed to tailor common regional policies to the particular needs and experiences of individual countries.[15] The National Action Plans require national governments to set priorities and put in place necessary legal and institutional mechanisms to combat trafficking. These plans are regularly revised and supplemented to address changing priorities and integrate subsequent regional agreements on information exchange, legal status of trafficked persons, and witness protection. While governments are formally responsible for formulating the plans, transnational actors have been directly involved in all stages of the process. Transnational actors have played both formal and informal roles in the institutional mechanisms created in Serbia and Montenegro to implement anti-trafficking policies. While the two nations face common top-down pressures, their institutional frameworks differ in their approach to trafficking, with Serbia stressing law enforcement and Montenegro a more holistic approach, as well as the type and extent of transnational involvement.

Both Serbia and Montenegro are primarily designated as transit countries in the human trafficking trade, primarily for sexual exploitation, although recently they have been viewed increasingly as source and destination countries. They are also bound by the 2000 UN Convention against Transnational Organized Crime and its supplementing protocols and are signatories of all regional conventions. Serbia and Montenegro were long considered laggards in anti-trafficking efforts, having been designated as Tier 3 countries by the U.S. State Department—that is, "countries whose governments do not fully comply with the minimum standards and are not making significant efforts to do so." By 2003 both states were redesignated as Tier 2 countries, deemed to be making "significant efforts to bring themselves into compliance" with these standards.[16] In broader terms, both entities confront a host of political and economic problems, including high unemployment, social dislocation, and rampant corruption. Their continued failure to cooperate with the International Criminal Tribunal for Former Yugoslavia (ICTY) in extraditing war criminals and to meet the minimum political and economic requirements necessary to enter EU accession negotiations makes EU membership a distant prospect for both states.

The Republic of Serbia is primarily a transit and destination country for the citizens of Romania, Bulgaria, Ukraine, and Moldova, who are trafficked toward Western countries and Kosovo. The 2005 National Strategy for Combating Trafficking in Serbia cites the most common forms of trafficking as women and children for the purpose of sexual exploitation. However, it also documents a rise in trafficking of children for the purposes of forced/organized begging, as well as increases in forced marriage and forced labor.[17] Serbia is becoming a country of origin, with a number of Serbian nationals trafficked abroad to countries such as Bosnia and Herzegovina, Kosovo, Italy, Montenegro, Romania, as well as trafficked internally.

Montenegro, like Serbia, is primarily a transit country. Women and girls from Serbia, Romania, Albania, and Kosovo are trafficked via Montenegro to the European Union. In recent years, Montenegro has become a destination country for women trafficked from Moldova, Ukraine, Georgia, and Russia as well as Serbia and Bosnia and Herzegovina.[18] Montenegrins have also been trafficked both abroad to Albania, Bosnia and Herzegovina, and Macedonia, as well as internally.[19] Similar to the trafficking situation in Serbia, most foreign and national victims of trafficking identified and assisted by IOM in Montenegro were trafficked for sexual exploitation. However, as in Serbia, trafficking for forced labor and begging is documented, with minors accounting for an increasing percentage of assisted victims in 2003 and 2004.

Despite sharing very similar trafficking problems, Serbia and Montenegro have implemented different anti-trafficking strategies. One set of differences concerns the domestic institutional framework for combating trafficking. In Serbia, the Ministry of the Interior is responsible for appointing a national coordinator who oversees all activities related to anti-trafficking. The national coordinator, a part-time position that is assumed by a highly ranked police officer, leads the National Team for Combating Trafficking in Human Beings.[20] The national team comprises four working groups: prevention and education, victim assistance and protection, legislation and law enforcement, and child trafficking. It is not a formal state body, but provides a forum where government, nongovernmental, and international organizations meet and discuss initiatives for combating trafficking.[21] In October 2004, the government appointed a formalized state body, the Council on Human Trafficking, whose main task is to review reports on trafficking developed by the relevant bodies of the international community and to propose measures for implementing recommendations given by international organizations in the area of combating trafficking.[22] While the national team continues to work as the operative body, the council now provides a formal channel to implement its policy recommendations.[23]

In Montenegro, the 2003 National Strategy for Combating Trafficking established an interministerial working group for the adoption and implementation of anti-trafficking policies. The working group, chaired by a national coordinator who is appointed by the prime minister, is composed of deputy prime ministers from the Ministries of Interior, Health, Justice, Education and Science, Labor and Social Welfare, and the deputy state prosecutor.[24] In 2005 the Ministries of Internal Affairs, Labor and Social Welfare, and Health and two NGOs signed a Memorandum of Understanding that defines the roles of individual actors in identifying and assisting the victims of trafficking. The memorandum creates special police units to combat trafficking, designates the Ministry of Health to lead victim assistance programs, establishes special units within the Ministry of Labor and Social Welfare to implement trafficking-related policies, and defines the role of NGOs in assisting victims and in disseminating information.

Another difference between the anti-trafficking strategies of Serbia and Montenegro is the degree and type of influence granted to transnational actors in each case. In Serbia, transnational actors serve in advisory roles; the OSCE, IOM, and UNICEF appoint representatives to a national advisory council. In Montenegro, transnational actors play a much more formal role, as representatives of the Council of Europe, the OSCE, IOM, and the U.S. consulate serve on the interministerial working group, the body which outlines national priorities, designates the responsibilities of each ministry, sets implementation targets, and proposes a budget. Prior to the creation of the interministerial working group, anti-trafficking efforts were coordinated by the National Anti-Trafficking Project Board, created by the OSCE in 2001. The project board includes representatives of numerous international organizations including the OSCE, IOM, UNICEF, the Council of Europe, Save the Children UK, and the UN Office of the High Commissioner for Human Rights (UNOHCHR), as well as local NGOs such as Women's Safe House, the Montenegrin Women's Lobby, and a Roma NGO, Women's Heart.[25]

Additionally, the pace in which Serbia and Montenegro have adopted and implemented legislation based on regional agreements varies. For instance, at a 2001 conference in Zagreb, all Balkan states agreed to create a regional information exchange mechanism, which was coordinated through the SECI office in Bucharest with the active cooperation of Europol and Interpol. In Serbia, a formal mechanism was developed in 2003 through a joint initiative of the OSCE and the Ministry of Labor, Employment, and Social Policy. The mechanism creates a state agency that identifies all actors with direct access to trafficking victims and a referral system that directs victims to the relevant institutions and organizations that can provide necessary medical, psychosocial, and legal assistance.[26] In Montenegro, on the other hand, no centralized mechanism exists for the screening, identification, and referral of trafficking victims. Rather, victims are referred on an ad-hoc basis based on institutional links and organizational relationships.[27] In 2003, each state signed a statement on commitments to witness protection, which obligates each government to develop special comprehensive measures for assistance and protection for witnesses who agree to testify in trafficking prosecution cases. Montenegro passed a law in 2005 that provides protection for all victims of crime, including trafficking, while Serbia has yet to pass victim protection legislation.

Table 4.1 summarizes the types of institutional mechanisms in place to adopt and implement anti-trafficking policies. Both states are signatories of the same laws and agreements, and open to the direct involvement of the same transnational actors. Yet some differences between the two cases are observable. The role of law enforcement, for example, appears stronger in the case of Serbia, where the appointed national coordinator is drawn from the senior police ranks. Issues of legislation and law enforcement are also combined in one working group in the Serbian national team, suggesting that most trafficking legislation is perceived to be

Table 4.1. Institutional Framework for Anti-Trafficking Strategies in Serbia and Montenegro

National strategy for combating trafficking	Serbia	Montenegro
Government authority	Ministry of the Interior	Office of the Prime Minister
National coordinator	Police officer of senior rank (part-time)	Prime minister appointee (full-time)
Implementing body	National Team for Combating Trafficking in Human Beings (2001) •National coordinator •Working groups 　—Prevention and education 　—Victim assistance & protection 　—Legislation & law enforcement 　—Child trafficking Council on Human Trafficking (2004)	Interministerial working group (2004) •Deputy Prime Ministers of Interior; Health; Justice; Education and Science; Labor and Social Welfare •Deputy State Prosecutor •Representatives of Council of Europe, OSCE, IOM (observer status) •U.S. consulate (observer status)
Advisory body	Advisory Council (2004) •National coordinator •Ministry of Interior representatives •National team working group chairs •Representatives of OSCE, IOM, and UNICEF	National Anti-Trafficking Project Board (2001) •National coordinator •Ministries of Interior; Education and Science, Labor, and Social Welfare •Governmental Office for Gender Equality •OSCE[1] •IOM, UNICEF, Council of Europe, Save the Children UK; UNHCHR •Local NGOs: Women's Safe House; Montenegrin Women's Lobby; Women's Heart (Roma NGO).
National referral mechanism	Agency of Ministry of Labor, Employment and Social Policy (2003) and OSCE Mission	Ad-hoc basis

Note: [1]The project board was first created and managed by the OSCE in 2001. In 2003 it was incorporated under the Inter-ministerial working group.

the responsibility of law enforcement. In Montenegro, in contrast, labor and social welfare institutions are equally represented in all stages of policymaking, suggesting a more integrated and human security–oriented approach to anti-trafficking. Curiously, however, Montenegro had not transferred these cooperative relations into a formal victim referral mechanism by 2006. In addition, as noted above, transnational actors and local NGOs play a more institutionalized role in Montenegro than in Serbia.

Interviews with key policy actors in both states offer some preliminary insights into why Serbia and Montenegro have created different anti-trafficking policy mechanisms. Montenegro tends to be more open to international influence in all policy areas, in order both to distance itself from Belgrade and to establish its legitimacy as a newly independent state. An exceptional factor is also evident: in a high-profile scandal in 2002, a Moldovan trafficked victim alleged that several high-ranking Montenegrin officials, including the deputy prosecutor, were involved in her trafficking and exploitation.[28] Corruption is rampant in both Serbia and Montenegro, with organized crime penetrating all levels of government. Yet this widely publicized case led to international shaming of the Montenegrin government that might, in turn, explain its willingness to allow more formal involvement of transnational and local actors in all stages of decision-making. Informants also pointed to the role of particular individuals in fashioning strategies. For instance, in Serbia, several high-ranking law enforcement officials took an early lead in placing anti-trafficking on the government agenda, pursuing prosecution and convictions of traffickers, and working with transnational and local NGOs to coordinate assistance. This might point to more bottom-up explanations for the disproportionate role played by law enforcement actors in the Serbian case and the ability of anti-trafficking actors in Serbia to formalize this existing cooperation into a victim referral agency. Given the traditionally highly adversarial relationship of Serbian police with local NGOs and transnational organizations, however, this more cooperative relationship in anti-trafficking efforts is quite exceptional.

Unintended Consequences of Implementing Anti-Trafficking Policies

Since the 2000 Trafficking Protocol and the subsequent drafting of National Action Plans, attention has turned to implementation. Inherent tensions and conflicts are emerging among the four approaches to anti-trafficking strategy: migration, law enforcement, human rights and economic. While transnational actors, working in close cooperation with states, have sought to pursue a coordinated approach that takes into account all four conceptualizations of the problem, in practice, focus on rule of law has often overshadowed human security concerns. The inherent tensions among these approaches can result in unintended consequences in the implementation stage. These unintended effects often, but not always, result in a feedback effect in which the problem might be reconsidered.

Recognizing the need for a more comprehensive and "objective" assessment of trafficking patterns resulted in the creation in 2003 of the RCP, under the auspices of the Stability Pact but led by IOM. The RCP has produced two comprehensive reports to date, one in 2003 and the other in August 2005.[29] The primary data source for both reports is the number of persons assisted in IOM shelters. The 2005 report supplemented this data with information provided from other governmental and nongovernmental sources. From 2000 to 2004, a total of 6,256 trafficked persons were assisted in the Balkans.[30] Concerning how trafficked persons were identified and assisted, the report explains: "Victims were voluntary returned to their countries of origin through assistance programs or identified in their countries of origin upon extradition and subsequently assisted. In addition, victims were identified through police operations and investigations and subsequently referred for assistance."[31] Albanians, Moldovans, and Romanians make up the greatest percentage of trafficked persons assisted *from* the region, together constituting over 75 percent of the overall total. Of the 477 persons assisted from *outside* the region, Ukrainians make up by far the largest number (357 persons, or 75 percent). The 2005 report also documents different forms of trafficking. While the largest percentage of persons is trafficked for purposes of "sexual exploitation" (74 percent), the report also documents trafficking in labor, begging, and children for adoption.

The RCP authors argue that the reports dramatically underestimate the scope of the trafficking trade. Indeed, the RCP report varied significantly from estimates published by IOM headquarters in Geneva in 2001, which claimed that one hundred thousand women are trafficked each year *through* the Balkans to the EU and further destinations and another seventy thousand women are trafficked annually *into* the Balkan region.[32] The RCP authors concede their data-gathering methods cannot account for the large number of women trafficked undetected through the Balkans to the EU and other markets. IOM officials also attribute low figures to victims being misidentified by law enforcement as illegal migrants who are immediately deported. In 2005, the RCP authors announced a new data-gathering clearinghouse based in Vienna, the Nexus Institute to Combat Human Trafficking, which will continue where the RCP left off but expand its data gathering beyond the territorial boundaries of the Balkans and incorporate a wider range of data sources.[33]

Governments, meanwhile, argue that the RCP and assistance agencies like IOM and local NGOs have numerous incentives to exaggerate the scope of trafficking, as their funding and *raison d'etre* depends on identifying human trafficking as a problem of crisis proportions. Law enforcement and government agencies are thus more inclined to accept the declining numbers as an objective assessment of the increasing effectiveness of anti-trafficking efforts.[34] Other critics accept IOM's claim that the RCP reports dramatically underestimate the scope of the trade, but are more inclined to attribute blame to IOM's migration approach to trafficking. For instance, Barbara Limanowska—a prominent independent expert who works closely with UN and OSCE agencies overseeing human rights in the Balkans—argues that the declining numbers of persons who seek assistance in IOM shelters are not attributable to a decreasing demand for assistance or to the difficulties of locating them. Rather, Limanowska argues that trafficked women have become increasingly aware that IOM assistance is conditional on "voluntary repatriation," and in recent years conditional on testifying against traffickers in prosecution cases, and thus in many cases *choose* not to seek IOM assistance. The perspective of trafficked women on the possible shortcomings of migration and law enforcement strategies is rarely considered, however, in formulating anti-trafficking policies.[35]

Law enforcement strategies have become a central focus of anti-trafficking strategies. Efforts to prevent, suppress, and prosecute traffickers have resulted in increased transborder cooperation among law enforcement agencies as well as high-profile operations such as Operation Mirage. The law enforcement approach has resulted in numerous traffickers being apprehended, convicted, and prosecuted. Yet critics argue that this approach has failed to significantly reduce the trade, as traffickers demonstrate great flexibility and ingenuity in eluding police by quickly changing transportation and distribution routes or moving the trade further underground. Critics also argue that the law enforcement approach has resulted in a re-victimization of trafficked persons. They suggest, for example, that operations like Mirage more often result in apprehending and charging women with illegal migration or prostitution than in identifying and assisting trafficked women and their traffickers. Moreover, aggressive policing has the unintended consequence of moving much of the prostitution trade to private apartments, often on the outskirts of cities and towns, where women are further isolated and vulnerable to violent abuse.[36] Helga Konrad, former chair of the SPTF, comments on the declining numbers of victims assisted in shelters: "We believe it's not a good sign, because it shows that the trafficking in human beings is going underground. It shows that the traffickers rapidly react to our responses in the fight against human trafficking. And it shows that the victims are no longer found in bars and brothels. Brothel raids caused traffickers to shift the victims to private locations where, of course, access is more difficult and where it becomes more difficult to provide assistance."[37]

Additionally, because the law enforcement approach rests on convicting and prosecuting *individual* traffickers (a condition of the UN protocol), prosecutors must rely largely on the willingness of victims to testify against their traffickers.[38] Since designated victims of trafficking are granted immunity from illegal migration or prostitution charges, refusing to testify can make them more vulnerable to threats of immediate deportation or prosecution. Moreover, as victim assistance programs, including emergency and short-term shelters, are increasingly being managed and funded by state agencies, assistance can be made conditional on trafficked persons cooperating with the prosecution. If a person does agree to testify, governments are legally required to provide witness protection. Yet in many cases the very same government and law enforcement agencies tasked with providing this protection have been implicated in the trafficking trade, as in the Montenegrin case. In sum, critics argue that when the principal concern of the law enforcement approach is to stop criminals, the interests of their victims become of secondary concern, often leading to their further exploitation.

Re-trafficking has been identified as an increasingly prevalent problem. The 2005 RCP report documents that anywhere from 3 percent to 50 percent of women repatriated from destination countries to their home countries from 2003 to 2005 were re-trafficked within a year. IOM attributes the high rates of re-trafficking to the predatory strategies of recruiters, who target highly vulnerable repatriated persons. Recruiters, unlike traffickers, are often embedded in particular cities and towns and thus are less vulnerable to being apprehended at border crossings or brothel raids. Yet IOM also acknowledges serious gaps in the repatriation and reintegration process, where women are returned home to face poverty, shame, and often abuse without adequate social support.[39] IOM's critics, however, argue that the high rates of re-trafficking raise fundamental questions about the long-term effectiveness of its migration approach to anti-trafficking, which makes repatriation and preventing illegal migration its central aim. Local and transnational networks of NGOs have taken the lead in addressing the re-trafficking issue, creating assistance and referral networks that track women being repatriated to their home countries. While informal monitoring and referral networks can provide some short-term assistance to repatriated women, advocates of an economic approach to anti-trafficking argue that the ongoing cycle of trafficking illuminates the underlying structural or economic nature of the problem. As the EU fortifies its borders against the migrant and crime-exporting states to its south and east and funds increased law enforcement initiatives in bordering regions like the Balkans, traffickers continue to profit from the limitless supply of unemployed and dislocated persons who become trapped in the trafficking cycle.

Shifting Focus on Trafficking

Anti-trafficking policies in which transnational actors are directly involved in development, diffusion, and implementation exemplify the growing prevalence of transnational policies in the Balkans. Like other transnational policies, anti-trafficking policies in the Balkans to date have been largely top-down. Ongoing conflicts among different actors over the framing and pursuit of different strategies point to the need to investigate sites of conflict and consensus in emerging transnational policy areas. Law-enforcement and migration approaches to combating trafficking currently dominate anti-trafficking strategies. Yet critics argue that this focus obscures structural factors underlying this trade and can also have the unintended effect of exacerbating the vulnerability and exploitation of trafficked persons.

A shift in focus may create more dynamic and effective transnational anti-trafficking policy. Including a wide range of relevant actors can make transnational anti-trafficking policy less unidirectional. For instance, creating mechanisms through which trafficked persons can be given a direct voice in policymaking can help overcome potential conflicts of interest when service providers—whether local NGOs, governments, or transnational actors—have incentives to interpret their firsthand accounts to further a particular agenda. Such mechanisms could help to resolve the dispute between IOM, which claims that declining shelter numbers can be attributed to law enforcement policies, and its critics, who argue that IOM's migration approach is to blame. In addition, the increasing awareness of re-trafficking highlights the limitations of policing, whether of borders or sex work, and turns our attention toward the underlying economic and social causes of trafficking. Easing strict visa regimes or granting extended or even permanent resident status to trafficked persons are two immediate solutions to reduce re-trafficking.[40] The EU might also rethink the accession model for the Western Balkans as it now stands, which stresses legal harmonization above, and often at the expense of, more development-oriented priorities. The process could also be more reciprocal, so that states meeting conditions on combating crime and corruption are offered rewards in return. Liberalizing trade, especially in highly protected sectors such as agriculture and textiles, providing substantial physical and social infrastructure assistance, and easing visa restrictions are some concrete ways in which the EU—as an increasingly central actor in the Balkans—can help ease some of the underlying factors that contribute to trafficking.

5

PEACEKEEPING AND RULE BREAKING

United Nations Anti-Trafficing Policy in Bosnia and Herzegovina

MARTINA E. VANDENBERG

A March 2005 report released jointly by the Organization for Security and Cooperation in Europe (OSCE), the UN Office of the High Commissioner for Human Rights (UNOHCHR), and UNICEF analyzed two mutually exclusive hypotheses on trafficking into the Western Balkans. Statistics gathered by border police, governments, police anti-trafficking units, and shelters indicated that trafficking to the region had plummeted in recent years. Nongovernmental organization leaders and some experts within the United Nations countered that human trafficking had not declined. Instead, they argued, trafficking had shifted its guise and moved underground.[1]

If the nongovernmental experts were correct, human trafficking in the Western Balkans had come full circle. In early 1998, human trafficking to Bosnia and Herzegovina did not officially exist. Trafficking inhabited an invisible netherworld—unacknowledged, unreported, and unnamed. Cases of trafficking in 1998 seemed as rare as those reported in official police documents in 2003.[2] These competing interpretations of the facts raise provocative questions. Do the largely empty trafficking shelters in 2003 and 2004 signify the success of regional anti-trafficking policies, rather than the increased sophistication of traffickers? Or did the international community fail trafficking victims in the Balkans, inadvertently undermining the rule of law and imposing an ineffective criminalization model?

This chapter critically examines the history of trafficking into the Western Balkans, focusing on the case of Bosnia and Herzegovina. Based on field work conducted in the Balkans for Human Rights Watch in 1998, 1999, and 2001; additional field work conducted in 2006; and on documents obtained through Freedom of Information Act (FOIA) requests, I analyze the initial responses to trafficking in the region and the evolution of anti-trafficking policy and approaches.[3] Human trafficking is situated firmly in the context in which it flourished in this region: international peacekeeping operations.

The Status of International Peacekeepers in the Balkans

The United Nations Department of Peacekeeping Operations (DPKO) has only recently acknowledged the stain that allegations of peacekeeper involvement in trafficking in persons have left on United Nations missions around the globe. A December 2004 DPKO publication stated, "Peacekeepers' use of trafficking victims for sexual and other services has been a source of major embarrassment and political damage to UN PKOs [peacekeeping operations]. Despite the fact that PKO involvement is usually not widespread, the political and moral stigma attached to this behavior can taint entire missions."[4] Similarly, in December 2006, UN Secretary General Kofi Annan reiterated his "zero tolerance" policy toward sexual exploitation and abuse by peacekeepers, admitting that UN personnel had committed crimes including "rape, pedophilia, and human trafficking" in missions around the world.[5]

In Bosnia and Herzegovina, allegations that "peacekeepers" had engaged in trafficking prompted international outrage. But the catch-all term "peacekeeper" glossed over the highly complicated mosaic of international military and civilian personnel deployed in conflict and post-conflict zones. The ranks of peacekeepers in Bosnia and Herzegovina, loosely defined, included United Nations civilian personnel, military troops,[6] contractors accompanying military forces, and international civilian police officers. The relevant status of forces agreements in Bosnia and Herzegovina provided each category of peacekeeping personnel with varying levels of immunity from prosecution for crimes committed while serving in these post-conflict zones. Under the terms of the Dayton Agreement, United Nations International Police Task Force officers serving in Bosnia and Herzegovina enjoyed complete immunity—akin to diplomatic immunity—from prosecution, as outlined in the 1946 Convention on the Privileges and Immunities of the United Nations.[7] NATO military and civilian personnel, in contrast, retained only functional immunity, as defined by the provisions of the Convention on the Privileges and Immunities of the United Nations relating to experts on missions. On a practical level, the immunity afforded to members of the peacekeeping community had profound implications when allegations of peacekeeper involvement in trafficking in persons for forced prostitution into the region emerged. In the eyes of the local population, the media, and human rights organizations documenting trafficking, immunity translated into impunity.

Differences in legal status merely echoed the vast differences between these various communities in terms of mobility and contact with the local population. While concerns about protecting the forces kept military service members largely confined to their bases in the Balkans,[8] other groups such as U.S. Department of Defense contractors rented apartments in local communities, traveled in civilian vehicles, and faced few restrictions on their freedom of movement. Similarly, United Nations International Police Task Force officers lived in local housing and circulated freely in the communities where they found themselves stationed. While most of these individuals served honorably, a handful engaged in criminal activities, including trafficking-related crimes. Such cases have critical implications for these peacekeeping missions and rule of law in the region.

Post-Conflict Bosnia and Herzegovina

Soon after the conclusion of the Dayton Agreement, some sixty thousand peacekeepers, as well as thousands of UN personnel, international organization staff members, and civilian and military contractors flooded into Bosnia and Herzegovina.[9] Flush with deutsche marks, the currency of choice, this influx of internationals immediately set down roots, renting apartments, hiring staff, and setting up offices and bases. With the infusion of cash came a rush of local entrepreneurship.[10] Indeed, would-be businesspeople hoping to peddle goods—legal and illegal—to the newly-arrived "international community" viewed the entry of NATO-led forces as a boon. Not only did the soldiers and civilians generate demand, the funds they released into the economy through salaries and purchases increased local demand for goods and services, including prostitution.[11] A flood of trafficked women and girls, brought to Bosnia and Herzegovina for the purpose of forced prostitution, soon followed.

The U.S. military, adopting the Wilsonian open trade model as a reconciliation tool, created the Arizona Market in 1996 as a gathering place for Serbs, Croats, and Bosniacs to buy and sell goods.[12] It worked, but the market soon became a hub for the trafficking of women, as well as the sale of washing machines, soap powder, stolen goods, and pirated CDs. Mara Radovanovic, director of Lara, a women's rights organization in Bijeljina, Republika Srpska, reported in 2001 that traffickers purchased women and their passports in the Arizona Market, as well as in several other "inter-entity" markets such as "Virginia," near Kalesija and the bar "Black Spider" in Orasje.[13]

According to Radovanovic, trafficked women—many from Russia, Moldova, Romania, and Ukraine—most often entered Bosnia and Herzegovina illegally, by car or boat. The traffickers simply bribed any border guards they confronted on the way.[14] By July 2000, official police reports indicated that 309 foreign "dancers" had found employment at forty-eight nightclubs in Republika Srpska alone.[15] Each of these women registered with the foreigners' department of the local police; in many cases the police kept the women's passports at the station.[16] As trafficking emerged, opportunities for corruption burgeoned.

Despite the ever-swelling numbers, trafficking remained largely invisible. In an interview with the OSCE human rights officer based in Bijeljina in 1998, researchers asked about the existence of brothels in Republika Srpska. The officer knew of multiple brothels, all full of foreign women. Similarly, researchers met with a group of young U.S. soldiers based in Republika Srpska as Joint Commission Observers (JCOs). The soldiers rattled off a long list of brothels located in Bijeljina, also full of "Russian women." One of the soldiers confided that the women could not leave the brothel, a fact he had learned after inviting the women to a party at the soldiers' rented house. Neither the human rights officer nor the soldiers called the situations that they observed "trafficking." The OSCE human rights officer had never included any information on trafficking in the weekly human rights status reports he submitted to headquarters in Sarajevo. The soldiers continued to visit the nightclubs in order to "collect intelligence," having found that local mafia figures and local leaders spent time at these establishments. While the military's nonfraternization rules purportedly prevented the soldiers from having sex with the prostitutes, their interpreter, a U.S. civilian contractor, admitted that he had purchased sexual services from the nightclubs.[17]

These anecdotes merely highlighted the prevailing trend in the international community's anti-trafficking approaches in post-conflict Bosnia and Herzegovina at the time: willful blindness. Trafficking remained largely invisible until reports began to emerge in the local press, particularly in *Dani*. Dzenana Karup Drusko, a local journalist with excellent local police contacts, began writing articles about trafficking of women from Russia, Ukraine, and Moldova into forced prostitution. Her articles documented cases in which trafficked women escaped the nightclubs, only to be prosecuted by local authorities for their status as undocumented migrants in Bosnia and Herzegovina or for engaging in illegal employment.[18] Madeleine Rees, director of UNOHCHR in Sarajevo, began monitoring the sporadic reports of cases that emerged around the country and translating local press reports.[19] Additionally, NGOs began attempting to provide services for victims, including emergency shelter.

For the vast majority of women and girls trafficked into Bosnia and Herzegovina, however, the increased attention to trafficking made little difference. Real and perceived corruption among local police officers, combined with the presence of internationals in the clubs, convinced some trafficking victims that escape would be futile. Because local police officers were moonlighting as guards at local brothels, receiving free sex from trafficked women held in those brothels, and collecting bribes, women had little faith that they could expect assistance from the police. As some U.S. Department of Defense contractors purchased women from brothel owners as chattel,[20] along with their passports, the perception of complicity of the international community took root.

As public attention increased and more cases emerged, trafficking finally became visible in early 1999.[21] In fact, by early 2000, human trafficking for forced prostitution had become blatant and notorious. But this visibility did not result in coherent anti-trafficking policies. Instead, for the next two years, the international community adopted an ad hoc approach, one that depended largely on international staff members in the field to identify and care for trafficked women. United Nations International Police Task Force (IPTF) officers now kept records on trafficking cases and attempted to accompany local police on brothel raids. Women identified as trafficking victims, however, generally faced criminal charges, imprisonment, fines, and "deportation" across the inter-entity boundary line (IEBL).[22] While members of the UNOHCHR often tried to intervene to have the women released from prison, their efforts did not always succeed.[23] Local Bosnian government officials continued to treat trafficking victims without proper immigration documents as illegal migrants, as criminals, or both.

During one brothel raid conducted in March 1999, local police and IPTF officers jointly identified four potential trafficking victims, but no one on the police teams spoke Russian, Ukrainian, or Romanian, the languages of the women found.[24] The women, one of whom believed that she was pregnant, requested assistance in returning to their countries of origin. The logistical tangle that ensued, however, only highlighted the lack of coherent policy. The women spent the night in a local police station without an interpreter or assistance from nongovernmental organization representatives. Although the women eventually returned to their countries of origin, they did not receive any victim assistance or remedy for the harm that they had suffered in Bosnia. As one of the first repatriations handled by the international community, the episode exposed the need for additional resources. Fearing for the women's safety, UNO-HCHR had previously requested Stabilisation Force (SFOR) escorts for the trafficking victims. SFOR refused.[25]

In the absence of anti-trafficking policy, some IPTF officers resorted to purchasing women under the guise of "rescuing" them.[26] The attempted "rescues" pointed to a fact perfectly obvious to local Bosnians. IPTF officers frequented the brothels, and, in some cases, used the services of the trafficked women.[27] The presence of internationals, particularly international police officers, in the brothels undermined the credibility of the United Nations Mission in Bosnia and Herzegovina (UNMIBH). The ad hoc purchases of women by international police from brothels only increased the local perception that the internationals could operate outside of the law. Indeed, since no one interviewed the women at the center of these purchases, it could not be known whether the women had received their freedom or simply traded one "owner" for another. In an interview in 1999, a local translator, forced to accompany his foreign bosses to brothels to interpret, expressed his disgust at the illegal activities he witnessed at the clubs.[28] The presence of members of the international community in the venues of the gray economy did not pass unnoticed.[29]

Ad hocism permeated the entire UNMIBH approach to trafficking. In guidance issued to IPTF officers in September 2000, UNMIBH instructed officers to bring trafficking victims requesting voluntary repatriation to Sarajevo by 6:00 p.m. If victims could not be transported by that time, they were to be housed in a "safe location." The memo, which enumerated local police stations, IPTF stations, and hotels as permissible "safe locations" stated, "Any expenses incurred in housing the individual in a safe location may be reimbursed if funds donated by the International

Community are available."[30] Funds were never available. This continued well into 2001, even after the International Organization for Migration had created a shelter in Sarajevo. As one IPTF officer told researchers: "We deal with the victims, and I try to help them. We dip into our own pockets. We kept them here [in the IPTF station] for a little while. . . . We feed them, get them coffee, and get them cigarettes. . . . The UN gives us no funds and no money to take care of them...We have to dip into our own pockets or show them the street. We make it possible for the UN to do nothing."[31] Similarly, in a 1999 case, two Romanian trafficking victims appeared at a local IPTF station in Brcko. A small group of IPTF officers, unable to house the women, chipped in personal funds to send the two women home by bus. After their departure, allegations of local police involvement in the brothel where they had been held could not be adequately investigated, as there were no witnesses.[32]

The absence of policy, combined with blanket immunity, created an atmosphere of impunity for international personnel. While most UN-MIBH and international organization staff members served with honor, allegations emerged, including in the *Washington Post*, that some IPTF officers had engaged in sexual misconduct, including trafficking-related offenses.[33] Critics suggested that the United Nations never properly investigated the allegations, instead sending all those involved home quietly.[34]

Allegations that the United Nations had covered up IPTF involvement in trafficking had emerged in the local Bosnian press long before the international press corps began to publish articles. In November 2000, Czech SFOR officers, together with IPTF officers based in Prijedor, raided three brothels owned by Milorad Milakovic and his family. The raids resulted in the release of thirty-four women and girls who claimed that they had been trafficked into Bosnia for forced prostitution. Milakovic retaliated with protests and public statements accusing one U.S. IPTF officer of conducting the illegal raids after Milakovic refused to pay him a bribe.[35] Milakovic's protests and those of his fellow bar owners attracted national press attention. Members of the bar owners' association gathered to hold a press conference after the raids wearing "SFOR Go Home" T-shirts.

The episode became an attack on the international community, which Milakovic portrayed as both corrupt and complicit. Local press coverage featured explicit photographs of men, supposedly American military and police, cavorting with nude women in the nightclubs. Whether or not these photos were legitimate, the incident further damaged the credibility of the UN mission with the local population. The IPTF officers, officially accused of improperly raiding the brothel, returned home quietly with little fanfare. Thirty-three of the thirty-seven women freed in the November raid claimed that they had been trafficked for forced prostitution.[36] Several provided testimony to UNMIBH internal affairs officers that the UN police officers who conducted the raids and drove them to Sarajevo had been their clients. Although at least one of the IPTF officers, a Spaniard, appeared to have engaged in witness tampering (by telling one of the victims not to speak of their sexual contact); none of the officers implicated in the women's accounts faced criminal charges upon their return to their countries of origin.[37] The United Nations internal investigation, conducted after the officers had already returned to their countries of origin, was thin at best.

Yet even a robust UN internal investigation would not have provided accountability, at least in the case of the U.S. officers. Indeed, prosecution of the three U.S. IPTF officers repatriated after the incident was a legal impossibility due to a gap in U.S. extraterritorial jurisdiction.[38] In an internal memorandum sent to the Secretary of State on December 10, 2001, State Department officials reported:

> One of the officers confessed that he had engaged the services of at least one of the trafficked women and implicated the other five [accused IPTF officers]. One of the Americans made a confession to another IPTF officer but later recanted it. We believe that these accusations played a role, probably the primary role, in the IPTF Commissioner's decision to seek [the] resignations [of the IPTF officers]. We do not believe that the uncorroborated allegations by one of the nightclub owners that he was asked to pay bribes and supply women to one of the Americans involved were a factor.

The memorandum also recounted an unrelated case involving a U.S. IPTF officer fired from the mission. The summary stated:

> In a fairly clear-cut case, an American officer was fired after he admitted that he had "bought out the contract" of a 19-year-old woman trafficked from Russia with whom he co-habitated for six months. This officer also admitted bringing sensitive documents about forthcoming IPTF raids to his residence, where this woman may have had access to them.[39]

This fundamental lack of accountability was even more pronounced among the U.S. officers, in large part because the United States has nearly eighteen thousand separate police forces scattered throughout the country. Due to this lack of central control over police officers serving as U.S. contractors abroad in the UN mission in Bosnia, few officers faced any professional repercussions for the purchase of human beings and engagement in trafficking-related activities. This lack of accountability did not only apply to U.S. police officers. In June 2002, U.S. State Department officials reported that the acting head of the Civilian Policing Unit of the UN Department of Peacekeeping Operations in New York admitted that some UN police officers suspected of illegal activities in one mission nevertheless had been deployed to other peacekeeping missions around the world.[40]

In contrast with the complete lack of accountability for internationals suspected of involvement in trafficking, infrequent law enforcement anti-trafficking actions undertaken by the Bosnian government resulted in the detention, incarceration, and deportation of trafficked women. According to the U.S. Department of State, "Trafficked women are routinely charged with offenses including prostitution and illegal residency." On the rare occasions when trafficking prosecutions occurred in the courts, "trafficking victims and witnesses [faced threats] to prevent their testimony."[41]

This pervasive ad hocism also served to render trafficking a vehicle for other agendas. European governments, convinced that Bosnia and Herzegovina served as a transit country for human trafficking and smuggling into Western Europe, reacted by pouring funds into border control. Trafficking experts criticized the efforts to secure the external borders, undertaken in earnest in late 2000, as a further step in the direction of "Fortress Europe."[42] Instead of dealing with the root causes of trafficking or providing significant support for victims of trafficking in Bosnia and Herzegovina, countries of destination shored up their borders, apparently fearing a flood of refugees and economic migrants. While some of these fears seemed to some extent legitimate—for example, the fear that Bosnia and Herzegovina had become a transit country for thousands of migrants decamped near Tuzla—the use of trafficking as a political fig leaf angered some in the anti-trafficking NGO community.[43] According to one Department of State cable, twenty-five thousand aliens (mostly from Turkey, China, Sri Lanka, and Iran) transited through Bosnia and Herzegovina en route to Western Europe between June 2000 and December 2001. While a significant market for trafficked females existed in Bosnia and Herzegovina, only a slender body of evidence indicated that traffickers used the country as a gateway for transfer to Western Europe. A December 2001 State Department cable concluded, "Bosnia is an increasingly significant transit point for economic migrants en route to the West and *a major destination for trafficked women*. According to credible local and international estimates, as many as 10,000 foreign nationals—overwhelmingly young women —have been trafficked to or through Bosnia for voluntary or involuntary employment in the sex trade."[44] Only one recent study pointed to the use of Bosnia as a transit country for trafficking victims.[45] Indeed, in 2003 and 2004, the vast majority of trafficking victims interviewed in Bosnia and Herzegovina knew that the country would be their final destination. Compared to destinations such as Serbia, Montenegro, and Kosovo, the women viewed Bosnia as an "acceptable" country of destination.[46]

Reeling from negative publicity alleging UNMIBH complicity in trafficking, the Special Representative to the Secretary General, Jacques Paul Klein, introduced new personnel and new policies. In July 2001, he announced the creation of a specialized anti-trafficking unit within the UN IPTF, known as STOP, the Special Trafficking Operations Program. STOP

operated in great secrecy, completely independent of local Bosnian authorities. Their strategy of disrupting the operation of the brothels met
with harsh criticism. As one commentator wrote, "[T]he STOP teams
typically smashed down the door of a brothel, entered with great flour-
ish (on occasion, with television cameras in tow), and then asked if the
females present had been trafficked."[47] UNMIBH faced some embarrassment when a spokeswoman admitted that one of the STOP team leaders,
a local police officer, would be de-authorized (fired) for allegations relating to trafficking.[48] By the end of the United Nations mission in 2002, this
law enforcement approach had fallen from favor. According to local NGO
and international experts, the aggressive policing model, while garnering
excellent press reports for Special Representative Klein, drove trafficking
underground, with most young girls and foreign trafficking victims now
housed in apartments.[49] According to Barbara Limanowska, the raids also
bordered on farce, as the teams raided the same bars and interviewed the
same women week in and week out.[50] A UN Department of Peacekeeping Operations (DPKO) training manual issued in 2004 concluded that
the STOP model should not be replicated in other missions.[51] Specifically,
the DPKO manual faulted the STOP program for working in isolation;
failing to integrate criminal justice, legislative reform, and victim support
programs; overly aggressive raids; and the lack of capacity building for
local counterparts.[52]

The Role of Corruption and Victim Protection

In spite of coordination meetings, high-level conferences, and joint task
forces, cooperation on anti-trafficking policy between the Bosnian government and UNMIBH officials progressed only in fits and starts. What
cooperation UNMIBH and government officials achieved at the national
level seemed to evaporate outside of Sarajevo. Corruption charges
against local police officers continued to emerge throughout this period.
In one case, two police officers who allegedly received bribes to regularize papers for trafficking victims purchased by U.S. military contractors
in Tuzla joined the Bosnian government's contingent of UN police officers serving in East Timor.[53] Allegations of involvement in trafficking

flowed in both directions, and local Bosnian prosecutors chafed under the Dayton-imposed immunity for contractors and IPTF personnel that prevented prosecutions in Bosnia and Herzegovina.[54]

In addition to the security implications of involvement in trafficking,[55] corruption provided a backdrop to the ongoing dilemma of victim protection. If local police were involved in trafficking, how could they be trusted to transport women from city to city, shelter to shelter? Similarly, if IPTF officers purchased women from brothels or paid owners to use the sexual services of trafficking victims, how could the women trust them to provide protection and escort?[56] These two underlying questions highlighted an obvious conundrum. Much of the international community measured policy success in terms of trafficking indictments and prosecutions. In order to secure those outcomes, trafficking victims had to testify before an investigative judge, and potentially at a full trial. Traffickers and brothel owners often forced the women to provide free services for police officers, and reminding them that the police officers would protect the traffickers, not their victims.

The criminal enforcement approach adopted by UNMIBH over the course of the mission only exacerbated the corruption dilemma. The approach did not take the victims' needs or human rights into account. Nor did the approach incorporate an understanding of human security. Instead, international police officers interrogated the women for hours following a raid. The goal of the interviews, according to IPTF human rights officers, was to determine whether or not each one of the women qualified as a trafficking victim. But before changes to the trafficking victim identification criteria made in late 2001, women who admitted to voluntarily entering the sex industry (but had suffered the same abuses) were automatically excluded from services offered to "trafficking victims."[57]

Madeleine Rees, other staff at UNOHCHR, workers at local NGOs, and other experts eventually prevailed in creating a far more humane and victim-centered interview process. Instead of immediately meeting with police, trafficking victims received a short period of rest and time for reflection in shelters. Shelters offered broader psychological and medical services.[58] Additionally, in at least one case, the International Organization for Migration director succeeded in arranging for third-country re-settlement for a trafficking victim with credible fear of retaliation.[59]

Failure and Reform

Whether one ascribes to the "trafficking has declined" theory or the "trafficking has gone underground" hypothesis, there is now general agreement that the model that ultimately evolved in Bosnia and Herzegovina failed to protect the human rights of trafficking victims adequately. The law enforcement–centered approach, applied in a region suffering from widespread corruption, failed to generate the large numbers of prosecutions that proponents had hoped to achieve. Similarly, the internationally sponsored anti-migration approach did little to combat the root causes of trafficking and may have exacerbated conditions for individual trafficking victims. As a rule, the expansion of border controls not only makes it more necessary for would-be migrants to turn to traffickers, but it also increases the cost of transportation, driving up the trafficking victims' level of indebtedness.

At a fundamental level, the model implemented in Bosnia and Herzegovina failed to ensure accountability. Internationals accused of involvement in trafficking-related activities enjoyed impunity. Similarly, corrupt local officials managed to evade prosecution in most cases.

Inexplicably, trafficking caught the United Nations completely unprepared and flat-footed in Bosnia and Herzegovina. Without a game plan or strategy, the UNMIBH officials appeared to make up policy as they went along. Where they ultimately arrived—a law enforcement approach with little involvement by civil society—both undermined the rule of law and left a lasting legacy of distrust.

Ironically, a decline in the number of trafficking victims transported into Bosnia and Herzegovina may have less to do with the anti-trafficking strategies adopted by the local and international authorities and much more to do with the withdrawal of international forces and personnel from the country altogether. As of January 2006, the European Union Police Mission, which replaced the UN International Police Task Force in January 2003, included only 198 international personnel.[60] Similarly, the European Union Force in Bosnia and Herzegovina (EUFOR), which took over from SFOR in December 2004, includes only 6,300 troops.[61] Unlike the U.S. forces, EUFOR relies to a far lesser extent on contractors. These factors all result in a significantly diminished international presence in Bosnia and Herzegovina, leading to the inevitable conclusion that the traffickers will again follow the market and move their trafficking hub to another destination with a significant military presence. As the United States prepares to redeploy some 70,000 troops from Western Europe, Romania has concluded an agreement with the U.S. government permitting the use of Romanian bases for U.S. forces.[62] As Romania prepares for the arrival of U.S. troops and contractors, the country should also develop a strategy for the arrival of trafficking victims.

As for the United Nations, the seed of such a strategy has only just started to emerge. One might have hoped that the trafficking scandals in Bosnia and Herzegovina led to extensive reform and effective prevention of similar abuses in other missions. That hope would be in vain. Despite the United Nations' much-ballyhooed zero tolerance for sexual exploitation, extensive allegations of child prostitution, rape, and sexual abuse by UN peacekeepers in Liberia, the Democratic Republic of the Congo, and Haiti erupted in 2005 and 2006.[63] Moreover, the implementation of the recommendations outlined in an extensive report by the Secretary General's Special Adviser on Sexual Exploitation and Abuse by United Nations Peacekeeping Personnel in 2005 remains very much a work in progress.[64] Yet there is room for some optimism. In mid-2006, a UN group of legal experts issued a report on the accountability of UN staff and experts on missions, along with a draft convention on the criminal accountability of United Nations personnel.[65]

The key lesson from Bosnia and Herzegovina is that as long as there is impunity, the abuse will continue.

6

HUMAN TRAFFICKING AND DEMOCRATIC TRANSITION IN ALBANIA

VASILIKA HYSI

Albania's transition from dictatorship to a pluralistic system of government has been fraught with challenges—chief among them the emergence of a powerful human trafficking industry. Albania has been an origin, transit, and destination country for the trafficking of women and children for many years.[1] The constant presence of poverty, unemployment, low levels of education within families, an absence of reliable information about trafficking, and meager support from state and social institutions has fostered an environment in which Albanian women and children become easy prey for Albanian criminal gangs. The lucrative trafficking of Albanians, as well as foreigners, has been facilitated by the erosion of social controls in society and the chronic weakness of the state. The government has proved incapable of projecting its authority to fight crime, protect crime victims, control its borders, and curtail corruption among its security forces. The issue of human trafficking reveals that the most important rights of Albanian citizens, such as the right to life and recompense in cases of victimization, have been seriously violated.

Socioeconomic and political changes during the 1990s heightened the risks of being trafficked for portions of Albanian society and facilitated the transition of criminal elements into the trafficking of Albanians and foreigners alike. The legal and institutional reforms adopted by the Albanian government to address human trafficking combined law enforcement and public awareness measures, but these efforts have been belated at best and have lacked the resources necessary for an efficient response.

Women, Society, and Human Trafficking in Albania

Albanian law, from its early origins in unwritten law and the Code (Kanun), has addressed the role of women and their position in family and society. Though the Albanian woman was once considered the property of and subject to her husband, and was responsible for the care of the children and house, the Code also identified rules that punished violations of a woman's honor and dignity. The husband was compelled to protect his wife not only from the sexual harassment of other men but also from offense and violence.[2] Violation of a woman's honor was punished in early history with the murder of the culprit and in later periods with exile or forgiveness through reconciliation.[3]

After World War II, the traditional role and position of women changed in Albanian society. Instead of the humble domestic of earlier historical periods, the Albanian woman came to represent someone who was at the service of the country through her contribution in various fields of life. Such service strengthened her position in the family and society.[4] Under Albania's authoritarian system, the modern trafficking phenomenon and sexual exploitation for prostitution did not exist. Prostitution and bordellos were present in urban areas, but rather than facilitating trafficking they offered material benefit and work mainly for girls that had run away from their families.[5] Family violence existed, but for the sake of preserving the family and avoiding problems for other members of the family, women tried to keep the issue within the walls of the house.

Prostitution and trafficking of women for sexual exploitation sur-

faced as challenges to Albania in the 1990s. The country was just emerging from a long period of isolation and was extremely poor and eager for
development, welfare, and money. However, Albania also was unprepared
to face the rise of savage and new forms of criminality. In urban and rural
areas throughout the country, traffickers bought and sold young girls and
women as if they were commodities. Albania became an origin and transit point for trafficking into the lucrative markets of Western Europe.

Many of those trafficked were exploited in motels, hotels, and apartments in various Albanian cities. Because of the country's location—
situated between the countries of the Former Yugoslavia and Western
Europe, and especially next to Italy and Greece—local and regional criminal gangs increasingly used Albania as a transit point. Traffickers moved
women from Eastern European countries such as Bulgaria, Moldova, and
Romania through Albania into Western Europe. Towns such as Vlora,
Durrësi, and Shengjini became gateways as traffickers took advantage
of the short distance between the Albanian and Italian coasts. Albanian
criminal groups collaborated with Italian and other groups in the region,
buying and selling girls and women multiple times to evade police and to
reach more lucrative markets in Italy and Greece. Collaboration between
criminal groups facilitated networks for transportation, acquisition of
fraudulent visas and passports, and employment.[6]

In the mid-1990s, however, few in Albania believed that the warnings
of a rise in human trafficking were real.[7] The absence of legal provisions
and, in turn, official statistics on trafficking inhibited recognition of the
problem. In 1995, legislators added penalties for prostitution and operation of facilities for prostitution to the Criminal Code of the Republic
of Albania, but did not include a definition of trafficking. Amendments
in 2001, however, began to bring Albanian law in line with the UN Protocol to Prevent, Suppress and Punish Trafficking in Persons, Especially
Women and Children (Trafficking Protocol), and subsequent steps in
2004 furthered that process. In 2001, the Albanian Council of Ministers
reported that approximately 100,000 Albanian women and girls had been
trafficked abroad during the 1990s, and official police statistics noted over
18,200 persons rescued from trafficking in 2000 and 2001 alone.[8]

Albania's role in trafficking appears easy to attribute to the difficult political and economic transition from an authoritarian to a pluralistic system. Other factors than changes to the system of governance, however, facilitated the rise of trafficking in Albania. After a period of extreme isolation, Albanians could move freely in and out of the country. Dreams of better lives, jobs, and education for their children were overwhelming for many Albanians. Others sought reunification with family members that had already migrated to Western countries. By 1991 and 2002, for example, an estimated 25 percent of Albania's population had emigrated, mainly to Italy and Greece.[9] Tight immigration regulations of European Union and other destination countries limited access to visas and thus increased patterns of illegal migration and the potential for these migrants to become victims of criminal groups. While some Albanians traveled on ferries, most of the time they boarded overcrowded vessels known as *death ships* to reach Italy and Greece. Others journeyed days and nights through the mountains to get to Greece. Many became victims of fatigue and of police violence against illegal immigrants.

Economic conditions also contributed to the rise in trafficking. In the mid-1990s, many Albanians fell prey to widespread financial fraud perpetrated by pyramid schemes. Initially seen as a source of profit and well being, the prospect of lucrative financial returns from investment in pyramid companies created a mass euphoria. Albanians sold their houses and other properties to generate investment funds. When the pyramid companies collapsed in 1997, however, a state of anarchy followed. For some Albanians who had lost property, human trafficking, and particularly the exploitation of women, became a way of re-accumulating the wealth they lost. For others, trafficking was considered as a solution to end their poverty and suffering.

Changing economic conditions in Albania were not limited to the impact of pyramid schemes. The economic costs of the country's transition away from dictatorship were extensive and had their greatest impact in rural areas and small towns. Negative growth in the country's gross domestic product and high levels of inflation contributed to conditions of poverty.[10] According to a Living Condition Survey (LCS) carried out in 1998, approximately 29 percent of Albanians were poor, and half of Albanians lived in extreme poverty. Poverty levels were six times higher in rural than urban areas.[11] Increasing unemployment and rural to urban migration—trends linked in part to patterns of privatization and the rise of the market economy—increased pressure on Albanian families. From 1995 to 1999, official unemployment increased from 12.9 to 18.3 percent, with unofficial rates believed to be much higher.[12] Women faced the greatest impact of unemployment as well as the additional burden of maintaining their families as their spouses sought employment through emigration. Under such circumstances, women and children became increasingly vulnerable. These factors emerged as a common theme in studies and interviews of victims repatriated from situations of trafficking and especially for women who turned to prostitution with the intent of only doing so temporarily. Although the trafficking of women and children are in many ways similar, the two differ in patterns of recruitment and exploitation.

While political and socioeconomic factors contributed to the rise in trafficking of Albanian women and young girls for sexual exploitation, geography and the slow response of the government to organized crime facilitated Albania's rise by the mid-1990s as a transit country for foreign women. The diversification of Albanian networks into the handling of foreign women further reflected growing threats of retaliation against traffickers from the relatives of exploited Albanian women and young girls. In this context, Albanian criminals increased their preference for dealing with girls imported from Bulgaria, Moldova, Romania, Russia, and Poland.

Albanian traffickers turned to various routes in the 1990s, including movement through Montenegro to final destinations of Italy and Greece. By 2002, the main trafficking routes were by sea to Italy. As border controls increased along the Italian coast, traffickers turned to passage overland into Greece. By 2004, the route of choice began in Gjirokastra in southern Albania, and continued on to Kakavija on the Albania-Greece border before finally moving into Greece, Italy, and other Western European countries.[13] Along these routes, cooperation among criminal groups and corrupt government authorities included the provision of visas, border crossings, transportation, and reception. Such cooperation helps to explain the trafficking of Moldovan and Romanian girls through Serbia and Montenegro into Albania and, in turn, into Italy and Greece (as well as the trafficking of Albanian girls into Kosovo).[14] Although maritime border security and control have recently been increased, the land borders with Montenegro, Greece, and Kosovo remain less secure and open to irregular migration.

During the transition from dictatorship, Albania was not only a transit country for the trafficking of human beings, but also a source country. Trafficking of Albanian women and young girls was, and continues to be, widespread. As small Albanian industrial towns built during the socialist years started to fail economically, the hope and the security of their citizens for employment and normal living standards also eroded. The prospect of migration to Western Europe offered hope even though many families had no access to information about the social position or sources of living for those who had already emigrated. In some cases, parents without hope for the future of their daughters pushed strongly for them to marry émigré Albanian young men. These factors contributed to a growing vulnerability of women and girls to the recruiting tactics of human traffickers.

Trafficked Albanian women and girls come from all across the country, from north to south and from urban and rural areas.[15] According to a study by the Women in Development Association, cities like Vlora, Berat, Fieri, Lushnja, Elbasani, and Korca have the highest rate of victims; towns like Puka, Lezha, and Skrapari also are involved though not as extensively as the southern cities. Tirana, the capital of Albania, is the center of money laundering and the residence of the trafficking bosses, while port cities like Vlora, Durres, and Shkodra are hot spots where the traffickers have established temporary accommodation and transportation facilities.[16]

Studies like this one reveal that criminal groups have used various methods to draw women and young girls into trafficking networks. The methods include deception and promises of marriage, a job, or a better life. In some cases, traffickers used force and kidnapping.[17] Once deceived into trafficking situations, some young girls are compelled by violence to engage in prostitution. Others turn to prostitution in Albania or abroad for economic reasons. Families, in ways contrary to Albanian custom, also play a role in the trafficking process. Women and young girls, mainly from rural areas, become involved in trafficking through the influence of family members including their parents or spouses. Studies reveal the role of so-called fiancés or uncles who act as go-betweens in finding husbands. Limited awareness of trafficking methods and the erosion of traditional value systems facilitate this process. Women and young girls are seen as a source of income, without consideration of the consequences of their being trafficked.

Albanian women are trafficked and exploited in various Western European countries where Albanian criminal groups are active, such as Italy, Greece, Germany, France, Belgium, and England. Insights into these patterns come from the foreign media as well as interviews of those repatriated back to Albania. Although Albanian girls are found in many countries of Europe, the numbers of repatriated women are highest from Greece and Italy.[18]

Children have been the primary victims of human trafficking during the Albanian transition to democracy. Since the 1990s, street children and their exploitation have been a problem of concern for Albania and other Central and Eastern European countries. Although their numbers recently appear to be decreasing, children remain visible in the streets begging, cleaning car windows, and selling cigarettes, phone cards, and other items. While there is insufficient data to determine whether these children are exploited by criminal groups or other elements, it is clear that they are being used by their parents to earn money. According to the Multiple Indicators Cluster Survey 2002 conducted by INSTAT (the Albanian National Statistical Institute), 32 percent of children aged sixteen to eighteen are working in various ways and one-third of them work in the street or other trade activities.[19]

Albania lacks complete data on the number of trafficked children. Prior to the approval of the National Strategy to Combat Trafficking in

Human Beings in 2001, the available data were very controversial and continue to be so. According to the Ministry of Public Order, approximately four thousand children were trafficked from 1992 to 2002, mainly into neighboring countries for sexual exploitation and jobs including begging and street work.[20] In November 2001, at a conference organized by the Ministry of Labor and Social Affairs, ministry representatives reported that six thousand Albanian children were in Italian centers for children and between one thousand and two thousand were in children's centers in Greece.[21]

Child trafficking relies on methods of recruitment and involvement that, according to scholars, nongovernmental organizations, and governmental organizations, often are identical to those used in the trafficking of women. Nevertheless, traffickers have turned to methods better suited to exploiting the young age and the limited capability of children to understand and prevent their involvement. In most cases, the parent knows the trafficker of his child. The trafficker might be someone who promises money or a monthly payment for the exploitation of the child; in effect, the child becomes an object as a result of the accord between the parent and the trafficker.[22] Cases reveal that parents, responding to extreme poverty, agree to sell their children for a small amount of money or even a television set.[23]

Most trafficked children come from rural areas and poor families, and often are the children of the Roma minority population. To provide income for their families, the children are allowed to migrate irregularly with the consent of the parents, especially to Greece, without concluding their compulsory education and without any access to care from the host countries. Trafficked children often come from large families and are frequently abandoned by parents who are uneducated, divorced, facing difficult economic conditions, and addicted to alcohol. Trafficked children also tend to come from families where physical or psychological violence is present. Patterns of exploitation are determined by age, ethnicity, social position, and level of education. Sadly, through trafficking, these children face situations of even greater violence in Albania and abroad than those they endured at home.

The risks to children abroad are widespread. For example, most Albanian children have been trafficked into Greece to beg, steal, and distribute drugs. According to a study conducted by the INSTAT and the International Labor Organization's Program on the Elimination of Child Labor (IPEC-ILO) on child trafficking and Albania, 17 percent of 71 child trafficking cases involved sexually exploited children in Italy, Greece, and Belgium, while the remainder were exploited as beggars and in other street jobs.[24] According to the Vatra Center, out of 303 cases of trafficking victims assisted by the center in 2004, 48 of the victims were girls under the age of eighteen.[25] Reports by NGOs and human rights organizations note exploitation of Albanian and other children in Greece, including the disappearances of approximately 500 Albanian street children from the Agia Varvara shelter in Athens between 1998 and 2001.[26] Italian media sources have reported that trafficked Albanian children have been killed by their pimps. Similarly, children who have survived and grown up in Italy and Greece tell of cases of maltreatment and violence when they tried to flee.[27]

Newborns also have been unable to escape human traffickers. The first cases of foreign citizens violating laws in adopting Albanian babies became public in 1990. Albania initially lacked both the legal framework and resources to track the different paths of child trafficking, including trafficking through the adoption process. In 1992, Albania established the Albanian Adoption Committee, which specified rules for foreign citizens seeking to adopt Albanian children. Despite these laws, the phenomenon of selling newly born babies (mainly from Roma families or gypsies) is evident in Albania though reliable information on this practice remains difficult to obtain.[28]

The victimization of children in Albania has increased for several reasons beyond those noted above. The Albanian government has neglected solutions to the poverty faced by a significant portion of the Albanian population, and the absence of social programs and social service centers for children in need have placed children at risk from criminal groups. Similarly, the internal migration of families to different areas in Albania has not been accompanied by the establishment of necessary social structures and services. Moreover, despite some recent progress, the absence of an accurate census, especially for the children of minority Roma and Egyptian families, continues to be a bitter Albanian reality.

Legal and Institutional Responses to Trafficking

Albanian efforts to define and introduce legislative measures against organized crime emerged slowly during the 1990s.[29] Part of the delay reflected shifting economic conditions. Specifically, the approval of the law on privatization in 1991 accelerated the privatization of the Albanian economy, and 75 percent of the trade network and services units were converted into private property by 1992.[30] Albania's lack of experience and transparency in the process of privatization, however, contributed to a rise in economic and other crime. Albanian authorities focused predominantly on these challenges and the need for broader political and legal reform. In this context, the trafficking of women and children was not a high-priority issue.

The velocity of the spread of organized crime and the increasing number of its victims, however, made taking action against human trafficking imperative. Initially, anti-trafficking policies aimed to improve Albanian criminal law. Later, especially after the approval of the 2001 National Strategy to Combat Trafficking in Human Beings, anti-trafficking policies became multifaceted. Steps included the improvement of the legal framework, institution of specialized structures and improvement of national capacities, and development of prevention programs. The strategy for prevention combined repatriation and reintegration programs as well as public awareness campaigns. In February 2005, the Council of Ministers of Albania approved the Strategy for the Fight against Trafficking in Children and the Protection of Child Victims of Trafficking. The drafting and implementation of these anti-trafficking policies resulted from the efforts of many actors, including members of the Albanian government, civil society, and various intergovernmental and nongovernmental organizations.

On the whole, the responses by the Albanian government to organized crime in general and trafficking in particular have signaled progress. The response to trafficking increased and improved after 2001. Legal changes have been combined with the establishment and consolidation of counter-trafficking structures, and structural changes have taken place at the national and local levels. In addition to measures focused on trafficking prevention and enhanced border control, the government has introduced measures focused on issues related to trafficking such as money laundering, witness protection, and steps to strengthen the judiciary. Criminal sentences have become harsher, not only in terms of imprisonment but also in combining incarceration with financial penalties. However, while progress has been made in the efficiency of counter-trafficking bodies, the steps have not reached the levels required to fully address the problem of human trafficking.

Legal reform has been an important first step against trafficking. From the outset, legal reform in Albania was oriented toward severe punishment of traffickers and protection and rehabilitation of trafficking victims. In addition to changes in criminal legislation and procedure, reforms have included the approval of laws regulating entities empowered to fight human trafficking. Albania also has ratified a series of international instruments for combating trafficking.

Albanian reforms initially reflected a lack of experience and knowledge regarding human trafficking. Changes in the legislation were often broad and did not fully anticipate the need for measures addressing trafficking prevention. In most cases, changes reflected the need to reconcile Albanian criminal legislation with European measures or international conventions. One of the shortcomings of such an approach was that in many instances, the new laws were not accompanied by related legal frameworks, establishment of new institutional structures, or training of personnel. Despite this lack of experience, within a relatively short time important legal and structural steps were taken to alter Albanian legislation, increase cooperation with other countries in the region, increase professionalism, expand public awareness, and implement protection programs to more effectively address the human trafficking problem.

Initial steps to amend the Albanian criminal code in 1992 added provisions, under Article 94, on kidnapping a person or child. In 1995, the government approved a new criminal code, prepared with international assistance, which mandated punishment of individuals involved in prostitution and also parents who abandoned their children to traffickers. The new code, however, did not contain provisions dealing with kidnappers, traffickers, or facilities linked to trafficking. In December 1996, Act Number 8175 made several changes in the criminal code relevant to trafficking.[31] Article 114 of this act criminalized activities such as recruiting, inducing and/or coercing a person for the purpose of prostitution, and engaging in prostitution for purposes of material gain. The act also established the following as separate crimes: the exploitation of children for purposes of prostitution (Article 114a), the exploitation of prostitution committed by criminal organizations (Article 114b), and the intermediation of prostitution services (Article 115).[32] Under Article 116, in addition to punishing offenders, the premises used for prostitution could be seized.[33]

The legal changes in 1996 emphasized, for the first time, the problem of exploitation of children and women for domestic and international prostitution by criminal gangs. One year later, in Act Number 8204 of 1997, Albania amended the criminal code to add Article 89a, which included measures against the illicit trade of organs for transplant as well as all activity related to the exchange of body organs.[34] Additional measures introduced under Article 109 designated kidnapping and taking hostage of persons under the age of fourteen as serious offenses. Article 109 was modified further in 2001 and 2004 to add provisions for cases of kidnapping, hostage taking, incitement and threats, and use of violence.

Without denying the importance of the changes during the 1990s, it was only in 2001 that the Albanian criminal code explicitly treated the smuggling of human beings, the trafficking of women for sexual exploitation, and the trafficking of children as separate criminal offenses.[35] Following the adoption of the criminal code in 1995, it took more than six years for the Albanian government to draft a national strategy to combat trafficking.

Changes in Albania's codes of criminal procedure have focused largely on the broader challenges posed by organized crime. In 1995, the government approved the new Penal Procedure Code (PPC) of the Republic of Albania. The PPC introduced provisions regarding jurisdictional relationships with foreign authorities in cases of extradition of convicted persons, as well as provisions for the exchange of information and evidence between Albanian and foreign authorities in cases under investigation, with the exception of situations where state sovereignty, security, or state interests are at risk. Moreover, the PPC permitted the interception of conversations, phone communications, and other forms of telecommunication in cases of intentional crimes that are punishable with no less than seven years of imprisonment and in cases of contraventions involving insult and threats by phone.[36] The PPC also stipulated that such evidence will be accepted when there are enough facts to prove the case and when there is no infringement upon the free will of the person. These provisions have offered a useful foundation to more effective investigations of human trafficking.

A substantial portion of Albanian efforts aimed at preventing and combating organized crime has related to the enactment of various institutional reforms. These reforms have affected preexisting state structures, such as the police and prosecutors, and have established specialized sections to combat organized crime as well as training of personnel. Albania also has taken several specific initiatives to tackle trafficking in human beings.

In 1998, the Anti-Trafficking Task Force (ATTF) was founded within the Ministry of Public Order (today known as the Ministry of Interior). As a result, each Albanian police commissariat has an anti-trafficking unit and special anti-trafficking units have been created at the airports and seaports and along several land borders. Act Number 8737 of 12 February 2001 instituted special anti-trafficking and organized crime sections in the General Prosecutor's Office and in some district prosecution offices.

Thorough reform of the state and judiciary police was enforced with the passage of Act Number 8291 in 1998 and Act Number 8677 in 2000. The police also began cooperating with other state-run bodies—including signing cooperation agreements—to prevent organized crime and its resulting money laundering. On 9 September 2002, the minister of finance, minister of public order, head of the National Informative Service, and general director of the Bank of Albania signed a memorandum of understanding to prevent money laundering. By early January 2003, the general director of state police, general director of the tax office, and general director of customs had developed action plans to prevent crime, particularly organized crime. The Court of Serious Crimes, authorized in 2002 under Act Number 8813 and functioning by 2004, also has addressed the actions of organized crime groups.

Although special anti-trafficking units exist in the police and judiciary, these units to date have not shown special attention to the protection of victims of trafficking. This pattern reflects long-standing operational philosophies in which the police are seen as an organ of violence, and programs of victim protection lack the human and financial capacity to function. Institutional steps to identify and protect victims of trafficking began to take place in 2001. Administrative Instruction Number 132, issued by the Ministry of Public Order on 8 February 2001, was directed to all police commissariats of Albania and established a pre-screening procedure for detained foreigners. In addition, on 25 April 2002, the Ministry of Public Order and the Ministry of Labor and Social Affairs signed an agreement designating locations to be reconstructed and transformed into shelters for victims of trafficking. In 2003, the Ministry of Public Order set up a center for trafficking victims in Tirana.[37]

To facilitate greater institutional cooperation, the government approved the National Strategy to Combat Trafficking in Human Beings in 2001. In October 2003, the government approved the short-term Anti-Trafficking Action Plan, which focused on interdepartmental action and coordination on trafficking issues. By 2005, the government extended these efforts with the National Strategy for Combating Trafficking in Human Beings, 2005–2007, and the Strategy for the Fight against Trafficking in Children. Coordination was facilitated further with the introduction in 2005 of the interministerial State Committee for the Fight against Trafficking in Human Beings, the Office of National Anti-Trafficking Coordinator/Deputy Minister of the Interior, and the national Anti-trafficking Unit.[38] Although there has been progress, monitoring the implementation of these measures remains important. Monitoring is not only an internal necessity, but also an obligation in the framework of the European Union's Stabilization and Association Process.

Albania has ratified several international conventions aiming to combat organized crime and human trafficking.[39] In July 2002, the Albanian Assembly ratified the United Nations Convention against Transnational Organized Crime and accompanying protocols against migrant smuggling and human trafficking. In July 2004, the Albanian parliament ratified the Council of Europe Conventions on victim compensation and cybercrime. The approval of these conventions, and others addressing issues of human rights, demonstrates that the legal framework of the fight against the trafficking of human beings, and especially that of children and women, is almost complete. The ratification of these conventions has facilitated more effective regional and international cooperation in the efforts against organized crime and constitutes a concrete step in the process of making Albanian legislation compatible with international standards. Unfortunately, even as there is progress in the implementation of such steps, difficulties remain in practice in the areas of infrastructure, training, logistics, equipment, and corruption.

Albania has improved its cooperation with international police forces since the late 1990s. Earlier in the decade, the government had turned to bilateral agreements with neighboring countries, beginning with Italy in 1991. Albania added agreements with Macedonia and Turkey in 1992 to strengthen the fight against organized crime. In 1995, Albania focused on multilateral cooperation by joining other South East European countries, Turkey, Russia, and the Caucasus in the Black Sea Economic Cooperation (BSEC) Pact on Cooperation in the Fight against Organized Crime. In 2000, Albania expanded its regional cooperation by ratifying the Charter of Organization and Operation of the SECI Regional Center for the Combating of Trans-Border Crime. South Eastern European Cooperative Initiative (SECI), based in Bucharest, Romania, supports efforts at the national level in combating trafficking in human beings, drugs and stolen cars, commercial fraud, and financial crime and in enhancing customs evaluation.[40]

Albania has participated in several other initiatives in cooperation with neighboring countries and their law enforcement agencies. The Vlora Anti-Trafficking Center (VATC) was established in 2001, as a common initiative with Greece, Italy, and Germany.[41] Training programs for Albanian police and the Office of the Prosecutor have been offered by international organizations and by foreign police missions. The list here is extensive and includes the Mission of Advisor Police Europe (MAPE), Police Assistance Mission of the European Community to Albania (PAMECA), the Italian Interforca police mission, the Organization for Security and Cooperation in Europe (OSCE), International Organization for Migration (IOM), and the International Catholic Migration Commission (ICMC). The United States also has provided assistance through the International Criminal Investigative Training Assistance Program (ICITAP) and the Overseas Prosecutorial Development Assistance and Training (OPDAT) program.

Training has been provided to the police and prosecutors by organizations such as IOM on investigative procedures for trafficking in human beings. But most international assistance has offered expertise to more broadly combat organized crime and enhance border control. For example, ICITAP and PAMECA have supported the Directorate for Organized Crime in the Albanian State Police and, with OPDAT, the creation of the Albanian Organized Crime Task Force (OCFT). ICITAP programs in Albania began in 1997 and more recently have included data support networks such as the Total Information Management System.[42] In addition to training, ICITAP has contributed to the improvement of security at the border by installing surveillance cameras at the Mother Theresa International Airport and the Durrës and Vlora seaports.

Despite these avenues for international cooperation, international assistance for the Albanian Government has not been well coordinated. Since December 2001, the International Consortium (IC) has sought to improve the coordination of international assistance to the government of Albania by ensuring complementarities, avoiding duplication, and facilitating the effective use of resources. The IC is composed of members of the government of Albania and the international donors who offer assistance in the area of law enforcement and rule of law. The IC has a steering committee composed of executive level representatives of the Ministry of Public Order, delegates from the European Commission, PA-MECA, Interforca, and ICITAP.[43]

As noted, the trafficking of women and children for sexual exploitation became explicitly prohibited in Albanian criminal law in 2001. Although the Albanian courts subsequently began punishing traffickers, the number of those punished remains small. Ministry of Justice statistics for 2002 reveal the prosecution of 119 cases of prostitution but not one instance of adjudication on charges of trafficking women and children for sexual exploitation. During 2003, the Albanian courts heard three cases on the trafficking of human beings, eighty cases on prostitution, fourteen cases on trafficking of women for sexual exploitation, and four cases on trafficking of children. The following year marked an increase in both the volume of cases handled by the courts and number of persons punished for trafficking of children and prostitution. According to the annual report of the Ministry of Justice for 2004, ninety-two cases were tried for prostitution, four for trafficking of women for prostitution, and five for trafficking of children; of these, guilty verdicts were issued, respectively, to one hundred, twenty-seven, and fourteen persons.[44] In 2005, the Albanian courts heard twenty-three cases on trafficking of women. Despite the increase over earlier years, the number of adjudicated cases remains scarce when compared with the number of trafficking victims.

The treatment of trafficking victims and steps to prevent new victims also reveal slow progress. The Albanian criminal justice system still is not oriented toward victims' protection. Victims continue to face considerable difficulties during criminal procedures, such as intimidation by traffickers or their relatives. There have been cases where the trafficking victims were killed by their pimps after reporting the crime to the police. Albania's Witness Protection and Compensation of Victims Law is difficult to apply due to the absence of related legal measures and financial resources. The practical implementation of victims' protection programs also faces difficulties, but this can be overcome by strengthening regional cooperation.

Albanian civil society has played an important role in victims' protection and in raising awareness on the issue of human trafficking. Civil society and especially NGOs working in the field of human rights and women's rights have had an impact in areas such as legal counseling and constructive criticism of government policy. Such criticism has assisted in the development of draft laws related to specialized structures in the fight against crime. NGOs were the first in Albania to provide assistance to trafficking victims. They have contributed to the process of establishing and operating reintegration programs for trafficking victims, operating shelters, offering free legal assistance, and providing psychosocial support.[45]

Despite these efforts, by 2004, activities directed toward the prevention of human trafficking were not widespread. Only a few organizations dealt with prevention and provided assistance for victim integration. Problems of capacity and limited coordination with the Albanian government also inhibited the success of NGO efforts.[46] The efforts of Albanian civil society in counter-trafficking initiatives have been facilitated by the support of foreign donors, but these donors often have their own areas of focus. To facilitate greater coordination, and with the support of the U.S. Agency for International Development (USAID), Albania introduced the Coordinated Action against Human Trafficking (CAAHT) in 2004. Under this program, Albanian NGOs, locally registered international NGOs, and private voluntary organizations that work in trafficking prevention and victims' assistance as well as reintegration can receive grants to facilitate anti-trafficking efforts.[47]

Public awareness programs as part of prevention campaigns have occupied an important place in Albania. In 2002, national and international NGOs, in cooperation with the Albanian government, joined to create All Together Against Child Trafficking. In the area of child trafficking, organizations including the OSCE, Terre des Hommes, IOM, International Social Service, Help for Children, and Save the Children have implemented programs focused on improving education, establishing youth centers for children at risk so that they can obtain information and training, and working with families in educating and treating their children.[48]

Although public awareness campaigns are a necessary part of prevention, addressing the factors that promote trafficking remains important. Since such factors persist in Albania it remains difficult to measure the impact of awareness campaigns and other prevention programs. For example, centers for street children—those that have abandoned school and live on begging (such as gypsies) and are at risk for child trafficking— are estimated to be successful but insufficient. These centers are managed by NGOs such as Children of the World Albania, which operates in the suburbs of Tirana, or other local NGOs in other cities of the country.[49] These and other programs need to be permanent and sustainable, and the Albanian government should take on this responsibility for at least two reasons. Currently, civil society's assistance to victims is dependent on donors' support, and this support is limited. Moreover, the task of the state is to offer victim protection programs and cooperate with private social structures and NGOs.

Despite the role of civil society, victim support—ranging from psychosocial to economic and employment assistance—continues to suffer. Not only do programs face challenges in sustainability, but trafficking victims' poor opinion of societal structures keeps them from utilizing such programs. As a result, victims often find themselves at risk of being retrafficked. This issue has been especially evident in dealing with trafficking victims repatriated to Albania.

It is difficult to determine how many of the Albanians abroad illegally in other countries are victims of human trafficking as opposed to irregular migration. Many trafficking victims are never identified and remain threatened and exploited as prostitutes and in more sophisticated ways in nightclubs and private dwellings. Since 2002, the number of trafficked women and children repatriated from EU countries has been limited. According to international NGOs such as Terre des Hommes, which facilitates the return of children from Greece and works for their reintegration, and local NGOs such as the International Social Service, which supports Albanian children returning from Italy, the number of trafficking victims among children remains small.[50]

Nevertheless, both returnees and repatriated women and children face obstacles to reintegration. In addition to the effects of poverty and limited prospects for employment, the opportunities for reintegration of trafficking victims into Albanian society remain scarce. In 2001, USAID funding and support from Save the Children facilitated the first shelters for victims of trafficking, one at the police commissariat in Fier and another in Vlora.[51] A shelter for foreign victims of trafficking was established and operated by IOM and ICMC. A few Albanian NGOs also offer reintegration and assistance services.[52] While centers such as Vatra and IOM programs exist for reintegrating young Albanian girls, reintegration of children in general is more difficult. Some are taken home by their families and thus do not benefit from reintegration programs. For this reason, organizations like Save the Children have implemented regional projects that aim to provide psychosocial, legal, and material support to the trafficked children once they have returned home.[53]

The success of reintegration programs that deal with education, families of trafficking victims, and community sensitivity to trafficked women also remains limited. Despite efforts in these areas, the mentality of a considerable portion of Albanian society constitutes a strong obstacle to the acceptance and reintegration of victims. Consequently, the reentrance of women and children into trafficking is still a real problem. This phenomenon is quite often noticed with girls repatriated from Italy treated at Vatra Center, as well as in the case of children repatriated from Greece who are soon back in Greece. In many cases, family members have been involved in the trafficking process and thus make minimal efforts to find their children and bring them back to Albania.[54]

Based on the bilateral readmission agreements signed by the Albanian governments and European countries such as Italy, the United Kingdom, and Belgium, many Albanian emigrants illegally residing abroad or having failed in asylum applications are being forced to return to Albania. For emigrants that choose to return voluntarily, there are programs such as vocational training and education assistance through IOM and local NGOs. For those formally expelled, however, there is neither assistance nor screening programs to determine whether the migrants were victims of trafficking. Consequently there are few chances for trafficking victims to benefit from reintegration programs.[55] The signing of readmission agreements is an expression of the goodwill of the Albanian political class toward meeting EU conditions. Given general socioeconomic conditions and especially employment issues, however, Albanian society is not able to offer the support necessary for a massive readmission of women and children trafficking victims. Parallel to very careful policies that EU countries should follow, the Albanian government needs to identify and implement programs necessary to smooth the potential social problems of readmission.

Overcoming the Challenge

The trafficking of women and children has been a massive challenge for Albanian society. Economic and social problems have constituted a permanent threat for weak social groups and increased the likelihood that the members of these groups will become victims of trafficking both inside and outside of the country. Security and elementary human rights have been threatened, and victims and their families remain at risk.

Reducing the factors that lead to the victimization of women and children must continue to be the main focus of Albanian anti-trafficking programs. Since poverty is one of the preeminent factors in the trafficking of children, economic development programs targeted at improving conditions for families should be a top priority. In addition, greater respect toward women in the family and improved education for children will greatly reduce the factors that drive them into the hands of traffickers. Albanian civil society, NGOs, and local and international organizations have contributed to anti-trafficking initiatives. The Albanian government should coordinate further with these organizations so that their joint actions have the greatest impact.[56] Civil society initiatives to raise awareness among young people about trafficking and its risks remain vital. Coordination and implementation of a series of programs to reduce school dropout rates are imperative. Assistance should be provided to families with economic and social problems by offering educational and training programs for the children that have already abandoned school. Public awareness campaigns, schools, and families can play important roles for these children. Social and psychological support programs for families suffering from physical and psychological violence can offer a means of intervention, decreasing the risk that members of vulnerable groups will become victims of trafficking.

The Albanian government has taken a series of steps to institute organized crime control policies, but they remain insufficient. This is especially the case in terms of human trafficking. Counter-trafficking measures have undermined human rights through practices of surveillance, searches, and increased security measures at border crossings. Although criminal and procedural laws have improved, the Albanian experience clearly shows that updated legislation and specialized structures are inadequate if these initiatives are not supported and implemented by professionally trained staff. It is important in this context to not only draft action plans, but also monitor their implementation. The approval of the law on the protection of victims of trafficking, witnesses, and informants who provide information in the investigation of criminal organizations is essential in the fight against organized crime.

Clear vision and strategy are necessary not only on paper, but also in practice. They must be translated into concrete activities of the government and include plans for adequate funds for justice and victim protection programs and poverty reduction. Victim identification and support are necessary steps and must be part of the government response to trafficking.[57] Increasing transparency, public access, and the efficiency of the criminal justice system will reduce the chances of traffickers preying on victims for the second time. Victims' reintegration programs remain one of the greatest difficulties faced by Albanian society. Albanian civil society groups, educational institutions, and specialized organizations should continue to implement such programs.

Essential to this fight is the guarantee that police and other state organs are not themselves involved in criminal activity. Further training of the police and judiciary is needed, particularly within the Court of Serious Crimes. It is also necessary to strengthen the state security and intelligence agencies so that they become more capable of controlling and infiltrating criminal groups to collect firsthand information. Law enforcement and judicial bodies, such as the police, prosecution offices, and courts also need to improve coordination and cooperation with each other, as well as with their counterparts in other countries. Bilateral and multilateral cooperation should be strengthened even further. Cooperation is necessary not only in the exchange of information but also in undertaking joint operations, especially considering the reality that the majority of trafficked Albanian women and children are still in Western European countries.

Introducing legislation and practice in accordance with European Union standards remains imperative and is an important step toward the eventual free movement of people across borders. Liberalization of EU policies on Albanian migration will have a positive influence on reducing the supply of victims for criminal gangs and in the prevention of other criminal practices. Regional cooperation will continue to increase the efficiency of efforts to prevent trafficking. Trafficking has become less visible since 2002, but no one can affirm that this is solely an indicator of success against trafficking rather than a sign of criminal groups adopting less detectable strategies. Thus, cooperative efforts to prevent trafficking in women and children remain essential. Their implementation should be viewed as a means to guarantee stability and security in the region and beyond.

Last but not least, there is a continuing need for social and criminological research to critically assess organized crime, trafficking in human beings, and the effectiveness of organized crime control policies in Albania. Academics and scientists will continue to occupy an important place in this effort.

POLICY RESPONSES TO HUMAN TRAFFICKING IN THE BALKANS

GABRIELA KONEVSKA

Trafficking in human beings is a complex and multidimensional crime that has expanded worldwide. Human trafficking has become the world's third largest criminal business, after trafficking in drugs and weapons. South Eastern European countries are particularly affected as countries of origin, transit, and final destination of trafficked persons. Every year an estimated 175,000 persons—mainly women—are trafficked from, to, or through South Eastern European countries, including the countries of the Western Balkans, and held in conditions amounting to slavery.

There are social, legal, and economic reasons for the increase in trafficking involving South Eastern European countries. Trafficking is largely connected with social decline during the transitional period in the 1990s; high rates of unemployment; reductions in social services; increases in poverty, corruption, and organized crime; and the lack of relevant legal regulations and rule of law.[1] The main purposes of human trafficking are sexual exploitation and forced labor or services in various sectors. This modern form of slavery is an affront to human dignity, often involving psychological terror and physical violence. Trafficking encompasses issues of human rights and rule of law, law enforcement and crime control, inequality and discrimination, corruption, economic deprivation, and migration. Poverty, which is linked to social and economic dynamics, and political instability prepare the ground for human trafficking—not only for the international sex trade but also for forced and bonded labor, trafficking in children, forced marriages, and the illicit trade in human organs.

The United Nations provided the current definition of trafficking in the UN Protocol to Prevent, Suppress and Punish Trafficking in Persons, Especially Women and Children (Trafficking Protocol), adopted in Palermo in 2000 as a supplement to the UN Convention against Transnational Organized Crime. Therein, human trafficking is defined as:

> [T]he recruitment, transportation, transfer, harboring or receipt of persons, by means of the threat or use of force or other forms of coercion, of abduction, of fraud, of deception, of the abuse of power or of a position of vulnerability or of the giving or receiving of payments or benefits to achieve the consent of a person having control over another person, for the purpose of exploitation. Exploitation shall include, at a minimum, the exploitation of the prostitution of others or other forms of sexual exploitation, forced labor or services, slavery or practices similar to slavery, servitude or the removal of organs.[2]

The necessary steps to combat human trafficking lie in strengthening the capacities for cooperation and collaboration in different fields connected with the nature of the crime in order to cover its multinational and multidimensional aspects. Without an effective and comprehensive legislative framework, fighting against trafficking in human beings is fruitless. Legislation not only needs to address the incrimination of various forms of organized crime but also to provide the necessary procedural tools for their efficient investigation, prosecution, and trial. Additionally, legislation needs to be harmonized with European standards and international practice. After all, transnational crime needs a transnational approach.

Prevention, Protection, and Prosecution

According to the UN Convention against Transnational Organized Crime and the Trafficking Protocol, which have been signed and ratified by all Western Balkan countries, a comprehensive approach is necessary to combat trafficking in human beings. Such an approach entails the prevention of trafficking, protection of victims, and prosecution of those who commit or facilitate the crime.

Given the nature of human trafficking, prevention must take place on three levels. Primary prevention involves stopping things before they happen. Secondary prevention entails efforts to limit the numbers of cases that occur. Tertiary prevention involves limiting the extent of cases and their damaging impacts. Thinking about trafficking in these terms, primary prevention tackles both supply and demand for women in sex industries and the pattern of interactions between rich and poor countries. Important tools for prevention include stable economic policies that aim to increase employment opportunities for women and efforts to increase their status and standing in society. Secondary prevention involves interventions with high-risk groups such as young women in rural areas, uneducated women, and those seeking to migrate. To be efficient in prevention, an awareness campaign carried out through personal visits is highly necessary in villages, households, and schools in areas of high risk. Such a campaign should be conducted in a manner to assure that everyone understands the realities of trafficking, the nature of the crime, and the real threats that are present. Finally, tertiary prevention means stronger law enforcement, victim rehabilitation work, and strategies that prevent the re-trafficking of women or further victimization.

Victim protection is closely linked to other elements of a comprehensive anti-trafficking policy, such as legislation, law enforcement, relevant regulations on related migration issues, and the existence of victim support agencies. Therefore, victim protection has to be discussed within the overall framework of government policies on these issues. Protection can be effective only within a strong legal framework containing adequate regulations in the fields of substantive criminal law, criminal proceedings, migration laws, and police laws.[3] Moreover, effectiveness is achievable only on the basis of close cooperation between victim support organizations (particularly nongovernmental organizations), the police, public prosecutors, judges, and migration authorities. This cooperation requires adequate funding of NGOs as well as a common understanding of the problems to be solved, priorities, and the distribution of roles and responsibilities. Effectiveness also requires a culture of cooperation between NGOs and authorities that acknowledges the legitimate role of civil society. Victim protection has to cover a wide range of responses adjusted to different levels of risk. It is important to keep this need for diverse tools in mind.[4] Very often victim support organizations—mostly NGOs—will perform the crucial functions of victim protection, asking for the support of the police and for the cooperation and understanding of prosecutors and judges to the extent needed in an individual case. It is imperative that victim support organizations, specialized in giving victims of trafficking assistance and counseling, are in place and adequately funded by governments.[5]

There is a danger that the term *protection* disguises the crucial fact that in the end, it is the victim who will have to look after her own safety. The issue is the victim's safety, not her protection, and so the overall aim is to support the victim in recovering from trauma and to empower her until she is in a position to (again) ensure her own safety. Therefore, the issue should be addressed starting with the unconditional right of a trafficked person to safety, which is guaranteed under international law.[6] Within the complex overall structure of a comprehensive anti-trafficking strategy, it is the protection of the safety of persons in danger that has the first priority. Not only police officers but also all other actors—and particularly the judiciary—have to bear in mind the security issue whenever acting in the context of anti-trafficking measures. A temporary residence permit forms a crucial element of any effective victim protection policy. However, while granting the trafficking victim a regular residence status creates the basis for her support and protection, such a permit should not depend on the willingness (or ability) of the victim to cooperate with law enforcement authorities in the prosecution and trial of the trafficker.[7] Indeed, a policy connecting support for the victim to the prosecution of the offenders would tend to instrumentally use the victim for the achievement of the goals of law enforcement. Italy, in particular, provides a positive example by pursuing a policy based on the victim's need for protection rather than on her contribution to the state's prosecution efforts.[8]

Particular consideration has to be given to the risk of victims being confronted with traffickers during court proceedings. Obviously, such a confrontation can threaten the physical safety of victims, and will in many cases cause secondary victimization. As a result, confrontation can undermine the ability of the victim to participate actively in court proceedings. Basically, there are two different strategies to avoid such confrontation. The first is to secure a well-documented, preferably videotaped, statement of the victim before court hearings to be introduced into proceedings. The second is to involve the victim in court hearings while shielding her against secondary victimization.

A trafficked victim most often plays the double role of being a victim and a witness at the same time. A mere witness is, apart from possible psychological aspects, not a victim and in most cases did not suffer grave mental or physical injuries. A victim, on the other hand, should be granted special rights, taking into account the personal damage that s/he has suffered. Both groups need access to legal and other supportive mechanisms in order to feel safe and make informed decisions.

Fighting against trafficking in human beings always includes two major aspects: the issue of combating and controlling organized crime and the issue of severe human rights violations. It is important to consider both aspects with great care. Victims of trafficking have, in most cases, suffered harmful and multiple human rights abuses. Basic principles of human rights like human dignity, personal liberty, freedom of movement, privacy, self-determination, and the prohibition of slavery and slavery-like practices have been violated by the traffickers and have left traces in the victims' physical and mental dispositions, often clearly visible in post-traumatic stress syndrome.[9] States have the obligation to prosecute traffickers in order to prevent further violations and to provide trafficked persons with comprehensive support.[10] This means that the efforts to prosecute and to punish traffickers have to be implemented within a system that respects and safeguards the victims' human rights.

Measures to ensure appropriate and effective victim/witness protection may vary greatly in scope, cost-effectiveness, and accompanying security measures. Key players in the anti-trafficking field should discuss multilevel models that would be able to respond to the individual needs of all trafficking cases. Once a victim is identified as such, utmost priority must be given to her/his protection, which is at the core of each national referral mechanism. In the course of the investigation process, victim protection most often turns into witness protection since criminal investigations and prosecutions still heavily rely on the statements of trafficked persons. Guaranteed safety, shelter, access to independent advice and counseling, an opportunity for reflection delay, as well as effective witness protection are prerequisites to enabling trafficked persons to report the crimes and to consider cooperation with authorities. Only stabilized victims will be able to contribute to successful prosecution efforts as reliable witnesses.

Safe accommodation for trafficked persons contributes to both physical security and mental recovery by giving them the feeling that their needs are being looked after and their worries are being taken seriously. In most cases, trafficked victims stay in shelters or apartments that are run by NGOs. Sometimes the police provide apartments for victims/witnesses. The accommodations in both cases must provide appropriate safety measures for the women without giving them the feeling of being held in detention. In general, two models of safe accommodation for trafficked victims are used: a decentralized model with a number of small apartments that can be changed when needed, and a centralized model with only one permanent location for all clients of the program.

Giving testimony in court against the trafficker is a great burden for the victim and can, in the worst case, mean re-victimization. If the defense lawyer poses disrespectful questions or if the victim has to face the trafficker in the courtroom, the victim will again feel defenseless and exposed to his/her perpetrator. On the other hand, if the victim's rights are taken into account properly and carefully, the trial can be a chance for compensation and for gaining mental freedom from the traffickers. For this reason, emphasis must be put on treating the victim not merely as a source of evidence for the prosecution but as the main person in the trial whose needs have to be respected alongside the government's wish to prosecute and punish. A number of procedural provisions pay respect to the victim's difficult position and protect her/him from re-victimization. Of course, those rights also have to take into account the rights of the accused and the fair trial principle.[11]

Programs for witness protection are one of the main tools in the prosecution of cases of trafficking in human beings, serving as a key element of judicial proceedings. These programs establish the necessary standards of protection for the relevant persons during the entire criminal procedure and beyond; improve the efficiency of the prosecution; and determine the usage of information, data, and evidence in an appropriate manner. Such programs also establish minimum standards that might lead to broader cooperation between Western Balkan countries during the entire process from arrest to trial. Put simply, witness protection programs will enable Western Balkan countries to reach better efficiency in criminal procedures and an increased level of human security.

Governmental actors are crucial in this regard. These actors include members of the ministries of justice, judicial authorities (including public prosecutors and judges), and law enforcement authorities. Parliamentary commissions prepare, promote, and justify relevant legislation. European Union bodies work to preserve harmonization with EU legislation and standards. International institutions and organizations, including those competent to fight against organized crime and those engaged in legal coordination, are critical in delivering best practices.

The main imperatives for harmonization of witness protection programs on the regional level are: creating common regional definitions of terminology to avoid misinterpretation; establishing general principles in accordance with EU legislation and best practices; determining common levels of protection; and protecting human rights and respecting the discrepancies that exist between the individual as witness and as victim. To meet these imperatives, several activities on the national and regional levels in the Western Balkans should be taken. These activities include: establishing a domestic authority for witness protection in accordance with national legislation and the competencies of various institutions; considering EU admission procedures for witness protection; creating cooperation protocols between the competent authorities on the national level; ensuring appropriate understanding of the threats against witnesses; recognizing the rules for disclosure of identity of a protected witness and termination of the protection; establishing working groups for relevant aspects of witness protection; and cooperating with EU institutions and relevant international organizations.

Organized Crime and Human Security

Organized crime has gained a prominent and devastating role in South Eastern European countries, including the Western Balkans. Organized crime affects all levels of societies by undermining democratization, human rights, individual security, respect for the rule of law, and trust in investment and reform efforts, including social progress. It is essential to strengthen the capacities for fighting against organized crime in accordance with EU standards, confirm the strategy of regional ownership of anti–organized crime projects and initiatives, and establish close cooperation with the institutions of the EU. Such steps are necessary to facilitate the process of legal harmonization and judicial cooperation according to recognized standards.

Several international programs, initiatives, and projects have been developed to contribute to a climate of confidence and security throughout the Western Balkans by enhancing transparency and predictability in the area of justice and home affairs. The current anti–organized crime infrastructure in the South Eastern European region shows that several institutions, initiatives, and task forces exist in this respect, addressing different aspects and phenomena of organized crime, including trafficking in human beings. Their mandates are mainly to facilitate dialogue among international and regional representatives of the legal, academic, donor, and law enforcement communities. The South Eastern European initiatives assist joint projects regarding capacity building, awareness raising, and legislative reforms.

A key problem is that organized crime is intertwined with all political, economic, and social activities. To advance their aims, criminal networks foster a corporate identity based on ethnicity and clan structures. Some of them utilize their financial assets to fund local social facilities and infrastructure such as schools and roads. This in turn provides them with power, recognition, and support within their communities, making all prosecutorial efforts against them appear to be directed against the community as a whole. In the Balkans, many state-owned companies are being privatized, and local crime families are using their power and their knowledge to obtain control over these businesses. This process, sometimes referred to as "the last chance to get rich quickly," attracts members of organized crime because of the opportunity for money laundering. The funds invested in privatized, formerly state-owned enterprises have been illegally obtained through drug trafficking, cigarette smuggling, serial vehicle theft, extortion, and other illegal activities.

Any approach aimed at combating organized crime and reestablishing the rule of law in war-torn countries must begin with a thorough assessment of the remaining capabilities, structures, and instruments. It is paramount to analyze the relationship between organized crime and the remaining administration. Are they completely separate? Is organized crime tolerated by the administration? Is there even a cooperative relationship or, and this is the worst-case scenario, are key criminals and major players in government and administration identical?

From an operational and practical point of view, the improvement, coordination, and joint action between law enforcement agencies and relevant ministers in the Western Balkans depends on the more specific development of reforms in the judicial and law enforcement areas. Without these components, the fight against trafficking in human beings, organized crime, corruption, smuggling of excise commodities, and terrorism cannot be successful. The effectiveness of the system of prevention; the realization of organized crime connectivity between the Western Balkans, South Eastern European countries, and the EU; and the processes of transparency and common strategies should define the cost-benefit analysis of a mutual concept for fighting against organized crime.

Such considerations should provide a way to sell the concept of the EU to the residents of the Balkans, with the purpose of bringing the idea of integration closer. Up until now, European integration has been understood and implemented only as a program of the elite. Politicians have to recognize the need for the popularization of the idea. The whole concept of integration must be made more accessible, with emphasis on the scope for creating strong policies to prevent international, regional, or national crises and for realizing benefits such as functioning of the market economy, higher living standards, and enjoying the EU lifestyle.

In this respect, three actors are crucial for implementation of a common strategy along the lines of EU standards for combating organized crime and promotion of a better environment for economic growth—governments, the private sector, and civil society. Each actor has its importance and role in the achievement of the common goal, expressing a new dimension in traditional politics. Governments have the political leadership and expectations for the reform of the national integrity system through implementation of the rule of law, development of accountability systems, official competency, and efficient separation of powers supporting the independence of the judiciary. On the other side, the private business sector is the engine of the economy and promoter of the market interest. Civil society also is very important as it balances the perspectives of government and business with the real demands of the population, actively supporting the process of transparency.

Aside from the discrepancies between national and international/European legal standards on international police and judicial cooperation, as well as the differences on best practices, several main obstacles exist to new legislative steps against human trafficking.[12] These include: a lack of harmonization of criminal procedure instruments (such as standards on witness protection, seizure and confiscation of criminal assets, and the introduction of special investigation techniques); the incompleteness or absence of witness protection provisions, including the lack of specific technological devices to guarantee witness anonymity (such as video links for interviewing witnesses); and the absence of efficiency in confiscation systems. Other obstacles include: the lack of adequate legal limitations on the use of special investigative techniques, primarily in undercover operations and controlled deliveries; the lack of liaison magistrates, which inhibits efficient direct judicial cooperation; the absence of efficient joint investigative teams for direct police cooperation, as well as the absence of direct operative instruments; the lack of cooperation agreements with Europol, Eurojust, and the European Judicial network; and the lack of data protection rules as an imperative of an operative cooperation protocol with Europol.

In order to implement the UN Convention against Transnational Organized Crime and the Trafficking Protocol, a comprehensive approach and harmonized legal solutions are crucial for South Eastern European countries. As part of this approach, necessary stipulations should include provisions on criminal procedure, criminal offenses, prevention, cooperation, and border measures. The main directions for law enforcement in this area should be: harmonization of penalties for offenses, procedures and definitions incorporated into the law regarding principles of incrimination contained in the Trafficking Protocol; coordination on a national level according to international standards; confiscation of items and means of transport used in trafficking; suspension of economic activity derived from investments gained by human trafficking; and the protection of witnesses and victims with special preservation of their human rights.

Networks for Cooperation

A new era of regional leadership has started to address the problem of human trafficking. This leadership consists of governmental anti-trafficking coordinators; international, intergovernmental, and nongovernmental organizations; law enforcement bodies; prosecutors; and representatives from the judiciary. Some of the main intergovernmental actors working in close partnership in the Western Balkans to address human trafficking are: International Organization for Migration (IOM), International Labor

Organization, United Nations Office of the High Commissioner for Human Rights, United Nations Office on Drugs and Crime, United Nations Children's Fund, International Centre for Migration Policy Development (ICMPD), United Nations Development Fund for Women, and the International Criminal Police Organization. European actors working in partnership include: Council of Europe, Organization for Security and Cooperation in Europe, Europol, Stability Pact for South Eastern Europe, Southeast European Cooperative Initiative (SECI) Regional Center for Combating Trans-Border Crime, and the European Commission Expert Group. Nongovernmental organizations active in the region include ECPAT International (End Child Prostitution, Child Pornography and Trafficking of Children for Sexual Purposes), Anti-Slavery International, Terre des Hommes, Save the Children, and La Strada International.

The SECI initiative was designed to bring economic stability to the region of South Eastern Europe in hopes of attracting foreign direct investment. It quickly became apparent that economic stability was impossible to achieve if the SECI initiative did not also address the destabilizing impact of corruption, organized crime, and transborder crime. For this reason, the SECI Center was established in 2000. The concept of the center was that experienced nations would cooperate with member countries and share comparative advantages with the South Eastern European region to achieve EU and relevant international minimum standards. This level of cooperation would ease the accession process of each member country, particularly in the areas of justice and home affairs. The SECI Center has enjoyed critical successes and, notably, has achieved innovations in both the operational and legal areas.

Operationally, a total of eight task forces have been developed to address specific criminal activity threatening the region, including trafficking in human beings. The success of the SECI Center in facilitating information exchange by liaison officers requires comparable success in encouraging the prosecution and conviction of targets identified through the task forces. Without judicial convictions consistent with human rights and EU standards, the SECI Center cannot continue to applaud its own success. For this purpose, SECI's legal department has established formal cooperation with Interpol to support the exchange of information, several training programs related to the phenomena of human trafficking, a draft regional agreement on witness protection, and a compendium on necessary legislation on trafficking in human beings. These activities were undertaken with close collaboration with law enforcement authorities from the United States, especially the U.S. Federal Bureau of Investigation.

The vision of the SECI Center is to be a unique international entity, possessed by the region, and recognized as a professional, serious, and successful organization. Through the development of the SECI Center's capacity as a diplomatic mission, it shall facilitate the goals of the member countries to become economically viable and attractive EU member states. Thus the SECI Center is structured around two primary concerns. The operational aspect addresses, in a concrete way, the criminal threat to regional stability by encouraging communication and information sharing between the parties in the region. This aspect is further enhanced through the coordination of specific, short-term operations targeting a certain type of criminal activity. In addition, the legal aspect ensures that the proper framework is in place for the SECI Center to operate as an international legal entity and cooperate with other international organizations. This framework includes the Data Protection and Privacy Protocol, based upon EU Convention Number 108, which ensures that all information exchanged by the liaison officers of the SECI Center is handled in a manner consistent with EU expectations and standards. Having established the legal framework of the center and in the process of facilitating successfully viable task forces to address criminal activity, the legal department is currently focused on determining the prioritization of the following: the passage of needed legislation in the region; the development of model laws to assist regional legal harmonization with EU standards; the support of viable prosecutions resulting from SECI operations; the protection of witnesses in order to ensure the prosecution and conviction of criminal entities, not just individuals; the establishment of minimum standards for the collection of evidence to ensure its viability in the courts of law of each member country; the facilitation of extradition throughout the region; and the implementation of realistic mechanisms for efficient mutual legal assistance.

The SECI Center is not a law enforcement organization but a unique international organization with diplomatic status and a broader vision that, in addition to operational activities, includes efforts supporting regional harmonization of laws relevant to justice and home affairs at a standard consistent with EU expectations. For these reasons, the organizational structure must reflect the professional goals of the SECI Center and be flexible enough to grow with its successes. It is not necessary to itemize each position but more critical to set out the management positions and the competency of each. Of necessity, the organizational structure points toward both professional aspects of the SECI Center: operational and legal. The role of the management is to facilitate the work of both aspects of the SECI Center, encouraging the efficient use of human resources.

The SECI Center is a positive example of networking within the South Eastern European region in the fight against trafficking in human beings. Operation Mirage was SECI's first regionally coordinated and conducted activity. During this operation in 2002, law enforcement agencies, international organizations such as IOM and the Stability Pact for South Eastern Europe, and nongovernmental organizations worked together on a national and regional basis for the first time. All the participants understood and realized the dimensions of the phenomenon of human trafficking and totally involved themselves in this regional effort according to their particularities and specific needs. The results have been positive and encouraging, showing that this kind of operation should be organized and conducted more often in the future, being one of the most active and aggressive methods of combating trafficking in human beings and illegal migration.[13]

Connected to cases of human trafficking, the SECI Center turned to a project on witness protection and established a cooperation network of public prosecutors. The network led to recommendations emphasizing the rule of law, the process of harmonization of criminal procedures, and regional cooperation to increase the awareness of the role of public prosecutors among law enforcement personnel. Law enforcement is a powerful tool for fighting crime, but without a legal basis or the components of the protection of human rights, principles of democracy, and the rule of law, law enforcement can only be a naked power that easily can become totalitarian. In this respect, the public prosecutor functions as a public authority who, on behalf of the society, ensures the application of the law and protects the rights of the individuals and of the effectiveness of the criminal justice system.

The SECI Center's Regional Consultative Conference against Trafficking in Human Beings and Illegal Immigration and the European Conference against Trafficking in Persons served as a forum to express the problems of and suggest the possible strategies for cooperation in the field of prosecuting criminals and protection of victims of human trafficking from a legal perspective. Work in this area consists of addressing ratification of the UN Convention against Transnational Organized Crime and its relevant protocols, implementation of international legal standards and law enforcement practices through proposals for creating projects on the national and international level, and sharing references on international legal frameworks. In view of these goals, cooperation with the United Nations, IOM, ICMPD, the OSCE, Stability Pact, UNHCHR, and the OSCE Office for Democratic Institutions and Human Rights has been extremely useful.

Key Recommendations

Despite progress, trafficking in human beings remains a challenge for the Western Balkans and the broader region of South Eastern Europe.[14] Awareness must be raised on the issue of human trafficking and support provided for the development of appropriate responses. Support measures are needed to enhance existing national and regional anti-trafficking structures such as: creating multidisciplinary working groups; implementing National Action Plans, including plans for combating child trafficking; and strengthening national anti-trafficking governmental coordinators. Improving the role of law enforcement in combating human trafficking will require: promoting the mainstreaming of training for police, the judiciary, and prosecutors on human trafficking; supporting the development of special sections on child trafficking for inclusion into the existing training curricula; facilitating judicial and law enforcement cooperation; supporting capacity building and cooperation of law enforcement bodies with local and regional NGOs; and providing technical assistance.

Steps also must be taken to address the needs of trafficking victims. Recommended measures here include: supporting the implementation of temporary residence programs for victims of trafficking; supporting the implementation of victim/witness protection programs; and supporting the further exploration of the labor dimensions of human trafficking (trafficking for forced and bonded labor and services) within the Western Balkans.

Close cooperation between the law enforcement and judicial authorities is essential. Facilitating such cooperation will necessitate the creation of mutual working plans, training, programs, and activities covering legal, infrastructural, and operational aspects of combating human trafficking. This remains a weak point for all Western Balkan countries since they do not recognize in a real sense the close linkage between law enforcement and judicial authorities within the area of justice and home affairs.

Judicial reform will require changing the procedural and material laws to incorporate the main principles of independence of judicial authorities and respect for rule of law. The main judicial tools that are missing from implementation or need improvement are: legislation on specialized investigation techniques (such as undercover operations, controlled deliveries, and electronic surveillance); recognition of electronic evidence, especially important for combating money laundering; personal data protection; and witness protection, including measures for victims as a primary point for the preservation of human rights.

Implementing national programs for combating trafficking in human beings will require an explicit systematic and comprehensive approach supported by an action plan. In working toward compliance with relevant EU and international standards, Western Balkan countries must understand that implementation is crucial. The process of ratification is important as well, but only as a first step. More imperative is the creation of relevant national legislation supported by sub-legislation, which will have operational impact.

Anti-trafficking efforts and economic development are inextricably linked. Fighting trafficking in human beings is a crucial precondition for achieving better economic development, attracting foreign investments, and achieving better standards of living.

Cooperation with civil society, and especially NGOs, also is very important in the fight against trafficking. Western Balkan countries acknowledge the need for but have not fully implemented consortiums between law enforcement and NGOs; if they do so, the NGO presence will be very helpful.

Finally, regional cooperation is a key element for a comprehensive approach to human trafficking. The countries of the Western Balkans must recognize that first they have to cooperate with their neighbors, then with the extended region and the EU.

8

HUMAN TRAFFICKING AND HUMAN SECURITY

H. RICHARD FRIMAN and SIMON REICH

According to the 2005 *Human Security Report* released by the Human Security Centre, human trafficking is "so widespread and so damaging to its victims that it has become a cause of human insecurity" on a global scale.[1] The report's conclusion is based on information from and arguments of leading government agencies and intergovernmental organizations many of which are discussed in this volume, such as the U.S. State Department, UN Office on Drugs and Crime, and the International Organization for Migration.[2] However, with few exceptions, these same agencies and organizations have failed to facilitate, and at times have impeded, steps toward the realization of a human security approach to human trafficking.[3] Their arguments for enhancing measures of prevention, protection, and prosecution in the fight against human trafficking suggest a multifaceted, integrated approach based on principles of human security: addressing freedom from want, freedom from fear, and establishing and strengthening the rule of law. Responses to human trafficking in practice, however, have tended to privilege state security through an emphasis on enhanced

136

border control and law enforcement. The contributors to this volume reveal the flawed legacy of such an approach.

Theory, Policy, and the Search for a Coherent Agenda

First coherently articulated in 1994 when the United Nations Development Program issued its annual report,[4] the concept of human security is still at an early stage of development, and its meaning is still contested. Indeed, it remains amorphous as a concept, not yet having consolidated into a series of contending, well-articulated definitions. Proponents of the human security agenda generally coalesce around the idea that the threats involved are direct ones to the health, welfare, and, indeed, the lives of civilian populations. But beyond that, the definition is contested in at least two dimensions. One issue concerns its relative breadth. To some, the definition of human security should be bounded by threats constituted through direct physical violence. To others, it extends beyond the scope of physical safety to issues such as human dignity and the root causes of conflict, many of which are attenuated from actual conflicts themselves. In this latter group are included a variety of (purportedly) universalistic economic, political, and social factors such as poverty, the deprivation of human rights, and various forms of discrimination,[5] many of which are reflected in the United Nations Millennium Development Goals.[6]

The debate is further complicated by the broad swath of interdisciplinary approaches employed in the study of human security, coupled with the need to bridge the work of academics and policymakers. This creates a potential cleavage between *those who do* and *those who study what is done* in a variety of ways. In terms of human security's utility as a concept, the necessary rigor of the definition may therefore differ markedly for academics and policymakers. Academics seek greater analytic precision in their understanding for the purposes of explanation while policymakers often prioritize prescriptions for specific policy goals.

Academics, therefore, require a definition they can study and measure; policymakers need one they can employ and implement. The two sets of objectives need not be in tension. Indeed, one can argue that a meticulous analytic approach is the foundation for effective policy formulation and implementation. But complementarities are often, in practice, elusive under the pressures of time and scarce resources. Interestingly, the concept of human security is a rarity; it originates from the policy community, perhaps explaining its relative lack of theoretical and analytic precision. Attempts by academics to wrestle with the concept over the course of the last decade have produced uneven results and contrasting conclusions about the substance of and appropriate tools employed in studying issues from a human security perspective.[7]

So what can we conclude from these diverse views? Advocates of the human security agenda contrast their perspective with those who hold traditional notions of state security. Proponents of the state security view often focus on threats to state integrity, noting that the threat to civilian populations is often indirect—such as death as a result of famine or disease in the context of civil war. To use the popular term, human casualties constitute *collateral damage* under the rubric of state security, even when civilians die in large numbers. It is the state's capacity to govern, to project force abroad, and to monopolize force at home that is critical to this traditional approach.

An ironic illustration of this perspective is provided by the famous television movie *The Day After*, first broadcast in the 1980s. In the final frames of the movie, which depicted events in the aftermath of a large-scale nuclear war between the Soviet Union and the United States, a group of survivors have gathered outside a hospital in Lawrence, Kansas. Their fate has been effectively sealed: contaminated by radiation, they will endure a slow and painful death. But as they huddle around a radio, they hear the voice of the American president proclaiming that the government is intact, and thus the United States has survived. The sardonic fact that there is no civilian population to govern is not lost on the viewer.

This extreme, indeed caricatured, version of the justification for the human security agenda finds a more conventional and thus more alarming formulation in the context of current warfare. According to the *Human Security Report*, more people died from intrastate than interstate wars in the 1990s, and more people generally died from the indirect causes of war—such as famine and disease—than direct combat in interstate conflicts.[8] The exemplar of this trend is reflected in the current conflict in the Democratic Republic of the Congo (DRC), dating from 1998. Often called, perhaps paradoxically, Africa's first World War because it has been a vortex into which so many of the DRC's neighbors have been dragged, this fighting has claimed the lives of an estimated four million people, the majority of whom died not as a result of conflict under arms, but of famine and disease.

The result of all this discussion is consistent to a large degree with a situation of controlled chaos. A colloquium published by *Security Dialogue* in 2004 revealed that even ten years after the term *human security* was first coined, senior scholars and policymakers could reach no consensus about the scope, domain, or application of the term.[9] With pluralism—if not fragmentation—therefore ruling, we are left with a definition of security that is the lowest common denominator and is therefore vague. This definition reads something like: human security is akin to the absence of threats and the reduction of vulnerabilities caused by exogenous factors such as unanticipated crises that are targeted at civilian populations. Yet we know that the definition of human security, which clearly has interdisciplinary components, must have policy applicability rather than being too abstract.

The difficulty in defining human security has, predictably, created an agenda with distinct, potentially discrete, components. One set of issues captured under the human security rubric focuses on the proximate causes of violence, and is characteristically advocated by middle powers, such as Canada and the smaller European states. Work in this area largely focuses on peacekeeping and peace building, and is often reliant on regional organizations and the United Nations to adjudicate and implement measures designed to feed and protect civilian populations from the violence, famine, and disease that result from war. The most notable example of this area of policy work was the debate regarding the "responsibility to protect" initiative, the core elements of which addressed the conditions under which external, multilateral forces could intervene in the context of wide-scale threats to civilian populations.[10] In the parlance of the United Nations, these kinds of initiatives are associated with the freedom from fear component of the human security agenda. Part of this debate has expanded into a high-level policy discussion, promulgated by Kofi Annan at the uppermost levels of United Nations governance, of not only the rights but also the responsibilities associated with state sovereignty.[11]

Another component of the agenda is characterized by the UN literature as *freedom from want,* perhaps best encapsulated in the central themes of the UN's Millennium Development Goals: extreme poverty and hunger, infant mortality, and diseases such as HIV and malaria.[12] Those who work on this agenda largely focus on redistributive measures. Freedom from want issues are composed of vulnerabilities rather than threats in a traditional security sense. Yet advocates of the importance of these policy areas point to both their broad and destructive force, and to how these problems both lay the conditions for, and are the consequences of, societal violence. Perhaps not surprisingly, the most vocal proponents of this part of the human security agenda are located in the Global South. The governments of Heavily Indebted Poor Countries (HIPC), for example, have focused on the need for economic justice dating back to the New International Economic Order initiative of the 1970s. By also adopting the freedom from fear component of human security, proponents can pursue a comparable agenda in a different guise. While not recognized as such, the goals of the debt relief initiatives promoted by celebrities such as Bob Geldof and Bono, as well as foundations formed by philanthropists such as Bill Gates, are consistent with this dimension of the human security agenda.

An additional element of the human security agenda is often characterized as the vaguest and most amorphous, *freedom to live in dignity.* While some of the more radical and universalistic formulations of this aspect stress the abrogation of human rights as a result of racial, social, and economic discrimination, a more conventional formulation emphasizes the importance of civil and political rights—often captured under the rubric of the rule of law.

While the United States does not openly subscribe to any of the three dimensions of human security agenda, paradoxically it is among the most vocal supporters of the concept of the rule of law. The United States actively advocates democratization, transparency, and account-ability, all key components of the concept of the rule of law. From the sponsorship of nongovernmental organizations that educate judges and lawyers as a way of assisting the formulation of independent judiciaries in fragile and transitional states, to the broadest political support for vel-vet revolutions around the world, American governments have spent de-cades working both at the micro- and multilateral organizational levels to promote the expansion of political and civil rights. The unpopularity of any concept emanating from the United Nations in the United States, however, precludes legitimating such policies in terms of the human se-curity agenda.[13]

Finding Coalescence in the Discord about Human Trafficking

It would not be surprising if these fissures regarding the definition of human security, the contrasting levels of abstraction embedded in the differing definitions, and the distinct policy themes articulated by the various advocates were to take policymakers off into diverse areas. It is not hard to imagine that those focusing on economic justice would want to deal with policymaking in a different realm from those interested in the rule of law. Contrasting spheres of policymaking—in scope and do-main—have confounded attempts to consolidate human security beyond an agenda (or in the case of many academics, a research program) into a legitimate field of public policy in which the assumptions, methods, and tools are debated within recognized boundaries.

Yet, surprisingly, the interdisciplinary and diffuse character of that agenda often proves to be a source of strength when it comes to both the study of particular problems and the generation and implementa-tion of feasible, tenable policy solutions. This latter point is illustrated by the case of human trafficking. Clearly a global phenomenon extending well beyond the Western Balkan region, the nonvoluntary use of human labor is embedded in a degree of impoverishment that motivates both sellers and smugglers and leads victims into situations of risk. Human trafficking also challenges the rule of law, as criminal networks of differing degrees of organization both undermine the enforcement capacity of the state and rely extensively on its corruption, and as governments risk criminalizing the victims of trafficking in the name of securing national borders.[14] The case of human trafficking further reveals the ironies of the international community's efforts to address the proximate causes of insecurity. The representatives of the international community charged with restoring order have—through their very presence and practice—increased the demand for sexual exploitation and forced labor, and emerged as buyers, sellers, and smugglers of trafficking victims.[15] In effect, human trafficking is a multifaceted challenge to human security that requires a multifaceted, integrated response.

On the surface, such a response informs the international community's steps against trafficking. The 2000 UN Convention against Transnational Organized Crime and its Protocol to Prevent, Suppress and Punish Trafficking in Persons, Especially Women and Children (Trafficking Protocol) came into force in 2003. It constitutes a significant step toward a global prohibition regime against trafficking.[16] The Trafficking Protocol addresses the linkage between trafficking and freedom from want through prevention measures—calling for "social and economic initiatives" that address "factors that make persons, especially women and children, vulnerable to trafficking, such as poverty, underdevelopment and lack of equal opportunity."[17]

In addition to offering a legal definition of trafficking, the Trafficking Protocol requires signatories to strengthen the rule of law through measures including the criminalization of trafficking, enhancing border controls to "prevent and detect" trafficking, and steps to enhance the protection of trafficking victims. The latter steps consist of measures ranging from the provision of assistance and services with "full respect for their human rights" to provisions allowing for victims to remain in the receiving state.[18] Victim protection measures also illustrate the linkages between trafficking and achieving freedom from fear, a linkage more broadly illustrated by the Trafficking Protocol's justification for its creation as essential to protect persons "vulnerable to trafficking" by means of a "comprehensive international approach."[19]

The Toolkit to Combat Trafficking in Persons, released by the United Nations Office on Drugs and Crime's Global Programme against Trafficking in Human Beings (GPAT) in October 2006, seeks to facilitate implementation of the protocol. The Toolkit offers examples of how to: introduce criminalization and enforcement measures; facilitate victim identification, protection, assistance, and repatriation; and address trafficking prevention through education and awareness campaigns, anti-corruption measures, discouraging demand, and promoting the economic rights and gender equality of women.[20]

The United States has played an influential role in the realization of the Trafficking Protocol and in the broader emergence of the global prohibition regime against human trafficking.[21] The Trafficking Victims Protection Act of 2000 (TVPA), reauthorized in 2003 and 2005, is the legislative centerpiece of U.S. efforts and serves as the basis for the criteria used by the Department of State in its annual *Trafficking in Persons (TIP) Report* to assess foreign compliance with anti-trafficking efforts.[22] Although the TVPA defines human trafficking more broadly than the United Nations to include prostitution and other commercial sex acts, the U.S. operative regulations on trafficking narrowly focus on its more "severe" forms—those that entail the use of "fraud, force or coercion."[23] The language of the TVPA and *TIP Report* focuses on promoting the integrated dimensions of prevention, prosecution, and protection. Though not couched explicitly in terms of human security, these dimensions illustrate human security arguments.

For example, the TVPA links freedom from want and human trafficking, noting that those most at risk of trafficking are "women and girls, who are disproportionately affected by poverty, the lack of access to education, chronic unemployment, discrimination, and the lack of economic opportunities in countries of origin . . . and children [bought] from poor families."[24] Prevention thus hinges not only on instilling a greater awareness among potential victims of the risks of trafficking but on promoting "economic alternatives to prevent and deter trafficking" through measures aimed at education and business skill training for women and children and enhancing the participation of women in "political, economic, social and educational roles."[25] More explicit reference to prevention by addressing sources of demand for trafficking victims, including demand for commercial sex acts, appears in the 2005 TVPA reauthorization.[26]

Similarly, provisions on prosecution and protection address freedom from fear and strengthening the rule of law. The TVPA and *TIP Report* assessments require the criminalization of severe forms of human trafficking, the introduction of levels of punishment sufficient to deter its practice, and the vigorous implementation of enforcement measures, including steps against public officials that "participate in or facilitate severe forms of trafficking."[27] Trafficking victims also are to be protected, including being "safely integrated, reintegrated or resettled as appropriate." The extent to which these protection provisions illustrate a human security approach, however, should not be overstated. The TVPA links protection to the extent of the victim's cooperation in the investigation of trafficking cases. For example, foreign victims of trafficking discovered in the United States are to be provided protection as well as medical and other assistance, although provisions for continued presence and temporary U.S. residence are based largely on the victim's cooperation with law enforcement authorities.[28]

The European Union has moved toward a more comprehensive, human rights–oriented approach across member states to address human trafficking. Intended to "complement" the UN Trafficking Protocol, the 2002 EU Council Framework Decision on Combating Trafficking in Human Beings (Framework Decision) follows the UN definition of human trafficking. The Framework Decision calls upon member states to criminalize trafficking and related offenses, introduce "effective, proportionate and dissuasive criminal penalties," and establish enforcement measures.[29] Despite the broad language of protecting human rights included in the preamble, the Framework Decision prioritizes rule of law more extensively than considerations of freedom from fear or want. Victim protection is couched primarily in terms of allowing for investigations of trafficking cases without requiring a "report or accusation" by the trafficking victim, and victim assistance is noted only in the context of victims who are children and their families.[30] Council Directive 2004/81/EC of 29 April 2004, added provisions for third-country victims of human trafficking to receive temporary residence permits, medical assistance, education, and employment, during a "reflection period" as determined by individual member states. Similar to United States provisions, Council Directive 2004/81/EC links these provisions to victims' cooperation with law enforcement authorities.[31]

A more multifaceted approach is envisioned by the goal underlying the European Union itself, noted by the European Council in Tampere in 1999, to establish an area of "freedom, security and justice." As recommended by the Council, the EU's migration policies would work to address: "political, human rights and development issues in countries and regions of origin and transit. This requires combating poverty, improving living conditions and job opportunities, preventing conflicts and consolidating democratic states and ensuring respect for human rights, in particular rights of minorities, women and children."[32] Steps against human trafficking as envisioned by the council in 1999 included criminalization of human trafficking, enforcement against trafficking networks, enhanced border controls, and facilitation of voluntary returns, while taking steps to ensure the human rights of trafficking victims.[33] Progress toward such an approach has been more evident since 2003 in the work of the European Commission's Expert Group on Trafficking in Human Beings, and in conferences and the commission's efforts toward an EU Plan of Action.[34] Measures to protect the human rights of human trafficking victims are the centerpiece of these efforts.

The 11 October 2005 recommendations of the experts group called for prioritizing "victim protection, assistance and compensation" through measures such as a minimum three-month "reflection period" during which victims would receive housing, medical, and legal assistance; extensive assessments of risk and support networks for victims prior to returning them to their home countries; and measures to protect victims in "all investigation and prosecution activities." The recommendations further called for greater preventative efforts, including the need to focus on linkages between trafficking, migration, and the "informalisation of the workplace," as well as to confront the root causes of trafficking by addressing issues of economic development, discrimination, and weak democratic institutions and practices.[35]

The 18 October 2005 recommendations by the Commission to the European Parliament and Council reiterated the call for an "integrated . . . human rights centered approach" in EU policy efforts at home and abroad. Policy recommendations included many of those advocated by the experts group as well as calls for greater cooperation with "source, transit and destination countries" in promoting victim protection and assistance and targeting EU development funds as the root causes of trafficking such as poverty, lack of education, and discrimination.[36]

The initiatives of the United Nations, United States, and European Union all suggest extensive support for a multifaceted response to human trafficking, and policy initiatives have taken place in the areas of freedom from want, freedom from fear, and strengthening the rule of law. In practice, however, considerations of state security still hold sway. Broader steps toward prevention are often thin at best. The *TIP Report's* process in assessing foreign compliance with the minimum standards for steps against trafficking set by the TVPA, for example, "does not focus on government efforts that contribute indirectly to reducing trafficking, such as education programs, support for economic development, or programs aimed at enhancing gender equality, although these are worthwhile endeavors."[37] Moreover, as observed by the U.S. Government Accountability Office (GAO) in 2006, even U.S. foreign aid decisions regarding those efforts that contribute directly to addressing trafficking have not been coordinated with the *TIP Report* ranking process.[38]

Victims' protections are also limited, illustrated best in the practice of linking victim protection and assistance to cooperation with enforcement authorities. In 2006, the European Commission's assessment of compliance with the Framework Decision also revealed that few member states provided relevant information on victim protection and assistance provisions, making implementation "difficult to evaluate." In contrast, the assessment described extensive reporting by member states on their steps toward criminalization and the introduction of prohibitive sanctions on human trafficking.[39] For those states seeking membership in the EU, the Stabilisation and Association Process and actual accession agreements also have placed greater emphasis on issues of enforcement and border control than on linking human trafficking to issues of victim protection and broader root causes.[40]

Central Lessons from the Western Balkans

The experience of anti-trafficking efforts in the Western Balkans exposes the gap between the international community's rhetoric of a multifaceted, integrated approach and the reality of uneven prioritization and implementation. The experience also reveals the challenges posed by socioeconomic conditions, the challenges of unintended results of anti-trafficking measures, and broader lessons for efforts to realize human security.

Extensive steps have been taken against human trafficking in the Western Balkan region. Regional and national initiatives have been backed to varying degrees by the United States and EU, both directly and working with intergovernmental organizations such as the OSCE, Council of Europe, IOM, and the United Nations, as well as multiple nongovernmental organizations.

Initiatives have emphasized law enforcement as well as broader aspects of prevention and protection. For example, the Stability Pact for South Eastern Europe Task Force on Trafficking in Human Beings (SPTF) has prioritized broader regional coordination and cooperation in South Eastern Europe in areas of "prevention, raising awareness, victim assistance and protection, return and reintegration of victims, legislative reform, law enforcement cooperation, as well as training, exchange of information and capacity building."[41] Although emphasizing a comprehensive approach and facilitating regional cooperation, SPTF efforts to obtain support, especially financial support, for programs directed at the socioeconomic root causes of trafficking have been less successful.[42] Another major regional initiative, the South Eastern European Cooperative Initiative (SECI) Center and Task Force on Human Trafficking and Migrant Smuggling has been more narrowly focused, and more successful, in facilitating law enforcement cooperation, increasing action against traffickers, and improving identification of trafficking victims.[43] In this context, it is not surprising that by 2004, multifaceted human trafficking prevention programs extending beyond a narrow focus on the repression of "migration, organized crime and prostitution" were not a priority for "governments or international organizations" in the region.[44]

Nicole Lindstrom's chapter in this volume reveals the tension between and among governments, intergovernmental organizations, and transnational and local NGOs active in the Western Balkans. These actors have conceptualized the trafficking problem through at least four major approaches: first, as an issue of unregulated or irregular migration, best addressed through rescue of trafficked persons and repatriation to their home countries; second, as a criminal activity, best addressed through law enforcement suppression of illegal migration, traffickers, and the sex industry; third, as a human rights challenge, best met by an expansion of legal and socioeconomic rights protections geared toward the empowerment of women; and fourth, as an economic issue, best met by addressing the structures and conditions of poverty in source countries through economic and political development. Although elements of all four conceptual approaches have found their way into the regional initiatives and National Action Plans adopted by individual Western Balkan governments, the contributors to this volume reveal that the prioritization of trafficking as a migration/criminal problem traditionally has held sway.[45] This prioritization has led to unintended results eroding rather than enhancing human security.

Advocates of all of the four conceptual approaches noted by Lindstrom acknowledge that economics help to drive human trafficking. The observation is most commonly expressed by the international community in terms of the extensive revenues generated for traffickers and the socioeconomic dislocation and hardships that lead women into exploitative circumstances. Human trafficking does generate revenue. In

1997, the Global Survival Network estimated human trafficking as generating upwards of $7 billion annually for criminal groups.[46] By 2004, the U.S. Federal Bureau of Investigation estimated annual human trafficking revenue at closer to $9.5 billion.[47] Unlike the economics of consumable products such as drugs, the revenue streams in human trafficking are also enhanced by the ability of traffickers to sell and resell trafficking victims.[48] Drug and arms trafficking have long histories in the Western Balkan region and were intensified by the violent fragmentation of Yugoslavia. Organized crime networks already active in these areas expanded into human trafficking during the 1990s and into the new millennium, especially polycrime networks operating out of and through Albania and Macedonia.[49]

While such patterns are not unique to the Western Balkans, the region reveals a greater complexity in the socioeconomic sources of human trafficking. Lynellyn Long's chapter shows how politicized ethnic conflict during Yugoslavia's fragmentation distorted traditional exchange relationships in the region, including rural practices of arranged marriages within and across clans and ethnic and religious groups. Rather than being valued as "gifts" designed to build trust and cooperation, women (especially those from other ethnic or religious groups) became commodities more valued to warring factions when raped, kidnapped, and trafficked. Destroying the gift served to intensify interethnic conflict and reinforce practices of ethnic cleansing, while simultaneously generating revenue through the sale of sexual services and the women themselves. This denial of humanity persists in the region in the trafficking activities of local and transnational criminal groups, prostitution networks, and law enforcement officials.

More commonly explored socioeconomic conditions also lead women into the reach of trafficking networks in the region. Limited economic opportunities and discrimination, intensified by the impact of global economic forces, encourage migration from the countryside both to the cities and abroad. Restrictions on legal international migration in destination countries encourage potential migrants to seek out migrant smugglers that can move them across the border. A lack of education increases the risk of women being deceived by the recruitment practices of traffickers.

Interviews conducted by Human Rights Watch and IOM, discussed in this volume, again reveal complexity. Friends, family members, other nationals, and internationals play a role in recruiting women into trafficking networks through offers of employment abroad, marriage, or even well-paying prostitution on the women's own terms. The dynamics of trafficking in the Western Balkans also illustrate that women often are well aware of recruitment practices and the potential life of a trafficking victim. Nonetheless, they knowingly choose to accept the risks to escape from poor socioeconomic conditions.

The experiences coming out of the Western Balkans also suggest that socioeconomic conditions can be dramatically altered by the introduction of stabilization and relief efforts by the international community into conflict and post-conflict areas. The positive impact of such interventions, however, has been offset by unintended consequences of a large-scale international presence. The chapters by Martina Vandenberg and Julie Mertus and Andrea Bertone depict how the presence of thousands of peacekeepers and other internationals, although essential to the post-conflict stabilization of the Western Balkans, also expanded the commercial sex industry.

The international community, largely male and well-paid relative to the local economy, became the clientele of restaurants, bars, and clubs, as well as the gatekeepers to employment opportunities, housing, and social services. Organized prostitution and the trafficking of women into prostitution networks expanded in this context, especially in areas of international concentration such as Bosnia and Herzegovina and Kosovo. Over the past few years, high-profile exposés of the actions of international troops and staff in facilitating human trafficking have led to new regulations, education campaigns, and enforcement measures by the UN, NATO, and U.S. forces, but with limited results.[50]

The unintended results of anti-trafficking steps prompted by, and in some cases directed by, the international community, however, are broader than the socioeconomic distortions noted above. The increasing prioritization of human trafficking in the Western Balkans has led to a series of high-profile crackdowns against major trafficking networks. Subsequent falling numbers of arrests of traffickers and discovery of trafficking victims have led some to proclaim that the problem is diminishing. Yet, as several contributors to this volume note, such steps intended to eradicate trafficking have had the unintended effect of shifting traffickers to new routes and driving trafficking operations underground. Evidence shows that crackdowns against major networks in Serbia, Bosnia and Herzegovina, and elsewhere have had the effect of displacing the trafficking of women for prostitution from major to smaller cities and towns; shifting operations from bars and clubs to private apartments; and from visible direct contacts with clients to indirect contact through middlemen. Although conveying the impression of success by curtailing the more visible aspects of human trafficking, these shifts have had the cumulative effect of placing the victims of trafficking at an even greater risk of exploitation.[51]

Arrest data stemming from the disruption of high profile trafficking networks is only one of several metrics commonly used by governments, intergovernmental organizations, and nongovernmental organizations in the region to assess the effectiveness of anti-trafficking measures. Increasingly, the international community also has turned to standards of measure such as the numbers of new shelters for trafficking victims and the numbers of trafficking victims.[52] The Western Balkans region, however, reveals that such metrics can hide unintended effects. The prioritization and proliferation of shelters and a competition for funding to establish and maintain shelters between NGOs and governments risk diverting resources from other social service programs for women. Shelter utilization is uneven in terms of the numbers of persons who use them; the extent to which shelters are open to trafficked women who are repatriated from abroad; the numbers of women who voluntarily seek out shelter services; or the numbers of women who are offered shelter access when cooperating with anti-trafficking law enforcement efforts. In some cases, shelters also have been used by trafficking networks to offload women who are no longer seen to be profitable.

The focus on shelters also reveals little about the extent to which re-integration of trafficking victims actually takes place. Problems of community acceptance of formerly trafficked women and children back into society remain common throughout the region. Those who return need access to economic and educational opportunities, as well as protection from trafficking networks. In the case Albania, for example, Vasilika Hysi's chapter notes that these problems are compounded by social support programs that are more accessible to those who return voluntarily than those who are forcefully repatriated. The chapters by Long and Lindstrom also reveal that the failure of reintegration leads to problems of re-trafficking. Despite the efforts of NGOs working to establish assistance and social safety networks for returnees, these problems persist.

A relative emphasis on enhancing the rule of law—criminalization of trafficking and related practices and enforcement that place victims at risk while focusing on organized trafficking networks and border control—is unlikely to resolve the challenge of human trafficking. A multifaceted, integrated approach that better addresses the root causes of human trafficking, addressing factors that influence patterns of demand and supply for exploited persons, holds greater promise. Yet rhetoric in this regard continues to outstrip practice. The problem is not the absence of ideas but the failure of these ideas to attract the requisite support for integrated implementation. Such a pattern is clearly not unique to human trafficking in the Western Balkans[53] or to the issue of human trafficking as a whole. Broad criminalization and patterns of selective enforcement dominate the international drug control regime despite calls for a greater emphasis on the broader socioeconomic roots of supply and demand.[54]

Peter Andreas and Ethan Nadelmann argue that global prohibition regimes "tend to mirror the criminal laws of countries that have dominated the global society."[55] Over the last century and into the new millennium, the United States has played this dominant role, supported and occasionally contested by the EU and its member states. In this sense,

the path toward the realization of a human security approach to the illicit global economy lies in influencing the policies and practices of the
United States.

Domestic and transnational nongovernmental organizations have
played, and will continue to play, a crucial role in this regard. Andreas and
Nadelmann point to the role of governments as well as nongovernmental "transnational moral entrepreneurs" in shaping the rise and influence
of global prohibition regimes. Moreover, conflicts between transnational
moral entrepreneurs, ranging from individuals to nongovernmental organizations, over the proper ways of conceptualizing the problem and the
proper solutions have shaped the structure and effectiveness of regimes
in reducing the incidence of the undesired activity. The intertwined issues
of human trafficking and prostitution, and the deep divide among transnational moral entrepreneurs as well as governments over the latter's prohibition in both policy and practice, lead Andreas and Nadelmann to see
limited possibilities for success in the global prohibition regime against
human trafficking.[56]

Yet a human security approach, by its multifaceted nature, holds out
a potential path to address human trafficking without necessarily becoming paralyzed by the debate over prostitution. Regardless of whether one
sees the potential for choice by those who engage in prostitution or sees
the very concept of sex work as immoral exploitation, a human security approach reveals that progress is still possible through taking steps
to ease freedom from want, freedom from fear, and the weaknesses of
rule of law that help to drive the practice of human trafficking. Transnational moral entrepreneurs have placed human security, with all of its
gray areas, on the global agenda. As Roland Paris writes, human security
has worked as a "rallying cry," uniting diverse coalitions and as the basis
for a global "political campaign" against issues such as land mines.[57] Human trafficking, more so than trafficking in drugs, endangered species, or
violations of intellectual property rights, reveals a human face. Like the
horrible images of injuries to children and noncombatants by land mines,
the images and stories of trafficked children, women, and men have the
potential to create pariahs among those who fail to act. To date, however,

the human security approach remains underutilized and its potential unrealized. The Western Balkans offers insights as to why a multifaceted, integrated approach to human trafficking is necessary, and why efforts toward such an approach have fallen short.

Notes

Chapter 1: Human Trafficking and the Balkans

1. Ivan Krastev et al., *Human Security in South-East Europe* (Skopje, Macedonia: United Nations Development Program, 1999), 9, http://www.ceu.hu/cps/bluebird/eve/statebuilding/krastev_humansecurity.pdf (accessed 24 January 2007).

2. For example, see Margaret E. Beare, "Illegal Migration: Personal Tragedies, Social Problems, or National Security Threats?" in *Illegal Immigration and Commercial Sex: The New Slave Trade*, ed. Phil Williams (London: Frank Cass, 1998), 11–42; Michele Anne Clark, "Trafficking in Persons: An Issue of Human Security," *Journal of Human Development* 4, no. 2 (2003): 247–63.

3. The Western Balkan region consists of Albania, Bosnia and Herzegovina, Croatia, the Former Yugoslav Republic of Macedonia, Montenegro (independent as of June 2006), Serbia, and the UN Administered Province of Kosovo.

4. Krastev et al., *Human Security*, 9; Clark, "Trafficking in Persons," 248; Barbara Limanowska, *Trafficking in Human Beings in South Eastern Europe: 2003 Update on Situation and Responses to Trafficking in Human Beings* (Warsaw and Sarajevo: UNICEF, UNOHCHR, OSCE/ODIHR, 2003), http://www.ceecis.org/child_protection/PDF/Traff2003.pdf (accessed 20 January 2007).

5. U.S. Department of State, "Introduction," *Trafficking in Persons Report*, 2006, http://www.state.gov/g/tip/rls/tiprpt/2006/65983.htm (accessed 20 January 2007). The extent to which these figures accurately reflect the extent of human trafficking remains a point of considerable contention, and thus must be approached with caution. For example, see U.S. Government Accountability Office (GAO), *Human Trafficking: Better Data, Strategy, and Reporting Needed to Enhance U.S. Antitrafficking Efforts Abroad*, GAO-06-825, July 2006, http://www.gao.gov/new.items/d06825.pdf (accessed 22 January 2007); and United Nations Office on Drugs and Crime (UNODC), *Trafficking in Persons: Global Patterns* (Vienna: UNODC, April 2006), http://www.unodc.org/unodc/en/trafficking_persons_report_2006-04.html (accessed 26 January 2007).

6. Phil Williams, "Human Commodity Trafficking: An Overview," in Williams, *Illegal Immigration and Commercial Sex,* 1–10; Siriporn Skrobanek, Chuitima Jantha-keero, Nattaya Boonpakdi, *The Traffic in Women: Human Realities of the International Sex Trade* (London: Zed Books, 1997); Gillian Caldwell, Steve Galster, Jyothi Kanics, and Nadia Steinzor, "Capitalizing on Transition Economies: The Role of the Russian Mafiya in Trafficking Women for Forced Prostitution," in Williams, *Illegal Immigration and Commercial Sex,* 42–73; Kevin Bales, *Disposable People: New Slavery in the Global Economy* (Berkeley: University of California Press, 1999), 34–79; Donna Hughes, "The 'Natasha' Trade: The Transnational Shadow Market of Trafficking in Women," *Journal of International Affairs* 53, no. 2 (2000): 625–51.

7. International Organization for Migration (IOM), *Victims of Trafficking in the Balkans: A Study of Trafficking in Women and Children for Sexual Exploitation to, through, and from the Balkan Region* (Geneva: IOM, 2001), xii, http://www.old.iom.int/documents/publication/en/balkan_trafficking.pdf (accessed 22 January 2007).

8. IOM, *Victims of Trafficking in the Balkans,* xii; Jean Philippe Chauzy, "Geneva-Report on the Extent of Trafficking in Women and Children for Sexual Exploitation to, through and from the Balkan Region," *IOM Press Briefing Notes,* 8 January 2002, http://www.old.iom.int/en/archive/PBN080102.shtml (accessed 30 May 2007); Ian Burrell, "From the Balkans to the Brothels in Soho," *Independent,* 21 January 2002; Barbara Limanowska, *Trafficking in Human Beings in South Eastern Europe: Current Situation and Responses to Trafficking in Human Beings* (Belgrade, Warsaw, Sarajevo: UNICEF, UNOHCHR, OSCE/ODIHR, 2002), 4, http://www.osce.org/documents/odihr/2002/06/1649_en.pdf (accessed 24 January 2007).

9. European Council, *European Security Strategy: A Secure Europe in a Better World,* Brussels, 12 December 2003, 5, http://www.consilium.europa.eu/uedocs/cmsUpload/78367.pdf (accessed 30 May 2007); Eric Jansson, "Human Trafficking in Balkans Growing, UN OSCE Say," *Financial Times,* 18 December 2003.

10. Human Rights Watch (HRW), *Hopes Betrayed: Trafficking of Women and Girls to Post-Conflict Bosnia and Herzegovina for Forced Prostitution* 14, no. 9 (D) (November 2002), http://www.hrw.org/reports/2002/bosnia/Bosnia1102.pdf (accessed 20 January 2007).

11. See HRW, *Hopes Betrayed;* Limanowska, *Trafficking in Human Beings* (2003); Barbara Limanowska, *Trafficking in Human Beings in South Eastern Europe: 2004—A Focus on Prevention* (Warsaw and Sarajevo: UNICEF, UNOHCHR, OSCE/ODIHR, 2005), http://www.unicef.org/ceecis/Trafficking.Report.2005.pdf (accessed 20 January 2007); and Rebecca Surtees, *Second Annual Report on Victims of Trafficking in South-Eastern Europe,* Regional Clearing Point, International Organization for Migration (IOM) (Geneva: IOM, 2005), http://www.iom.int/jahia/webdav/site/myjahiasite/shared/shared/mainsite/published_docs/studies_and_reports/second_annual05.pdf (accessed 20 January 2007).

12. For example, see Phil Williams, "Trafficking in Women and Children: A Market Perspective," in Williams, *Illegal Immigration and Commercial Sex: The New Slave Trade,* 147–70; Rey Koslowski, "Economic Globalization, Human Smuggling, and Global Governance," in *Global Human Smuggling: Comparative Perspectives,* ed.

David Kyle and Rey Koslowski (Baltimore: The Johns Hopkins University Press, 2001), 337–58; Sally Stoecker, "Human Trafficking: A New Challenge for Russia and the United States," in *Human Traffic and Transnational Crime: Eurasian and American Perspectives*, ed. Sally Stoecker and Louise Shelley (Lanham: Rowman and Littlefield, 2005), 13–28; Moises Naim, *Illicit: How Smugglers, Traffickers, and Copycats Are Hijacking the Global Economy* (New York: Doubleday, 2005), 86–91; Md. Shahidul Haque, "Ambiguities and Confusions in Migration-Trafficking Nexus: A Development Challenge," in *Trafficking and the Global Sex Industry*, ed. Karen Beeks and Delila Amir (Lanham: Lexington Books, 2006), 3–20.

13. Peter Andreas and Timothy Snyder, eds., *The Wall Around the West: State Borders and Immigration Control in North America and Europe* (Lanham: Rowman and Littlefield, 2000).

14. Penelope Turnbull, "The Fusion of Immigration and Crime in the European Union: Problems of Cooperation and the Fight against the Trafficking in Women," in Williams, *Illegal Immigration and Commercial Sex*, 189–213; Virginie Guiraudon and Christian Joppke, eds., *Controlling a New Migration World* (London: Routledge, 2001).

15. Limanowska, *Trafficking in Human Beings* (2003); Limanowska, *Trafficking in Human Beings* (2005).

16. Jane Gronow, "Trafficking in Human Beings in Southeastern Europe: An Inventory of the Current Situation and Responses to Trafficking in Human Beings in Albania, Bosnia & Herzegovina, Croatia, the Federal Republic of Yugoslavia, and the former Yugoslav Republic of Macedonia" (Sarajevo: UNICEF Area Office for the Balkans, 2000), 27–30, 94, http://www.unicef.org/evaldatabase/files/CEE_CIS_2000_Trafficking.pdf (accessed 20 January 2007); Limanowska, *Trafficking in Human Beings* (2002), 108, 126; Thomas Koeppel and Agnes Szekely, "Transnational Organized Crime and Conflict in the Balkans," in *Transnational Organized Crime and International Security*, ed. Mats Berdal and Monica Serrano (Boulder: Lynne Rienner, 2002), 129–40; Peter Andreas, "Clandestine Political Economy of War and Peace in Bosnia," *International Studies Quarterly* 48, no. 1 (2004): 29–52; Peter Andreas, "The Criminalized Legacies of War: The Clandestine Political Economy of the Western Balkans," *Problems of Post-Communism* 51, no. 3 (May/June 2004): 3–9.

17. Kevin Bales argues that a key distinction between old and modern slavery is: "the *legal* ownership of human beings" has been replaced with control through mechanisms of violence. See Bales, *Disposable People*, 5.

18. Eileen Scully, "Pre-Cold War Traffic in Sexual Labor and Its Foes: Some Contemporary Lessons," in *Global Human Smuggling: Comparative Perspectives*, ed. David Kyle and Rey Koslowski (Baltimore: The Johns Hopkins University Press, 2001), 74–106 (quote 83).

19. Peter Andreas and Ethan Nadelmann, *Policing the Globe: Criminalization and Crime Control in International Relations* (Oxford: Oxford University Press, 2006), 33.

20. Scully, "Pre-Cold War Traffic," 84–87; Andreas and Nadelmann, *Policing the Globe,* 33–34.

21. Scully, "Pre-Cold War Traffic," 84–87 (quoted material); Andreas and Nadelmann, *Policing the Globe,* 33–34. See also Williams, "Trafficking in Women and

Children," 147; and Diana Wong, "The Rumor of Trafficking: Border Controls, Il-
legal Migration, and the Sovereignty of the Nation-State," in *Illicit Flows and Criminal
Things: States Borders, and the Other Side of Globalization*, ed. Willem van Schendel and
Itty Abraham (Bloomington: Indiana University Press, 2005), 72–73.

22. Andreas and Nadelmann, *Policing the Globe*, 34–35. The authors define a global
prohibition regime as emerging where "the activity becomes the subject of criminal
laws and police action throughout much of the world, and international institutions and conventions emerge to play a coordinating role" (17–22). See also Ethan
Nadelmann, "Global Prohibition Regimes: The Evolution of Norms in International
Society," *International Organization* 44, no. 4 (Autumn 1990): 479–526.

23. "International Agreement for the Suppression of the 'White Slave Traffic,'" 18
May 1904, University of Minnesota Human Rights Library, http://www1.umn
.edu/humanrts/instree/whiteslavetraffic1904.html (accessed 22 January 2007);
"International Convention for the Suppression of the 'White Slave Traffic,'" 4 May
1910, University of Minnesota Human Rights Library, http://www1.umn.edu/
humanrts/instree/whiteslavetraffic1910.html. For a discussion of disputes over the
issue of repatriation, and efforts to block forced repatriation, see Scully, "Pre-Cold
War Traffic," 91–92.

24. Andreas and Nadelmann, *Policing the Globe*, 35.

25. Scully, "Pre-Cold War Traffic," 87.

26. The backlash against the conceptualization of white slavery had begun earlier,
at international conferences held in 1912 and 1913. Scully, "Pre-Cold War Traffic,"
88, 97.

27. Scully, "Pre-Cold War Traffic," 92–93 (quote 93); Andreas and Nadelmann,
Policing the Globe, 34–35.

28. United Nations Treaty Collection, "Convention for the Suppression of the
Traffic in Persons and the Exploitation of the Prostitution of Others," http://www
.unhchr.ch/html/menu3/b/treaty11a.htm (accessed 29 January 2007).

29. As of 2006, CEDAW had 98 signatures and 185 ratifications, accessions, and
successions. See United Nations Division for the Advancement of Women, "Convention on the Elimination of All Forms of Discrimination against Women: States
Parties," http://www.un.org/womenwatch/daw/cedaw/states.htm (accessed
29 January 2007).

30. For example, see Caldwell et al., "Capitalizing on Transition Economies,"
42–73; Gerben J. N. Bruinsma and Guus Meershoek, "Organized Crime and Trafficking in Women for Eastern Europe in the Netherlands," in Williams, *Illegal Immigration and Commercial Sex*, 105–18; Hughes, "The 'Natasha' Trade," 625–51; Sally
Stoecker and Louise Shelley, eds., *Human Traffic and Transnational Crime: Eurasian and
American Perspectives* (Lanham: Rowman and Littlefield, 2005).

31. Gillian Caldwell, Steven Galster, and Nadia Steinzor, *Crime and Servitude:
An Expose of the Traffic in Women for Prostitution from the Newly Independent States*
(Washington DC: Global Survival Network, 1997); Caldwell et al., "Capitalizing on
Transition Economies"; United Nations Development Program (UNDP), *Human

Development Report (New York: Oxford University Press, 1999), 89, http://hdr.undp.org/reports/global/1999/en/.

32. United Nations, *Protocol to Prevent, Suppress and Punish Trafficking in Persons, Especially Women and Children, Supplementing the United Nations Convention against Transnational Organized Crime* (Geneva: United Nations, 2000).

33. See United Nations Office on Drugs and Crime, "Signatories—Protocol to Prevent, Suppress and Punish Trafficking in Persons, Especially Women and Children, Supplementing the United Nations Convention against Transnational Organized Crime," http://www.unodc.org/unodc/crime_cicp_signatures_trafficking.html#U (accessed 29 January 2007). The Transnational Organized Crime Convention entered into force on 29 September 2003, and by 2007 had 147 signatories and 131 parties. See United Nations Office on Drugs and Crime, "Signatories—United Nations Convention against Transnational Organized Crime," http://www.unodc.org/unodc/en/crime_cicp_signatures_convention.html#U (accessed 29 January 2007).

34. Although U.S. reward and threat strategies have had an impact in furthering the global prohibition regime, the extent of their impact remains a point of contention. For example, see Janie Chuang, "The United States as Global Sheriff: Using Unilateral Sanctions to Combat Human Trafficking," *Michigan Journal of International Law* 27, no. 2 (2006): 437–94; and GAO, *Human Trafficking*.

35. UN, *Protocol to Prevent, Suppress and Punish Trafficking in Persons*, Article 3.

36. For example, see the shift beginning in the U.S. Department of State's 2005 *Trafficking in Persons Report*. On sex trafficking as modern slavery, see Bales, *Disposable People*.

37. Gronow, "Trafficking in Human Beings," 4. See also Kemala Kempadoo and Jo Doezema, eds., *Global Sex Workers: Rights, Resistance and Revolution* (New York: Routledge, 1998); Nora V. Demleitner, "The Law at a Crossroads: The Construction of Migrant Women Trafficked into Prostitution," in *Global Human Smuggling: Comparative Perspectives*, ed. David Kyle and Rey Koslowski (Baltimore: The Johns Hopkins University Press, 2001), 257–93; and Joyce Outshoorn, "The Political Debates on Prostitution and Trafficking of Women," *Social Politics* 12, no. 1 (Spring 2005): 141–55.

38. United Nations General Assembly, "Crime Prevention and Criminal Justice: Report of the Ad Hoc Committee on the Elaboration of a Convention against Transnational Organized Crime on the Work of Its First to Eleventh Sessions, Addendum, Interpretive Notes for the Official Records (*travaux preparatoires*) of the Negotiation of the United Nations Convention against Transnational Organized Crime and the Protocols Thereto," UN Document A/55/383/Add.1, 3 November 2000, http://www.uncjin.org/Documents/Conventions/dcatoc/final_documents/383a1e.pdf (accessed 29 January 2007).

39. For example, see Demleitner, "The Law at a Crossroads"; Council of the European Union, "Council Framework Decision on Combating Trafficking in Human Beings," 2002/629/JHA, Official Journal L 203 (1 August 2002), http://europa.eu/scadplus/leg/en/lvb/l33137.htm (accessed 22 January 2007).

40. See especially, Division A—*Trafficking Victims Protection Act of 2000* (TVPA), section 103, *Victims of Trafficking and Violence Protection Act of 2000,* Public Law 106-386, 106th Cong. (28 October 2000), 7, http://www.state.gov/documents/organiza tion/10492.pdf (accessed 20 January 2007); see also Chuang, "United States as Global Sheriff," 450.

41. Allen D. Hertzke, *Freeing God's Children: The Unlikely Alliance for Global Human Rights* (Lanham: Rowman and Littlefield, 2004), 327–55; Dorothy McBride Stetson, "The Invisible Issue: Prostitution and Trafficking of Women and Girls in the United States," in *The Politics of Prostitution: Women's Movements, Democratic States and the Glo-balization of Sex Commerce,* ed. Joyce Outshoorn (Cambridge: Cambridge University Press, 2004), 245–64.

42. Andreas and Nadelmann, *Policing the Globe,* 35.

43. U.S. Department of State, "Pathbreaking Strategies in the Global Fight against Sex Trafficking," Conference recommendations, 23 February–26 February 2003, http://www.state.gov/g/tip/rls/rpt/20834.htm (verified 20 January 2007).

44. Agence France-Press, "Balkan Summit in Macedonia to Discuss Security, Bor-der Controls," 23 May 2003, http://www.balkanpeace.org/index.php?index=article &articleid=11835 (accessed 22 January 2007); Aleksandra Ilievska, "Fighting Crime Together." *Transitions Online,* 9 June 2003, http://www.tol.cz/look/BRR/tolprint .tpl?IdLanguage=1&IdPublication=9&NrIssue=1&NrSection=1&NrArticle=9740 (accessed 22 January 2007).

45. Limanowska, *Trafficking in Human Beings* (2005), 24.

46. Limanowska, *Trafficking in Human Beings* (2002).

47. For example, see Frank Laczko, "Human Trafficking: The Need for Better Data," *Migration Information Source* (November 2002), http://www.migrationinfor mation.org/feature/display.cfm?ID=66 (accessed 20 January 2007); Frank Laczko and Marco Gramegna, "Developing Better Indicators of Human Trafficking," *Brown Journal of World Affairs* 10 (Summer/Fall 2003): 179–94; Nicole Suter, "Human Trafficking and Statistics: The State of the Art" (working paper no. 15, submitted by the International Organization for Migration to the Statistical Commission and UN Economic Commission for Europe, Conference of European Statisticians, 2 November 2004); GAO, *Human Trafficking;* UNODC, *Trafficking in Persons.*

48. Surtees, *Second Annual Report.*

49. Nicole Lindstrom, "Regional Sex Trafficking in the Balkans: Transnational Networks in an Enlarged Europe," *Problems of Post-Communism* 51, no. 3 (May/June 2004): 45–52.

50. Gronow, "Trafficking in Human Beings," 2.

Chapter 2: Trafficking Exchanges and Economic Responses

1. Trafficking occurs with children and both men and women. In this chapter, however, I focus on trafficking of women because of the importance of gender relations and the particular role and position of women in marriage exchanges in many societies in relation to trafficking; and the programs with which I worked and

the case histories I both heard in the course of my work as well as collected in most cases involved young women and girls (with a few exceptions).

2. Between 1815 and 1957, some three hundred international agreements outlawing slavery were promulgated. The current relevant international legislation includes: the UN Declaration of Human Rights (1948); the Convention for the Suppression of the Trafficking in Persons and the Exploitation of the Prostitution of Others (1949); the Convention against Transnational Organized Crime (2000); the UN Protocol to Prevent, Suppress and Punish Trafficking in Persons, Especially Women and Children (2000); the Protocol Against the Smuggling of Migrants (2000); the Convention on the Rights of the Child (1989); the Convention to Eliminate the Worst Forms of Child Labor (1999); the Supplementary Convention on the Abolition of Slavery, the Slave Trade, and Institutions and Practices Similar to Slavery (1956); The Hague Convention on the Protection of Children and Cooperation with Respect to Intercountry Adoption (1993); the Convention on the Consent to Marriage, the Minimum Age for Marriage and Registration of Marriages (1962); and the International Labor Organization Convention Concerning Abolition of Forced Labor (1957).

3. The UN Convention against Transnational Organized Crime and Trafficking Protocol subsequently came into force in 2003 but no date as yet has been established for the smuggling protocol. However, regionally, the European Commission has negotiated, and is negotiating, a series of readmission agreements. For a further discussion of the Palermo protocols, see Lynellyn Long, "Trafficking in Women and Children as a Security Challenge in Southeast Europe," *Journal of Southeast European and Black Sea Studies* 2, no. 2 (May 2002): 63.

4. Sujata Manohar argues that the Palermo trafficking protocols primarily deal with trafficking as organized crime while the subsequent South Asian Association for Regional Cooperation (SAARC) Convention on Preventing and Combating Trafficking in Women and Children for Prostitution, 2002, has a broader human rights focus that engages state responsibility, and cooperation, as well as promoting rehabilitation and focusing on trafficking for prostitution. In several regions, however, this focus has led to some of the current abolitionist and anti-prostitution approaches, which stigmatize sex workers and deny the agency of many trafficked women. Sujata Manohar, "Trafficking in Women and Girls" (paper prepared for United Nations Expert Group Meeting, Glen Cove, New York, 2002), http://www .un.org/womenwatch/daw/egm/trafficking2002/reports/WP-SujataManohar.PDF (accessed 24 January 2007).

5. See United Nations Office on Drugs and Crime, "UN Global Programme against Trafficking in Human Beings," www.unodc.org/unodc/en/trafficking_ human_beings.html (accessed 20 January 2007); and U.S. Department of State, "Fact Sheet on the U.S. Government's International Anti-Trafficking in Persons Initiatives," 12 July 2001, http://www.state.gov/g/tip/rls/fs/2001/4051.htm (accessed 20 January 2007).

6. Lynellyn Long, "EC Perspectives on the Albanian Readmission Agreement," in *Combating Irregular Migration in Albania and the Wider Region*, ed. International Organization for Migration (IOM) (Geneva: IOM, forthcoming).

7. This is based on research conducted for the Women-to-Work Initiative in Belgrade from 2004 to 2006 and on interviews with "trafficked women" being returned from Sarajevo in 2002.

8. Amy O'Neill Richard observes that in the major trafficking cases since 1990, the perpetrators tended to come from small crime groups, smuggling rings, gangs, and a loose network of corrupt individuals and that most were not up for other illicit activities. Amy O'Neill Richard, *International Trafficking in Women to the U.S.: A Contemporary Manifestation of Slavery and Organized Crime* (Washington DC: Center for the Study of Intelligence, 1999).

9. For example, see U.S. Department of State, *Trafficking in Persons Report*, 2005, http://www.state.gov/g/tip/rls/tiprpt/2005 (accessed 20 January 2007).

10. LaShawn Jefferson's critique that the criteria for tier movement are not explained continues to be the case in the 2005 report, which argues for abolitionist approaches with Secretary of State Condoleezza Rice describing trafficking as the "abolitionist movement of the 21st century." LaShawn R. Jefferson (executive director, Women's Rights Division, Human Rights Watch), "Letter to Colin Powell on the Trafficking in Persons Report 2003," Human Rights Watch, http://www.hrw.org/press/2003/06/us062703ltr.htm (accessed 20 January 2007).

11. A major schism over how best to deliver anti-trafficking assistance has also emerged between a group of feminists (e.g., Gloria Steinem, Patricia Ireland, and Kathleen Barry) and conservative religious leaders, who argue for abolitionist approaches for all forms of prostitution, versus labor, reproductive and sexual rights' advocates, and sex workers, who document a range of abuses within the sex industry with the goal of decriminalization and sex industry reform. For an explication of the debates, see Kathleen Barry, *The Prostitution of Sexuality* (New York: NYU Press, 1995); Jo Doezema, "Loose Women or Lost Women?" *Gender Issues* 18, no. 1 (Winter 2000): 23–50; Laura Agustin, "Migrants in the Mistress's House: Other Voices in the 'Trafficking' Debate," *Social Politics* (Spring 2005): 96–117; Human Rights Watch, "Anatomy of a Backlash: Movements and Moral Panics," in *World Report 2005* (New York: Human Rights Watch, 2005), http://www.hrw.org/wr2k5/anatomy/index.htm (accessed 20 January 2007); Trafficking Policy Research Project, "Trafficking Policy Research Project: Examining the Effects of U.S. Trafficking Laws and Policies," www.bayswan.org./traffick/trafficking.html (accessed 20 January 2007).

12. For discussion of the late-nineteenth- and early-twentieth-century anti-"white slavery" regimes and the parallels to contemporary counter-trafficking efforts, see Doezema, "Loose Women"; and Lynellyn Long, "Anthropological Perspectives on the Trafficking of Women for Sexual Exploitation," *International Migration* 42, no. 1 (2004): 5–31. For discussion of nineteenth-century "white slavery," see Ernest A. Bell, *War on the White Slave Trade* (Toronto: Coles, 1980).

13. See the Human Rights Watch critique that the *TIP Report* does not meaningfully evaluate anti-trafficking efforts: Jefferson, "Letter to Colin Powell."

14. Marcel Mauss's seminal discussion of the gift as opposed to the commodity describes how this kind of exchange invokes every aspect of society of which it

is a part and is the basis of societal relations. Marcel Mauss, *The Gift, the Form and Reason for Exchange in Archaic Societies* (New York: W. W. Norton, 1990). A longer discussion of marriage prestations and trafficking is found in Long, "Anthropological Perspectives."

15. Gayle Rubin, "The Traffic in Women: Notes on the 'Political Economy' of Sex," in *Toward an Anthropology of Women*, ed. Rayna R. Reiter (New York: Monthly Review Press, 1975), 157–210; and Rayna R. Reitner, "Introduction," in *Toward an Anthropology of Women*, 11–19.

16. For discussion of the ethno-religious forms of the violence, see Paul Mojzes, *Yugoslavian Inferno: Ethnoreligious Warfare in the Balkans* (New York: Continuum, 1994).

17. Anti Sex Trafficking Action (ASTRA), personal communication, Belgrade, April 2005.

18. This section is based on conversations and interactions with many different women survivors of domestic violence and trafficking in Sarajevo, Banja Luka, and Belgrade during the period of 2000 to 2002 and for shorter periods during 2004, 2005, and 2006. The discussion on the impact of rape and post-traumatic stress is based on my work and interviews with women in refugee camps in several countries in the region (Serbia, Montenegro, Croatia, Bosnia and Herzegovina, and Macedonia) during several trips and periods of stay from 1993 to 1996.

19. Some of the failures to address war crimes have also led to more frustration and violence throughout the region—and, most importantly, to a culture of impunity.

20. Madeleine Rees, Office of the High Commissioner for Human Rights and Amela Effendic, International Organization for Migration (IOM), personal communication, Bosnia-Herzegovina, 2001.

21. For a comprehensive analysis of the role of the international community in developing demand and patterns of trafficking and/or in refusing to address the phenomena and its own role in these operations, see Human Rights Watch (HRW), *Hopes Betrayed: Trafficking of Women and Girls to Post-Conflict Bosnia and Herzegovina for Forced Prostitution* 14, no. 9 (D) (November 2002), http://www.hrw.org/reports/2002/bosnia/Bosnia1102.pdf (accessed 20 January 2007).

22. Julie Mertus, personal communication, Pittsburgh, June 2005. Aida Hozic at the same meeting also noted that this pattern of bringing outside women to satisfy local demand (and protect local prestations, thereby segmenting the exchange) began earlier during the Sarajevo Olympics when women from Belgrade were imported to Sarajevo to provide sexual services.

23. A local Bosnian policeman, who does not care to be identified, reported this information in Sarajevo, spring 2001.

24. Interviews with women in shelters in Bosnia-Herzegovina during the period of 2000 to 2002; reports of other shelter programs, 2004, 2005.

25. Anti Sex Trafficking Action (ASTRA), personal communication, Belgrade, March 2005; see also Barbara Limanowska, *Trafficking in Human Beings in South Eastern Europe: 2004—A Focus on Prevention* (Warsaw and Sarajevo: UNICEF, UNOHCHR,

OSCE/ODIHR, 2005), http://www.unicef.org/ceecis/Trafficking.Report.2005.pdf (verified 20 January 2007).

26. Sandra Dickson, *Sex in the City: Mapping Commercial Sex across London* (London: The POPPY Project, Eaves Housing for Women, 2004), 10, 15.

27. For an evaluation of the impact of a conditional cash transfer program on school attendance in Mexico, see Elizabeth Sandoulet, Frederico Finan, Alain de Janvoy, and Renos Vakis, "Can Conditional Cash Transfer Programs Improve Social Risk Management? Lessons for Education and Child Labor Outcomes" (social protection discussion paper No. 0420, World Bank, December 2004).

28. For evaluation of cash transfers on child labor and school attendance in Brazil, see Eliana Cardoso and Andre Portela Souza, "The Impact of Cash Transfers on Child Labor and School Attendance in Brazil" (working paper 04-W07, Department of Economics, Vanderbilt University, 2004).

29. Sonja Drljevic, Association for Women's Initiative (AWIN) Women's Network, personal communication, Belgrade, April 2005.

30. Microenterprise and small and medium enterprise training and mentoring could be extended to more vulnerable groups of women. Several NGO programs, including Oxfam, International Catholic Migration Commission, Women-to-Work, Integra, and others, have tried this approach with some success.

31. For discussion of the need for legal migration regimes as alternatives to growing irregular migration, see Bimal Ghosh, *Managing Migration: Time for a New International Regime* (Oxford: Oxford University Press, 2000); and International Organization for Migration (IOM), "Ways to Curb the Growing Complexities of Irregular Migration," in *World Migration Report 2003*, 58–70 (Geneva: IOM, 2003). In light of security issues, migration experts also argue for international or global regimes although these seem very difficult to obtain. For example, see Ghosh, *Managing Migration*; and Rey Koslowski, "The Mobility Money Can Buy," in *The Wall Around the West: State Borders and Immigration Control in North America and Europe,* ed. Peter Andreas and Tim Snyder (Lanham: Rowman and Littlefield, 2000), 203–18.

32. Lynellyn D. Long, "From Handmaid to Entrepreneur" (report summary for Women-to-Work, London, 2005).

33. Richard Lewis Siegel, "The Right to Work: Core Minimum Obligations," in *Core Obligations: Building a Framework for Economic, Social, and Cultural Rights*, ed. Audrey Chapman and Sage Russell (Antwerp: Intersentia, 2002), 21–52.

34. See Martha Brady, "Laying the Foundation for Girls' Healthy Futures: Can Sports Play a Role?" *Studies in Family Planning* 29, no. 1 (1998): 79–82; and Martha Brady and Arjmand Banu Khan, *Letting Girls Play: The Mathare Youth Sports Association's Football Program for Girls* (New York: Population Council, 2002). The U.S. President's Council on Physical Fitness and Sports is also conducting long-term studies on the effects of athletic programs and team sports on girls' outcomes.

35. Sean Barrett, personal communication, London, November 2004.

36. Without entering too much into the longer discussion of whether sex work or prostitution is inherently exploitative, I would argue that criminalizing and making sex work illegal are likely to increase the violence and exploitation in these activities.

Carol Leigh suggests how a prostitute and rights' advocate approaches these issues: Carol Leigh, *Unrepentant Whore: Collected Works of Scarlot Harlot* (San Francisco: Last Gasp, 2004).

37. What some consider pornographic material, others consider erotic. All too often, religious and political leaders argue for censorship on religious grounds and invoke moral regimes, whereas traditionally, the major religions have inspired artistic erotic expression (particularly in imagery and movements).

Chapter 3: Combating Trafficking

1. This study includes in its scope the countries of Albania, Bosnia and Herzegovina, Croatia, the Former Yugoslav Republic of Macedonia, Serbia, Montenegro, and the UN Administered Province of Kosovo. Montenegro achieved independence in mid-2006.

2. International Organization for Migration (IOM), *Victims of Trafficking in the Balkans: A Study of Trafficking in Women and Children for Sexual Exploitation to, through and from the Balkan Region* (Geneva: IOM, 2001), http://www.old.iom.int/documents/publication/en/balkan_trafficking.pdf (accessed 22 January 2007).

3. U.S. Department of State, *Trafficking in Persons Report,* 2006, http://www.state.gov/g/tip/rls/tiprpt/2006/ (accessed 20 January 2007).

4. Amnesty International, "'So Does It Mean that We Have the Rights?' Protecting the Human Rights of Women and Girls Trafficked for Forced Prostitution in Kosovo," AI Index: EUR 70/010/2004, 6 May 2004, http://web.amnesty.org/library/Index/ENGEUR700102004?open&of=ENG-373 (accessed 20 January 2007).

5. IOM, *Victims of Trafficking in the Balkans.*

6. Amnesty International, "'So Does It Mean?'"

7. Human Rights Watch (HRW), *Hopes Betrayed: Trafficking of Women and Girls to Post-Conflict Bosnia and Herzegovina for Forced Prostitution* 14, no. 9 (D) (November 2002), http://www.hrw.org/reports/2002/bosnia/Bosnia1102.pdf (accessed 20 January 2007).

8. Amnesty International, "'So Does It Mean?'"

9. HRW, *Hopes Betrayed,* 17.

10. Amnesty International, "'So Does It Mean?'"

11. IOM, *Victims of Trafficking in the Balkans,* 58–59.

12. HRW, *Hopes Betrayed.*

13. Reports have been undertaken by the U.S. Department of State, U.S. Agency for International Development (USAID), United Nations Children's Fund, International Organization for Migration, Organization for Security and Cooperation in Europe/Office for Democratic Institutions and Human Rights, and the United Nations Office of the High Commissioner for Human Rights, among others. In addition to reports noted in the text, see United Nations Mission in Bosnia and Herzegovina/United Nations Office of the High Commissioner for Human Rights (UNMIBH/UNOHCHR), "Report on Joint Trafficking Project of UNMIBH/OHCHR," May 2000; Stability Pact for South Eastern Europe, "Statement on Commitments,

Legislation of the Status of Trafficked Persons" (statement presented at the Third Regional Ministerial Forum, Tirana, 2002); Counter-Trafficking Regional Clearing Point (CTRCP), *First Annual Report on Victims of Trafficking in South Eastern Europe* (Vienna: International Organization for Migration, Stability Pact for South Eastern Europe, International Catholic Migration Commission, 2003), http://www.iom.hu/PDFs/First%20Annual%20Report%20on%20VoT%20 in%20SEE.pdf (verified 22 January 2007); Organization for Security and Cooperation in Europe (OSCE), "Taking a Stand: Effective Assistance and Protection to Victims of Trafficking" (conference sponsored by the OSCE Special Representative on Combating Trafficking in Human Beings and the Anti-Trafficking Assistance Unit under the Aegis of the Alliance against Trafficking in Persons, Vienna, 2005).

14. Barbara Limanowska, *Trafficking in Human Beings in South Eastern Europe: 2004—A Focus on Prevention* (Warsaw and Sarajevo: UNICEF, UNOHCHR, OSCE/ODIHR, 2005), http://www.unicef.org/ceecis/Trafficking.Report.2005.pdf (accessed 20 January 2007).

15. IOM, *Victims of Trafficking in the Balkans.*

16. Global Alliance against Traffic in Women (GAATW), *Human Rights and Trafficking in Persons: A Handbook* (Bangkok: GAATW, 2001), 65–67, http://gaatw .net/books_pdf/Human%20Rights%20and%20Trafficking%20in%20 Person.pdf (accessed 22 January 2007).

17. Nicole Lindstrom, "Regional Sex Trafficking in the Balkans: Transnational Networks in an Enlarged Europe," *Problems of Post-Communism* 51, no. 3 (May/June 2004): 45–52.

18. Stability Pact for South Eastern Europe, Task Force on Trafficking in Human Beings, "National Programmes to Combat Trafficking in Human Beings (National Plans of Action) Background Paper" (Vienna: Stability Pact for South Eastern Europe, 2001); Stability Pact for South Eastern Europe, Task Force on Trafficking in Human Beings, "Guidelines for National Plans of Action to Combat Trafficking in Human Beings and National Programmes to Combat Trafficking in Human Beings (National Plans of Action) Background Paper" (Vienna: Stability Pact for South Eastern Europe, 2001).

19. Limanowska, *Trafficking in Human Beings* (2005), 3.

20. Rochelle Jones, "Prevention as the New Approach to Human Trafficking: AWID Interviews Barbara Limanowska," 19 August 2005, Association for Women in Development (AWID), http://www.awid.org/go.php?stid=1538 (accessed 22 January 2007).

21. Amnesty International, "'So Does It Mean?'"

22. Amnesty International, "'So Does It Mean?'"

23. Amnesty International, "'So Does It Mean?'"

24. HRW, *Hopes Betrayed, 35.*

25. HRW, *Hopes Betrayed.*

26. Amnesty International, "'So Does It Mean?'"

27. Amnesty International, "'So Does It Mean?'"

28. Wim Van Meurs, "Stabilizing the Balkans–US and EU Policies" (workshop lecture, American Institute for Contemporary German Studies Workshop, Washington DC, 26 September 2000). In 2000, for example, unemployment in Kosovo reached a high of 60 percent (Amnesty International, "'So Does It Mean?'").

29. International Organization for Migration (IOM), Counter-Trafficking Service, *Changing Patterns and Trends of Trafficking in Persons in the Balkan Region* (Geneva: IOM, July 2004), http://www.iom.md/materials/balkans_trafficking.pdf; Rebecca Surtees, *Second Annual Report on Victims of Trafficking in South-Eastern Europe*, Regional Clearing Point, International Organization for Migration (IOM) (Geneva: IOM, 2005), http://www.iom.int/jahia/webdav/site/myjahiasite/shared/shared/mainsite/published_docs/studies_and_reports/second_annual05.pdf (accessed 20 January 2007).

30. IOM, *Changing Patterns and Trends*, 5.

31. IOM, *Changing Patterns and Trends*, 5.

32. IOM, *Changing Patterns and Trends*, 16; Commission of the European Communities, *Research Based on Case Studies of Victims of Trafficking in Human Beings in 3 EU Member States, i.e. Belgium, Italy and the Netherlands* (Brussels: Commission of the European Communities, Payoke, On the Road, De Rode Draad, 2003), 172–73, http://www.ontheroadonlus.it/rootdown/RapIppocra.pdf (accessed 20 January 2007).

33. Surtees, *Second Annual Report*, 253n233, 248, 253.

34. Surtees, *Second Annual Report*, 118.

35. Sebastian Lăzăroiu and Monica Alexandru, *Who Is the Next Victim? Vulnerability of Young Romanian Women to Trafficking in Human Beings* (Bucharest: International Organization for Migration, 2003), 59, http://www.old.iom.int/DOCUMENTS/PUBLICATION/EN/Romania_ct.pdf (accessed 20 January 2007).

36. Limanowska, *Trafficking in Human Beings* (2005).

37. "Women Increasingly Migrate for Economic Reasons; Trafficking also Rising," *EuropaWorld*, 4 March 2005, http://www.europaworld.org/week214/women4305.htm (accessed 22 January 2007).

38. OSCE, "Taking a Stand," 5.

39. International Council on Human Rights Policy (ICHRP), *Human Rights Crises: NGO Responses to Military Interventions* (Versoix: International Council on Human Rights Policy, 2002), 6, http://www.ichrp.org/paper_files/115_p_01.pdf (accessed 16 April 2007).

40. Janice Helwig, "United States Mission to the OSCE: Statement on Trafficking in Human Beings" (paper delivered at the U.S. Helsinki Commission to the OSCE Human'Dimension Implementation Meeting, Warsaw, 27 September 2005), 1, http://osce.usmission.gov/archive/2005/09/HDIM_On_Trafficking_in_Human_Beings_09_27_05.pdf (verified 22 January 2007).

41. Amy O'Neill Richard, *International Trafficking in Women to the U.S.A.: Contemporary Manifestation of Slavery and Organized Crime* (Washington DC: Center for the Study of Intelligence, 1999), 1.

42. Jennifer Murray, "Who Will Police the Peace-Builders? The Failure to

Establish Accountability for the Participation of United Nations Civilian Police in the Trafficking of Women in Post-Conflict Bosnia and Herzegovina," *Columbia Human Rights Law Review* 34 (Spring 2003): 489n73.

43. Frank Laczko, "Human Trafficking: The Need for Better Data," *Migration Information Source* (November 2002), http://www.migrationinformation.org/feature/display.cfm?ID=66 (accessed 20 January 2007).

44. Journalist in the Balkan region (anonymous), telephone interview with author, 30 September 2005.

45. Limanowska, *Trafficking in Human Beings* (2005), 52.

46. Lynellyn Long (former IOM Chief of Mission in Sarajevo, 2000–2002), telephone interview with author, 26 September 2005.

47. Jones, "Prevention as the New Approach."

48. Limanowska, *Trafficking in Human Beings* (2005), xiv.

49. Barbara Limanowska, *Trafficking in Human Beings in South Eastern Europe: 2003 Update on Situation and Responses to Trafficking in Human Beings* (Warsaw and Sarajevo: UNICEF, UNOHCHR, OSCE/ODIHR, 2003), 204, http://www.ceecis.org/child_protection/PDF/Traff2003.pdf (accessed 20 January 2007).

50. Surtees, *Second Annual Report*, 44.

51. Limanowska, *Trafficking in Human Beings* (2005), 53.

52. Limanowska, *Trafficking in Human Beings* (2005), 55.

53. Lynellyn Long (former IOM Chief of Mission in Sarajevo, 2000–2002), telephone interview with author, 26 September 2005.

54. Surtees, *Second Annual Report*.

55. Surtees, *Second Annual Report*, 45, 46.

56. Limanowska, *Trafficking in Human Beings* (2005), 139.

57. Margaret Keck and Katherine Sikkink, *Activists Beyond Borders* (Ithaca: Cornell University Press, 1998), 2.

58. Lindstrom, "Regional Sex Trafficking," 50–51.

59. Limanowska, *Trafficking in Human Beings* (2003).

60. Limanowska, *Trafficking in Human Beings* (2003), xi.

61. Organization for Security and Cooperation in Europe/Office for Democratic Institutions and Human Rights, "Ensuring Human Rights Protection in Countries of Destination: Breaking the Cycle of Trafficking" (conference report, Helsinki, 23–24 September 2004), 7, http://www.osce.org/odihr/item_11_15919.html (accessed 20 January 2007).

62. NDI Regional Initiative for Central and Eastern Europe, "Delivering Democracy: Organizing Resources to Create Secure Societies National Democratic Institute Program for Women Political Leaders from Central and Eastern Europe" (seminar, Warsaw, 1–4 March 2002), http://www.ndi.org/ndi/library/1383_cee_women leaders_030102.txt (accessed 20 January 2007).

63. Geneva Global, "Sector Priorities: Human Liberty," http://www/geneva global.com/sector-priorities/human-liberty (accessed 4 June 2007).

64. Zonta International Foundation, "International Service Projects, 2002–2004, STAR Network of World Learning: The Bosnia-Herzegovina Anti-

Trafficking Community Mobilization Project," 2, http://www.zonta.org/site/DocServer?docID=4025 (accessed 20 January 2007).

65. Jones, "Prevention as the New Approach."

66. Laczko, "Human Trafficking."

Chapter 4: Transnational Responses to Human Trafficking

This chapter was prepared with the research assistance of Jelena Djordjevic, Anti Trafficking Center, Serbia and Montenegro, and University of Sussex, Brighton, UK.

1. Mitchell Orenstein, "The New Pension Reform as Global Policy," *Global Social Policy* 5, no. 2 (2005): 175–202.

2. This section draws on Nicole Lindstrom, "Regional Sex Trafficking in the Balkans: Transnational Networks in an Enlarged Europe," *Problems of Post-Communism* 51, no. 3 (May/June 2004): 45–52.

3. Frank Laczko and Marco Gramegna, "Developing Better Indicators of Human Trafficking," *Brown Journal of World Affairs* 10 (Summer/Fall 2003): 179–94.

4. Laczko and Gramegna, "Developing Better Indicators," 186–91.

5. Barbara Limanowska, *Trafficking in Human Beings in South Eastern Europe: 2003 Update on Situation and Responses to Trafficking in Human Beings* (Warsaw and Sarajevo: UNICEF, UNOHCHR, OSCE/ODIHR, 2003), http://www.ceecis.org/child_protection/PDF/Traff2003.pdf (accessed 20 January 2007); discussed in Lindstrom, "Regional Sex Trafficking," 47.

6. Lindstrom, "Regional Sex Trafficking," 48–49.

7. Helga Konrad, "Trafficking in Human Beings: The Ugly Face of Europe," *Helsinki Monitor* 13, no. 3 (March 2002): 263; Lindstrom, "Regional Sex Trafficking," 49.

8. Lindstrom, "Regional Sex Trafficking," 49; for an academic example of this kind of analysis, see Donna Hughes, "The 'Natasha' Trade: The Transnational Shadow Market of Trafficking in Women," *Journal of International Affairs* 53, no. 2 (2000): 625–51.

9. Lindstrom, "Regional Sex Trafficking," 49.

10. Global Alliance against Traffic in Women (GAATW), *Human Rights and Trafficking in Persons: A Handbook* (Bangkok: GAATW, 2001), 81, http://gaatw.net/books_pdf/Human%20Rights%20and%20Trafficking%20in%20Person.pdf (accessed 22 January 2007).

11. Lindstrom "Regional Sex Trafficking," 49.

12. Limanowska, *Trafficking in Human Beings* (2003), 23.

13. For a summary of the "feminization of poverty" in Central and Eastern Europe, see Rebecca Jean Emigh and Iván Szelényi, eds., *Poverty, Ethnicity, and Gender in Eastern Europe during the Market Transition* (Westport, CT: Praeger, 2001).

14. Lindstrom, "Regional Sex Trafficking," 51.

15. Stability Pact for South Eastern Europe, Task Force on Trafficking in Human Beings, "Guidelines for National Plans of Action to Combat Trafficking in Human Beings and National Programmes to Combat Trafficking in Human Beings (National

Plans of Action) Background Paper" (Vienna: Stability Pact for South Eastern Europe, 2001).

16. U.S. Department of State, *Trafficking in Persons Report,* 2004, http://www .state.gov/g/tip/rls/tiprpt/2004 (accessed 20 January 2007).

17. *National Strategy for Combating Trafficking in Human Beings of Serbia,* 2005, 3.

18. Limanowska, *Trafficking in Human Beings* (2003), 150.

19. Rebecca Surtees, *Second Annual Report on Victims of Trafficking in South-Eastern Europe,* Regional Clearing Point, International Organization for Migration (IOM) (Geneva: IOM, 2005), 397–98, http://www.iom.int/jahia/webdav/site/myjahiasite/ shared/shared/mainsite/published_docs/studies_and_reports/second_annual05 .pdf (accessed 20 January 2007).

20. *National Strategy,* 10.

21. Limanowska, *Trafficking in Human Beings* (2003), 146.

22. *National Strategy,* 10.

23. Barbara Limanowska, *Trafficking in Human Beings in South Eastern Europe: 2004—A Focus on Prevention* (Warsaw and Sarajevo: UNICEF, UNOHCHR, OSCE/ ODIHR, 2005), 147n255, http://www.unicef.org/ceecis/Trafficking.Report.2005.pdf (accessed 20 January 2007).

24. Limanowska, *Trafficking in Human Beings* (2005), 150.

25. Limanowska, *Trafficking in Human Beings* (2005), 151, 152.

26. Limanowska, *Trafficking in Human Beings* (2005), 147.

27. Surtees, *Second Annual Report,* 389.

28. Surtees, *Second Annual Report,* 400.

29. Counter-Trafficking Regional Clearing Point (CTRCP), *First Annual Report on Victims of Trafficking in South Eastern Europe* (Vienna: International Organization for Migration, Stability Pact for South Eastern Europe, International Catholic Migration Commission, 2003), http://www.iom.hu/PDFs/First%20 Annual%20Report%20 on%20VoT%20in%20SEE.pdf (accessed 22 January 2007); Surtees, *Second Annual Report.*

30. Surtees, *Second Annual Report,* 398.

31. Surtees, *Second Annual Report,* 32.

32. Surtees, *Second Annual Report,* 31; International Organization for Migration (IOM), *Applied Research and Data Collection on Trafficking in Human Beings to, through and from the Balkan Region* (Geneva: IOM, 2001).

33. Surtees, *Second Annual Report,* foreword.

34. Limanowska, *Trafficking in Human Beings* (2005), 117.

35. Rochelle Jones, "Prevention as the New Approach to Human Trafficking: AWID Interviews Barbara Limanowska," 19 August 2005, Association for Women in Development (AWID), http://www.awid.org/go.php?stid=1538 (accessed 22 January 2007).

36. The underground nature of trafficking is portrayed in Lukas Moodysson's 2002 film, *Lilja 4-Ever.* In this fictional account, a young Russian woman, unemployed and living in poverty in a Russian province, is recruited by an acquaintance with

the promise of working legally. She arrives by plane in Stockholm, is driven to a provincial Swedish industrial city, raped by her handler, and held captive in a private apartment in a nondescript housing bloc. *Lilja 4-Ever*, DVD, directed by Lukas Moodysson (2002; Newmarket Films, 2003).

37. "Balkan Human Trafficking Out of Control?" Radio Free Europe/Radio Liberty, *Balkan Report* 7, no. 35 (October 17, 2003), http://www.rferl.org/reports/balkan-report/2003/10/35-171003.asp.

38. Elizabeth Bruch, "Models Wanted: The Search for an Effective Response to Human Trafficking," *Stanford Journal of International Law* 40, no. 1 (Winter 2004): 1–45.

39. Surtees, *Second Annual Report*, 14.

40. Rey Koslowski, "The Mobility Money Can Buy," in *The Wall Around the West: State Borders and Immigration Control in North America and Europe*, ed. Peter Andreas and Tim Snyder (Lanham: Rowman and Littlefield, 2000), 203–18. See also Peter Andreas, "Introduction: The Wall After the Wall," in *Wall Around the West*, 1–14; and Milada Anna Vachudova, "Eastern Europe as Gatekeeper: The Immigration and Asylum Polities of an Enlarging EU," in *Wall Around the West*, 153–73.

Chapter 5: Peacekeeping and Rule Breaking

1. Barbara Limanowska, *Trafficking in Human Beings in South Eastern Europe: 2004—A Focus on Prevention* (Warsaw and Sarajevo: UNICEF, UNOHCHR, OSCE/ODIHR, 2005), 49–50, http://www.unicef.org/ceecis/Trafficking.Report.2005.pdf (accessed 20 January 2007).

2. Limanowska, *Trafficking in Human Beings* (2005), 105. In 2003, police identified and assisted only six trafficking victims at most.

3. For a full account of the findings of these research missions, see Human Rights Watch (HRW), *Hopes Betrayed: Trafficking of Women and Girls to Post-Conflict Bosnia and Herzegovina for Forced Prostitution* 14, no. 9 (D) (November 2002), http://www.hrw.org/reports/2002/bosnia/Bosnia1102.pdf (accessed 20 January 2007). In December 2003, the Department of Defense Office of the Inspector General published a report on its own investigation into trafficking in the Balkans. This report largely confirmed the findings of the Human Rights Watch report. See U.S. Department of Defense, Office of the Inspector General, "Assessment of DOD Efforts to Combat Trafficking in Persons," 2003, http://www.hrw.org/reports/2002/bosnia/ig.pdf (verified 27 January 2007).

4. United Nations Department of Peacekeeping Operations (DPKO), Best Practices Unit, *Human Trafficking Resource Package* (New York: United Nations, December 2004), 23, http://www.peacekeepingbestpractices.unlb.org/pbpu/view/viewdocument.aspx?id=2&docid=601&menukey=_7_23.

5. The United Nations' own statistics indicated that as of 2006, only 316 peacekeeping personnel had faced investigation in all missions. These investigations resulted in the summary dismissal of 18 civilians, repatriation of 17 members of

police units, and 144 repatriations or rotations home on disciplinary grounds. In comments made on 5 December 2006, Secretary General Annan did not point to any criminal convictions, and conceded that the United Nations lacked the authority to discipline 80 percent of 100,000 people working in its peacekeeping operations. BBC News, "'Zero Tolerance' for UN Sex Abuse," 5 December 2006, http://news.bbc .co.uk/2/hi/americas/6208774.stm (accessed 20 January 2007).

6. The Stabilisation Force (SFOR) in Bosnia and Herzegovina consisted of NATO-led forces from NATO and non-NATO countries. The SFOR replaced the Implementation Force (IFOR) in Bosnia and Herzegovina in 1996, under the authority of UN Security Council Resolution 1088. IFOR consisted of approximately sixty thousand troops and SFOR consisted of thirty-two thousand troops.

7. The convention entered into force on 17 September 1946. United Nations, *Convention on the Privileges and Immunities of the United Nations*, adopted by the General Assembly of the United Nations on 13 February 1946, http://www .unog.ch/80256EDD006B8954/(httpAssets)/C8297DB1DE8566F2C1256F2 600348A73/$file/Convention%20P%20&%20I%20(1946)%20-%20E.pdf (accessed 4 June 2007).

8. U.S. special operations personnel serving as Joint Commission Observers (JCOs) were one exception to this rule. The JCOs lived in local housing in communities in Bosnia and Herzegovina.

9. HQ SFOR Public Information Office, "History of the NATO-led Stabilisation Force (SFOR) in Bosnia and Herzegovina," SFOR, http://www.nato .int/sfor/docu/d981116a.htm (accessed 20 January 2007). U.S. forces first crossed over the Sava River into Bosnia and Herzegovina in 1996 with a force of twenty thousand personnel. See Major General James W. Darden, "Opening Remarks for Major General James W. Darden, USAR Deputy Director for Plans & Policy, United States European Command to the House Armed Services Committee Issue Forum, 'Winning the Peace under the Dayton Peace Accords: Military Lessons Learned and Sustaining the Peace in Bosnia,'" 12 July 2004, http://armedservices.house.gov/comdocs/openingstatementsandpress releases/108thcongress/04-07-12Darden.pdf (accessed 27 January 2007). On the civilian side, at maximum strength, the United Nations Mission in Bosnia and Herzegovina (UNMIBH) included 2,047 civilian police and military liaison personnel. As of 30 September 2002, UNMIBH included 1,414 civilian police personnel and 395 international civilian personnel. See United Nations Mission in Bosnia and Herzegovina, "Bosnia and Herzegovina: UNMIBH Background," http://www.un.org/Depts/dpko/missions/unmibh/background.html (accessed 22 January 2007).

10. It is by now an article of faith that the individuals who turned to trafficking in humans had trafficked drugs and arms during the war, committed war crimes, or engaged in war-profiteering. Because of the small number of prosecutions of traffickers, it is difficult to confirm these allegations.

11. A 2001 article in *Stars & Stripes* estimated that the NATO-led SFOR in Bosnia and Herzegovina infused between $600,000 and $800,000 each month into the local

economy. The article also suggested that U.S. defense contractors such as Brown & Root Services, TRW, and Sprint aided the local Bosnian economy by employing local nationals and spending approximately $1.1 million per year in rent for buildings and other property. Richelle Turner Collins, "Suggestions of U.S. Pullout Grab Attention in Bosnia," *Stars & Stripes*, 14 January 2001.

12. According to Retired Maj. Gen. William Nash, commander of the 1st Airborne Division and the first commander of Task Force Eagle, interviewed by the *Army Times* in December 2004, "We cleared a side of the road, took a few mines away and put some gravel down and allowed these shacks to be built to start some commerce, and the reason the commerce was there was because it was near a check-point so the area was secure so Serbs, Croats and Bosniacs could all come and do business without fear of ethnic violence from their respective police forces or armed forces because it was in the zone of separation and guarded by the NATO force, Americans. . . . Over the years the Arizona Market has had an up and down existence with some issues of black marketing, trafficking in literally drugs, sex and rock and roll." *Army Times*, "The Lessons Learned in Bosnia—and How They Apply to Iraq," December 2004, http://www.armytimes.com/print.php?f=1–292925–543796.php (accessed 10 May 2005, link no longer active).

13. Mara Radovanovic and Angelika Kartusch, *Report on the Combat of Trafficking in Women for the Purpose of Forced Prostitution in Bosnia and Herzegovina* (Vienna: Ludwig Boltzmann Institute of Human Rights, 2001), 12–13. The report cites an article published by journalist Dzenana Karup Drusko, "White Slaves in House of Sex," *Dani* 86 (12 October 1998), http://www.bhdani.com/arhiva/86/tekst186.htm (accessed 22 January 2007).

14. Radovanovic and Kartusch, *Report on the Combat of Trafficking*, 11.

15. The number of registered foreign women was merely the tip of the iceberg. Radovanovic and Kartusch estimated that twice as many women worked in the clubs illegally, without any official police registration. Of the 309 women registered, 171 hailed from Moldova, 76 from Ukraine, 56 from Romania, 4 from Russia, 1 from Belarus, and 1 from Cameroon. Radovanovic and Kartusch, *Report on the Combat of Trafficking*, 11.

16. Madeleine Rees (director, United Nations Office of the High Commissioner for Human Rights [UNOHCHR]), personal communication, New York, 1999.

17. [Name withheld], personal communication, Bijeljina, Republika Srpska, February 1998.

18. Dzenana Karup Drusko, interview with author, Sarajevo, February 1998.

19. Madeleine Rees (director, UNOHCHR), interview with author, Sarajevo, February 1998.

20. A United States Army Criminal Investigation Command report compiled in June 2000 documented the purchase of a trafficked woman and an Uzi by a U.S. contractor employed by DynCorp. The American military contractor confessed to U.S. Army investigators that he had purchased the weapon and the Moldovan woman as a package deal for 1,600 deutsche marks. Although the contractor claimed that he had purchased the woman, Oksana, to assist her in getting home, at the time

of the investigation, she was living in his quarters in Bosnia as "a housemate." U.S. Army, Criminal Investigation Command, CID Report 0075-CID597-49891, on file with author.

21. In a few cases, trafficked women managed to escape from the brothels. In one case documented by UN International Police Task Force (IPTF) officers in Doboj, the women went to the IPTF station for assistance, fearing that corrupt local police officers might return them to the brothel owners.

22. Jasminka Dzumhur, interview with author, Zenica, March 1999.

23. Madeleine Rees, interview with author, Sarajevo, March 1999.

24. The author participated in this raid as an observer and interviewed the victims in the brothel.

25. Madeleine Rees, interview with author, Sarajevo, March 1999. Note, however, that SFOR did become involved in anti-trafficking efforts with its participation in Operation Mirage.

26. In at least one case near Tuzla, a local IPTF officer purchased a woman from a brothel owner in order to "rescue" her, later sending her home to Ukraine. IPTF local interpreter, interview with author, Tuzla, March 1999.

27. HRW, *Hopes Betrayed*, 50.

28. IPTF local interpreter, interview with author, Tuzla, March 1999.

29. See, for example, Sarah Mendelson, *Barracks and Brothels: Peacekeepers and Human Trafficking in the Balkans* (Washington DC: Center for Strategic and International Studies, 2005), 65. Police interviewed near Tuzla, Bosnia and Herzegovina in 2001 indicated that they had video footage showing that a large proportion of the cars parked in the parking lots outside local brothels housing trafficked women and girls in the area sported SFOR contractor license plates.

30. United Nations Mission in Bosnia and Herzegovina/International Police Task Force (UNMIBH/IPTF), "Operating Procedures for Trafficking Victims," Guidance No. 9-A (revised), para. 4.2, 22 September 2000, cited in HRW, *Hopes Betrayed*, 45.

31. IPTF human rights officer, interview with author, Sarajevo, March 26, 2001, cited in HRW, *Hopes Betrayed*, 45.

32. HRW, *Hopes Betrayed*, 28nn110–11.

33. Colum Lynch, "UN Halted Probe of Officers' Alleged Role in Sex Trafficking," *Washington Post*, 27 December 2001, http://www.washingtonpost.com/ac2/wp-dyn?pagename=article&node=&contentId=A28267-2001Dec26 (accessed 20 January 2007).

34. UN internal affairs investigators themselves echoed these criticisms, reporting that they received minimal resources and little support to conduct investigations when allegations emerged. Canadian internal affairs investigator, interview with author, March 2001.

35. HRW, *Hopes Betrayed*, 50–51.

36. Milakovic was later prosecuted and convicted, receiving a prison sentence for his involvement in trafficking in women and girls for forced prostitution. Mara Radovanovic, interview with author, Sarajevo, July 2006.

37. HRW, *Hopes Betrayed*, 50.

38. This jurisdictional gap was not remedied until December 2005 with the passage of the Trafficking Victims Protection Reauthorization Act of 2005, H.R. 972, which created federal criminal jurisdiction for trafficking crimes committed abroad by U.S. civilian contractors.

39. U.S. Department of State, unclassified memorandum 200020567, 10 December 2001, obtained by Human Rights Watch through a FOIA request, http://www .hrw.org/reports/2002/bosnia/1201memo.pdf (accessed 27 January 2007).

40. U.S. Department of State, cable 2001USUNN02045, 25 June 2002, obtained by Human Rights Watch through FOIA request, http://www.hrw.org/reports/2002/ bosnia/Scan001.PDF (accessed 27 January 2007).

41. U.S. Department of State, cable 2001SARAJE01032, December 2001, obtained by Human Rights Watch through FOIA request, http://www.hrw.org/reports/ 2002/bosnia/0301cable.pdf (accessed 27 January 2007).

42. See, generally, BBC News, "Fortress Europe Raises the Drawbridge," 18 June 2002, http://news.bbc.co.uk/1/hi/world/europe/2042779.stm (accessed 20 January 2007); International Center for Migration Policy Development, "How to Halt Illegal Migration to, from, and through South East Europe?" Report on the activities of the Working Group on South East Europe of the Budapest Group, prepared by the Secretariat of the Budapest Group for the Meeting of the Working Group, Skoplje, 27–28 November 2000, http://unpan1 .un.org/intradoc/groups/public/documents/UNTC/UNPAN017488.pdf (accessed 20 January 2007).

43. Anti-trafficking NGO members, interviews with author, Sarajevo, March 2001.

44. U.S. Department of State, cable 2001SARAJE01032, December 2001 (emphasis added).

45. Rebecca Surtees, *Second Annual Report on Victims of Trafficking in South-Eastern Europe*, Regional Clearing Point, International Organization for Migration (IOM) (Geneva: IOM, 2005), 130, citing Alberto Andreani and Tal Raviv, *Changing Patterns of Trends in Trafficking in Persons in the Balkan Region* (Geneva: IOM, 2004), 49. For the report, see http://www.iom.int/jahia/webdav/site/myjahiasite/shared/shared/ mainsite/published_docs/studies_and_reports/second_annual05.pdf (verified 20 January 2007).

46. Surtees, *Second Annual Report,* 130.

47. Mendelson, *Barracks and Brothels,* 65.

48. HRW, *Hopes Betrayed,* 35.

49. Madeleine Rees, interview with author, October 2004.

50. Barbara Limanowska, *Trafficking in Human Beings in South Eastern Europe: 2003 Update on Situation and Responses to Trafficking in Human Beings* (Warsaw and Sarajevo: UNICEF, UNOHCHR, OSCE/ODIHR, 2003), 112, http://www.ceecis .org/child_protection/PDF/Traff2003.pdf (accessed 20 January 2007).

51. UN DPKO, *Human Trafficking Resource Package.*

52. UN DPKO, *Human Trafficking Resource Package,* 30.

53. IPTF officer, interview with author, Tuzla, March 2001. The author also

reviewed local police memoranda and documents confirming this allegation. Documents on file with Human Rights Watch.

54. In 2006, local police far more aggressively investigated allegations of trafficking that implicated members of the international community. In an interview with anti-trafficking police investigators in Sarajevo, the police officers reported that they had recently interviewed two suspected trafficking victims from the Russian Federation. The women had been brought to Bosnia and Herzegovina by a representative of an international organization. The police, less intimidated by internationals' immunity, planned to keep the case under investigation after the women denied that they were trafficking victims. Author interview with anti-trafficking unit police, Sarajevo, July 2006.

55. See Mendelson, *Barracks and Brothels.*

56. In one 2002 case in Kosovo, for example, an internal UN investigation uncovered the involvement of two U.S. UN civilian police officers in trafficking. According to a cable obtained by Human Rights Watch through a FOIA request, "One of the U.S. officers was involved with a known criminal and brothel owner and accepted gifts from him in the form of 'girls.'" Reflecting the United Nations' failure to investigate these and similar allegations, the cable also noted that the original internal affairs report on the incident was "lost" by the UN Mission in Kosovo (UNMIK) regional command. UNMIK initiated a full investigation only months later after the allegations had been leaked to the press. U.S. Department of State, cable 2001STATE141743, 25 June 2002, http://www.hrw.org/reports/2002/bosnia/Scan002.PDF (accessed 27 January 2007). For a discussion of trafficking into Kosovo for forced prostitution, see Amnesty International, "'So Does It Mean that We Have the Rights?' Protecting the Human Rights of Women and Girls Trafficked for Forced Prostitution in Kosovo," AI Index: EUR 70/010/2004, 6 May 2004, http://web.amnesty.org/library/Index/ENGEUR700102004?open&of=ENG-373 (accessed 20 January 2007).

57. HRW, *Hopes Betrayed,* 41–42.

58. Madeleine Rees, interview with author, March 2004.

59. Lynellyn Long, interview with author, March 2001.

60. European Union Police Mission in Bosnia and Herzegovina, "Weekly Establishment of EUPM Personnel by Countries—Member States," European Union Police Mission, http://www.eupm.org/Documents/Weekly.pdf (accessed 17 April 2007).

61. European Union Force in Bosnia and Herzegovina (EUFOR), "EU Military Operation in Bosnia and Herzegovina," http://www.euforbih.org/sheets/fs050103a.htm (accessed 22 January 2007).

62. BBC News, "Rice Signs US-Romania Bases Deal," 6 December 2005, http://news.bbc.co.uk/2/hi/europe/4504682.stm (accessed 20 January 2007).

63. BBC News, "Evidence of Sexual Abuse by UN Peacekeepers Uncovered," 30 November 2006, http://www.bbc.co.uk/pressoffice/pressreleases/stories/2006/11_november/30/un.shtml (accessed 20 January 2007).

64. United Nations General Assembly, "Letter Dated 24 March 2005 from the Sec-

retary General to the President of the General Assembly," UN Document A/59/710, 24 March 2005, http://daccessdds.un.org/doc/UNDOC/GEN/N05/247/90/PDF/ N0524790.pdf?OpenElement (accessed 20 January 2007).

65. United Nations General Assembly, "Note by the Secretary General, Ensuring the Accountability of United Nations Staff and Experts on Mission with Respect to Criminal Acts Committed in Peacekeeping Operations," UN Document A/60/980, 16 August 2006, http://daccessdds.un.org/doc/ UNDOC/GEN/N06/471/41/PDF/N0647141.pdf?OpenElement (accessed 20 January 2007).

Chapter 6: Human Trafficking and Democratic Transition in Albania

This chapter was translated into English by Ela Banaj. I would like to thank her for the support given in this process.

1. Albania's emergence as a destination country for human trafficking victims has been more recent and less extensive than patterns for transshipment or sourcing. For example, prostitution in Albanian motels and hotels related to the trafficking of foreigners is a new phenomenon emerging in some cities. Vatra Center, *The Girls and the Trafficking* (Tirana: Vatra Center, 2005), 31.

2. According to the Code of Leke Dukagjini (the Kanun), one's rifle and one's woman are not to be touched. Aleks Luarasi, *Family Relations* (Tirana: Luarasi, 2001), 150–53.

3. Ismet Elezi, *The Code of Laberia at a Comparative Plan* (Tirana: University Publishing House, 1994), 171.

4. Silvana Miria and Valdet Sala, "Women—Victims of Many Abuses," in *An Overview of the Written Contribution of the Women's Movement in Albania (1990–1998),* ed. Women's Center (Tirana: Women's Center, 1999), 97.

5. Miria and Sala, "Women—Victims," 98–99. According to Article 135 of the Penal Code of 1977, prostitution, incitement, or mediation for prostitution and payment for this activity were punishable by up to five years imprisonment.

6. International Organization for Migration (IOM)/International Catholic Migration Commission (ICMC), *Research Report on Third Country National Trafficking Victims in Albania: Inter-Agency Referral System (IARS) Project for Return and Reintegration Assistance to Victims of Trafficking* (Tirana: IOM/ICMC, April 2001), 4. http://iomtirana. org.al/en/E-Library/Reports/3rd%20country%20Research%20Report%202001.pdf (accessed 23 April 2007); Vatra Center, *Girls and the Trafficking,* 34–35.

7. Edison Heba, "The Economic Organized Crime and Fight Against It" (unpublished manuscript based on research carried out for GTZ [Deutsche Gesellschaft fuer Technische Zusammenarbeit, German Technical Cooperation], Tirana, 1997); Ndre Legisi (then minister of state to Albanian television), interview, 1997.

8. Albania, Council of Ministers, *The National Strategy for the Fight Against Trafficking of Human Beings: Appendix* (Tirana: Council of Ministers, 2001); Barbara Limanowska, *Trafficking in Human Beings in South Eastern Europe: Current Situation and Responses to Trafficking in Human Beings* (Belgrade, Warsaw, Sarajevo: UNICEF,

UNOHCHR, OSCE/ODIHR, 2002), 125, http://www.osce.org/documents/odihr/2002/06/1649_en.pdf (accessed 24 January 2007).

9. Human Development Promotion Center (HDPC), *Human Development Report: Albania 2002*, prepared for the United Nations Human Development Programme (Tirana: HDPC, 2002), 24, http://hdr.undp.org/docs/reports/national/ALB_Albania/Albania_2002_en.pdf (accessed 4 June 2007).

10. HDPC, *Human Development Report: Albania 2002*, 21.

11. Human Development Promotion Center (HDPC), *The Albanian Response to the Millennium Development Goals* (Tirana: HDPC, May 2002), 10, http://intra.undp.org.al/ext/elib/download?id=444&name=Albanian%20Response%20MDG%202002%20%28English%29%2Epdf (accessed 27 January 2007).

12. Ylli Cabri, et al., *Albanian Human Development Report 2000* (Tirana: United Nations Development Program, 2000), Annexes 3 (Table 26), http://hdr.undp.org/docs/reports/national/ALB_Albania/Albania_2000_en.pdf (accessed 4 June 2007).

13. Vatra Center, *Girls and the Trafficking*.

14. Council of Europe, *Organized Crime in Europe: The Threat of Cybercrime, Situation Report 2004* (Strasbourg: Council of Europe, Octopus Program, 2005), 33.

15. Miria and Sala, "Women–Victims," 109–13; Vatra Center, *Girls and the Trafficking*, 39–40.

16. Jeta Katro and Liri Shamani, *Prostitution and Trafficking of Women in Albania* (Tirana: Women in Development Association, 1999); International Organization for Migration (IOM)/Department for International Development (DFID), "A Report from the IOM and DFID Workshop on Trafficking of Women in Albania," 1999, http://www.stranieriinitalia.it/briguglio/immigrazione-e-asilo/1999/novembre/tratta-report.html (accessed 27 January 2007).

17. According to Interpol, for the period 1993 to 1998, 103 women were kidnapped. See Daniel Renton, "Child Trafficking in Albania" (Tirana: Save the Children in Albania, March 2001), 15, http://www.savethechildren.it/2003/download/pubblicazioni/traffickingAlbania/traffickingAlbania.pdf (accessed 23 April 2007).

18. This pattern of repatriation reflects several factors including: greater estimated numbers of trafficking victims in Greece and Italy, cooperative regional efforts against trafficking, ties between social service centers and other organizations in these countries with Albanian nongovernmental organizations, and mass repatriations of irregular migrants. Vatra Center, *Girls and the Trafficking*, 29–30.

19. Albanian Center for Economic Research, *Common Country Assessment: Albania*, prepared for the United Nations System in Albania (Tirana: UNDP, June 2002), 36–37, http://www.undp.org.al/download/cca2002.pdf (accessed 27 January 2007).

20. Albania, Council of Ministers, *National Strategy*.

21. Albanian National Statistical Institute (INSTAT) and the International Labor Organization-Program on the Elimination of Child Labor (ILO-IPEC), *Rapid Assessment of Trafficking in Children for Labor and Sexual Exploitation in Albania* (Tirana: INSTAT, ILO-IPEC, 2003), 4.

22. INSTAT/ILO-IPEC, *Rapid Assessment*, 22–25.

23. United Nations Children's Fund (UNICEF), *Rights of Women and Children in Albania* (Tirana: UNICEF), 86.

24. INSTAT/ILO-IPEC, *Rapid Assessment*, 22–25, 26–27.

25. Vatra Center, *Girls and the Trafficking*.

26. Fondation Terre des Hommes, *Children Trafficking from Albania to Greece, Report* (Lausanne, Switzerland: Foundation Terre des Homes, January 2003), 27; Organisation Mondiale contre la Torture (OMCT) et al., "State Violence in Greece, An Alternative Report to the UN Committee against Torture" (report presented at the thirty-third session of the Committee against Torture, Athens, 27 October 2004), 87, http://www.omct.org/pdf/procedures/2004/joint/s_violence_greece_10_2004.pdf (accessed 27 January 2007).

27. International Organization for Migration (IOM)/International Catholic Migration Commission (ICMC), *III Research Report on Third Country National Trafficking Victims in Albania* (Tirana: IOM/ICMC, 2002), 10, http://iomtirana.org.al/en/E-Library/Reports/3rd%20country%20Research%20Report%202002.pdf (accessed 27 January 2007); Vasilika Hysi, "Organized Crime in Albania: The Ugly Side of Capitalism and Democracy," in *Organized Crime in Europe, Concepts, Patterns and Control Policies in the EU and Beyond*, ed. Cyrille Fijnaut and Letizia Paoli (Dordrecht, The Netherlands: Springer, 2004), 550.

28. UNICEF, *Rights of Women*, 86.

29. Ismet Elizi, "On Criminology: Lectures for the Students of the Law Faculty Tirana University" (unpublished manuscript, Tirana University, 1994); Heba, "Economic Organized Crime"; Zamir Poda, *Organized Crime* (Tirana: SHBLU, 1998); Hysi, "Organized Crime," 541–44.

30. United Nations Development Program (UNDP), *Albanian Human Development Report* (Tirana: UNDP, 1998), 29.

31. Discussed in Hysi, "Organized Crime."

32. The latter focused on cases involving minors or persons in close relation (relatives or custodial relations) where intermediation took place in exchange for a material reward or where the victim was being prostituted abroad.

33. Act 8175 of 23 December 1996 (On Some Amendments of the Act No. 7895, 27 January 1995).

34. Act 8204 of 10 April 1997 (On Some Amendments of the Act No. 7895, 27 January 1995).

35. This article was amended in February 2004 to increase the severity of punishment by fine and imprisonment.

36. Regulations concerning the interception of conversations or verbal communication underwent important changes in 2002 and 2004.

37. Part of the Albanian government strategy also has been to improve the living conditions of the Roma minority and establish prevention programs against trafficking of Roma women and children.

38. Albania, Council of Ministers, *National Strategy*; Albania, Council of Ministers, Office of the Minister of State for Coordination, *Albanian National Strategy for*

Combating Trafficking in Human Beings: Strategic Framework and National Action Plan, 2005–2007, http://www.caaht.com/resources/NationalStrategy_2005-7_ENGLISH. pdf (accessed 5 June 2007); Albania, Ministry of Interior, Anti-Trafficking Unit, *Report on the Implementation of Albanian National Strategy for Combating Trafficking in Human Beings, January–June 2006,* Tirana, July 2006, http://www.osce.org/ documents/odihr/2006/10/20926_en.pdf (accessed 5 June 2007).

39. Albania has ratified most of the UN conventions and Council of Europe conventions in the field of criminal law and fighting organized crime. According to the Albanian Constitution, the ratification of these conventions makes them an integral part of Albanian law. Hysi, "Organized Crime," 976–77.

40. For additional information, see Southeast European Cooperative Initiative Regional Center for Combating Trans-Border Crime, http://www.secicenter.org.

41. However, the role of this center has been limited because of lack of consensus on its mission.

42. International Criminal Investigative Training Assistance Program (ICTAP), *Assistance to the Government of Albania* (Washington DC: ICITAP, November 2004), 2. Updated information on the program is available at http://www.usdoj.gov/ criminal/icitap/TextAlbania.html (accessed 27 January 2007).

43. ICITAP, *Assistance to the Government,* 7.

44. Albania, Ministry of Justice (MOJ), *Annual Statistics 2002* (Tirana: Ministry of Justice, 2003), 21; Albania, Ministry of Justice (MOJ), *Annual Statistics 2003* (Tirana: Ministry of Justice, 2004), 26; Albania, Ministry of Justice (MOJ), *Annual Statistics 2004* (Tirana: Ministry of Justice, 2005), 17. In 2004, Albania reported 588 penal offences, with 31 criminal groups and 105 persons implicated in the trafficking of women for sexual exploitation, trafficking in children, and trafficking in weapons. Albania, Ministry of Public Order, *Annual and Progress Report of Ministry of Public Order* (Tirana: Ministry of Public Order, 2005), 65. In the period 2003 to 2004, the Ministry of Justice also reported 891 offenses for false passports and visas with 1,279 persons punished. By comparison, there were no cases of such document fraud judged in 2002. MOJ, *Annual Statistics 2003,* 29; MOJ, *Annual Statistics 2004,* 26.

45. U.S. Agency for International Development (USAID), *The CAAHT Baseline Survey: A Summary* (Tirana: USAID, February 2005), http://www.caaht.com/ resources/CAAHTBaselineSurveyReports/Baseline.pdf (accessed 27 January 2007).

46. USAID, *CAAHT Baseline Survey,* 8–10.

47. For more information, see the CAAHT Web site at, http://www.caaht.com.

48. INSTAT, *Rapid Assessment,* 36–37.

49. USAID, *CAAHT Baseline Survey,* 67.

50. Barbara Limanowska, *Trafficking in Human Beings in South Eastern Europe: 2004—A Focus on Prevention* (Warsaw and Sarajevo: UNICEF, UNOHCHR, OSCE/ ODIHR, 2005), 101, http://www.unicef.org/ceecis/Trafficking.Report.2005.pdf (accessed 20 January 2007); Ministry of Public Order, *Annual and Progress Report,* 66.

51. IOM/ICMC, *III Research Report,* 15.

52. USAID, *CAAHT Baseline Survey,* 9.

53. Galit Wolfensohn, *Responding to Child Trafficking—An Introductory Handbook to Child Rights-Based Interventions Drawn from Save the Children's Experiences in Southeast Europe* (Tirana: Save the Children, May 2004), 29, http://www.childcentre.info/projects/traffickin/dbaFile11301.pdf (accessed 27 January 2007).

54. In February 2006, the Greek government signed a bilateral agreement with Albania on child trafficking including provisions for the return of trafficking victims. U.S. Department of State, "Introduction," *Trafficking in Persons Report,* 2006, http://www.state.gov/g/tip/rls/tiprpt/2006/65983.htm (accessed 20 January 2007).

55. Limanowska, *Trafficking in Human Beings* (2005), 102.

56. Editors' note: for example, see the 2006 recent bilateral agreement reached between Albania and Greece on child trafficking. U.S. Agency for International Development, Albania, "Albania and Greece Sign First Bilateral Agreement on Trafficking," 27 February 2006, http://www.usaidalbania.org/(z32chp551f3llz550 iaurk55)/en/Story.aspx?id=87 (accessed 5 June 2007).

57. Editors' note: for recent steps in this direction, see Albania, Ministry of Interior, Deputy Minister, "Short Term Priorities for the Prevention and Fight against Trafficking in Human Beings and Some of the Main Achievements in 2006," OSCE Office for Democratic Institutions and Human Rights, Legislationline, posted 26 April 2007, http://www.legislationline.org/legislation.php?tid=178&lid=7415& less=false (accessed 5 June 2007).

Chapter 7: Policy Responses to Human Trafficking in the Balkans

1. For example, see Ernesto U. Savona and Federica Curtol, *The Contribution of Data Exchange Systems to the Fight against Organized Crime in the SEE Countries* (Trento, Italy: Transcrime, 2004), http://transcrime.cs.unitn.it/tc/418.php (accessed 20 January 2007).

2. United Nations, *Protocol to Prevent, Suppress and Punish Trafficking in Persons, Especially Women and Children, Supplementing the United Nations Convention against Transnational Organized Crime* (Geneva: United Nations, 2000).

3. Article 25, paragraph 1 of the United Nations Convention against Transnational Organized Crime obliges state parties to take appropriate measures within their means to provide protection to victims of offenses covered by the convention, in particular in cases of threat of retaliation or intimidation. Accordingly, Article 6, paragraph 5 of the Trafficking Protocol obliges state parties to "endeavor" to provide for the physical safety of victims while they are within the state's territory.

4. See Article 8, paragraph 2 of the Trafficking Protocol. It has been argued that the protocol would restrict the obligation of state parties to protect the safety of victims to the time period while they are within the state's territory.

5. Article 9, paragraph 3 of the Trafficking Protocol obliges state parties to include in their policies and programs cooperation with NGOs.

6. The right to safety is based particularly on Article 9 of the United Nations Covenant on Civil and Political Rights and the European Convention on Human Rights.

7. Article 23 of the Convention against Transnational Organized Crime obliges state parties to criminalize the obstruction of justice, including the use of threats or intimidation in order to induce false testimony or to interfere in the giving of testimony or the production of evidence. Such comprehensive definitions shielding the victim against all forms of intimidation could prove an important tool of victim protection.

8. Article 7, paragraph 1 of the Trafficking Protocol urges state parties to consider adopting legislative or other appropriate measures that permit victims to remain in their territory, temporarily or permanently, in certain cases. In implementing this provision, state parties are asked to "give appropriate consideration to humanitarian and compassionate factors."

9. All of these basic principles are set forth in human rights documents such as the 1948 Universal Declaration of Human Rights, the 1966 International Covenant on Civil and Political Rights, and the 1956 Convention on the Elimination of Slavery.

10. Global Alliance against Traffic in Women (GAATW), Foundation against Trafficking in Women, and International Human Rights Law Group, *Human Rights Standards for the Treatment of Trafficked Persons* (Bangkok: GAATW, 1999), http://gaatw.net/books_pdf/hrs_eng2.pdf (accessed 20 January 2007).

11. For proposals on support/strengthening victim protections in addition to those in the Trafficking Protocol, see Radhika Coomaraswamy, "Integration of the Human Rights of Women and the Gender Perspective: Violence against Women" (report of the Special Rapporteur on violence against women, its causes and consequences, United Nations Economic and Social Council, Commission on Human Rights, 56th session, E/CN.4/2000/68, 29 February 2000), paragraph 116, http://www.unhchr.ch/Huridocda/Huridoca.nsf/TestFrame/e29d45a105cd8143802 568be0051fcfb?Opendocument (verified 20 January 2007); and NGO Voice, "Recommendations on the Framework Decision on Combating Trafficking in Human Beings," COM (2000) 854 final/2, part 4, 14 September 2001, http://www.ngovoice .org/activities/page/projects/traffickLetter/page_1_print.html (accessed 20 January 2007).

12. This section draws in part on Savona and Curtol, *Contribution of Data Exchange Systems*, 424–30, 464–70.

13. Editors' note: follow-up Mirage operations based on the 2002 model were conducted in 2003 and 2004, averaging ten days each. By late 2004, the SECI Center had shifted to more sustained efforts under the rubric of Task Force Mirage, the informal name for the Task Force on Combating Trafficking of Human Beings and Illegal Migration, with positive results. See Alexandru Ionas, *SECI Regional Center for Combating Trans-border Crime: Key Notes* (Bucharest: SECI, 2005), http://www .stabilitypact.org/rt/SECI%20Center%20Key%20Notes%20_SP%20WT%20III%20 Meeting%20Prague.pdf (accessed 20 January 2007); and "Task Force Mirage Regional Meetings," SECI Press Release, 9 October 2006 http://www.secicenter.org/ p180/_9th_of_October_2006 (accessed 20 January 2007).

14. This section draws in part on Savona and Curtol, *Contribution of Data Exchange Systems*, 464–70.

Chapter 8: Human Trafficking and Human Security

1. Human Security Centre, *The Human Security Report 2005: War and Peace in the 21st Century* (New York: Oxford University Press, 2005), part 2, 86, http://www.humansecurityreport.info/HSR2005_HTML/Part2/index.htm (accessed 20 January 2007). For a similar argument that human trafficking has reached the threshold of a "significant human rights crisis," see Michele Anne Clark, "Trafficking in Persons: An Issue of Human Security," *Journal of Human Development* 4, no. 2 (2003): 247.

2. Human Security Centre, *Human Security Report,* 86–89.

3. In addition to this contributors to this volume, see Gillian Caldwell, Steve Galster, Jyothi Kanics, and Nadia Steinzor, "Capitalizing on Transition Economies: The Role of the Russian Mafiya in Trafficking Women for Forced Prostitution," in *Illegal Immigration and Commercial Sex: The New Slave Trade,* ed. Phil Williams (London: Frank Cass, 1999), 69–70; Margaret E. Beare, "Illegal Migration: Personal Tragedies, Social Problems, or National Security Threats?" in *Illegal Immigration and Commercial Sex: The New Slave Trade,* ed. Phil Williams (London: Frank Cass, 1998), 11–42; and Clark, "Trafficking in Persons," 247–63.

4. United Nations Development Program (UNDP), *Human Development Report* (New York: Oxford University Press, 1994), 22–39, http://hdr.undp.org/reports/global/1994/en/.

5. For a discussion of this issue, see Fen Osler Hampson, Jean Daudelin, John B. Hay, Holly Reid, and Todd Martin, *Madness in the Multitude: Human Security and World Disorder* (New York: Oxford University Press, 2001).

6. United Nations, "United Nations Millennium Development Goals," UN Web Services Section, Department of Public Information, http://www.un.org/millenniumgoals/ (accessed 20 January 2007).

7. For example, see Roland Paris, "Human Security: Paradigm Shift or Hot Air," *International Security* 26, no. 2 (2001): 87–102; Kanti Bajpai, "Human Security: Concept and Measurement," *Columbia International Affairs Online (CIAO)* (August 2000), http://www.ciaonet.org/wps/baj01/ (accessed 20 January 2007; *CIAO* signup required).

8. Human Security Centre, *Human Security Report,* 1, 7, 128.

9. Taylor Owen, "Human Security—Conflict, Critique and Consensus," *Security Dialogue* 35, no. 3 (September 2004): 345–87.

10. Gareth Evans and Mohamed Sahnoun, *The Responsibility to Protect: Report of the International Commission on Intervention and State Sovereignty* (Ottawa: International Development Resource Centre [IDRC], December 2001), http://www.iciss.ca/pdf/Commission-Report.pdf (accessed 29 January 2007).

11. Kofi Annan, "Two Concepts of Sovereignty," *Economist,* 18 September 1999.

12. United Nations, "United Nations Millennium Development Goals."

13. For an extended recapitulation of these three elements of the human security agenda see Hampson et al., *Madness in the Multitude.*

14. Clark, "Trafficking in Persons," 247–63; Sakiko Fukuda-Parr, "New Threats to Human Security in the Era of Globalization," *Journal of Human Development* 4, no. 2

(July 2003): 173–74; Human Security Centre, *Human Security Report*, 86–89.

15. See Human Rights Watch (HRW), *Hopes Betrayed: Trafficking of Women and Girls to Post-Conflict Bosnia and Herzegovina for Forced Prostitution* 14, no. 9 (D) (November 2002), http://www.hrw.org/reports/2002/bosnia/Bosnia1102.pdf (accessed 20 January 2007); and Sarah Mendelson, *Barracks and Brothels: Peacekeepers and Human Trafficking in the Balkans* (Washington DC: Center for Strategic and International Studies, 2005).

16. Ethan Nadelmann, "Global Prohibition Regimes: The Evolution of Norms in International Society," *International Organization* 44, no. 4 (Autumn 1990): 479–526; Peter Andreas and Ethan Nadelmann, *Policing the Globe: Criminalization and Crime Control in International Relations* (New York: Oxford University Press, 2006), 17–22.

17. United Nations, *Protocol to Prevent, Suppress and Punish Trafficking in Persons, Especially Women and Children, Supplementing the United Nations Convention against Transnational Organized Crime* (Geneva: United Nations, 2000), Article 9, sections 2 and 4. Section 5 also briefly turns to the issue of demand: "States Parties shall adopt or strengthen legislative or other measures, such as educational, social or cultural measures, including through bilateral and multilateral cooperation, to discourage the demand that fosters all forms of exploitation of persons, especially women and children, that leads to trafficking."

18. See UN, *Protocol to Prevent, Suppress and Punish Trafficking in Persons*, Article 5 (criminalization), Article 11 (border), Articles 2, 6, and 7 (victims' protections), sections 2 and 4.

19. See UN, *Protocol to Prevent, Suppress and Punish Trafficking in Persons*, preamble.

20. The introduction to the Toolkit notes the basic premise that trafficking can only be addressed through "comprehensive strategies" that address human rights, the transnational nature of trafficking, the criminal activities and organized groups involved, and the impact on trafficking victims. The volume primarily offers "individual tools" intended to facilitate the development of comprehensive strategies, along with a few examples of comprehensive National Action Plans (p. ix). United Nations Global Programme against Trafficking in Human Beings, *Toolkit to Combat Trafficking in Persons* (New York: United Nations Office on Drugs and Crime, October 2006), http://www.unodc.org/pdf/Trafficking_toolkit_Oct06.pdf (accessed 20 January 2007).

21. Nadelmann, "Global Prohibition Regimes"; Andreas and Nadelmann, *Policing the Globe*, 17–22; Janie Chuang, "The United States as Global Sheriff: Using Unilateral Sanctions to Combat Human Trafficking," *Michigan Journal of International Law* 27, no. 2 (2006): 437–94.

22. Division A—*Trafficking Victims Protection Act of 2000* (TVPA), *Victims of Trafficking and Violence Protection Act of 2000*, Public Law 106-386, 106th Cong. (28 October 2000), http://www.state.gov/documents/organization/10492.pdf.

23. TVPA, section 103, especially the distinction in paragraphs 3 and 8; Chuang, "United States as Global Sheriff," 450.

24. TVPA, section 102(b)(4).

25. TVPA, section 106.

26. See TVPA, sections 107 and 108. Section 108(b)(3) of the 2000 TVPA had linked prevention broadly to the education of persons, both potential victims and the public, about trafficking's "causes and consequences." In response to a growing backlash over the role of peacekeepers and other internationals in facilitating trafficking while engaged in missions abroad, the 2005 reauthorization also added education measures to prevent such practices as part of the *TIP Report* review criteria under section 108(b)(3). See *Trafficking Victims Protection Reauthorization Act of 2005*, HR 972, 109th Cong., 1st sess. (4 January 2005), http://www.state.gov/g/tip/rls/61106.htm (verified 20 January 2007).

27. TVPA, section 108, section 112.

28. An exception would be hardship cases, such as aliens under the age of fifteen in the 2000 TVPA. Hardship under the 2003 reauthorization refers to aliens under the age of eighteen and to unmarried siblings, under the age of eighteen, of T Visa holders. *Trafficking Victims Protection Reauthorization Act of 2003*, HR 2620, 108th Cong., 1st sess. (7 January 2003), http://www.state.gov/g/tip/rls/61130.htm (verified 20 January 2007).

29. Council of the European Union, "Council Framework Decision on Combating Trafficking in Human Beings," 2002/629/JHA, Official Journal L 203 (1 August 2002), http://europa.eu/scadplus/leg/en/lvb/l33137.htm (accessed 22 January 2007).

30. Council of the European Union, "Council Framework Decision."

31. Commission of the European Communities, "Council Directive 2004/81/EC of 29 April 2004 on the Residence Permit Issued to Third-Country Nationals who are Victims of Trafficking in Human Beings or Who Have Been the Subject of an Action to Facilitate Illegal Immigration, Who Cooperate with the Competent Authorities," 32004L0081, Official Journal L 261 (8 June 2004): 19–23, http://eur-lex.europa.eu/LexUriServ/LexUriServ.do?uri=CELEX:32004L0081:EN:NOT (accessed 22 January 2007).

32. European Council, "Presidency Conclusions" (special meeting of the European Council, Tampere, Finland, 15–16 October 1999), http://www.europarl.europa.eu/summits/tam_en.htm#a (accessed 20 January 2007).

33. Tampere European Council, "Presidency Conclusions," numbers 22–27.

34. These steps draw on broader UN and European efforts against trafficking, including the 2005 Council of Europe Convention on Action against Trafficking in Human Beings, Commission of the European Communities, "Opinion of the Expert Group in Connection with the Conference 'Tackling Human Trafficking: Policy and Best Practices in Europe' and its Related Documents," paper presented in connection with the conference "Tackling Human Trafficking: Policy and Best Practices in Europe," 11 October 2005, http://ec.europa.eu/justice_home/doc_centre/crime/trafficking/doc/opinion_expert_group_11_10_05_en.pdf (accessed 22 January 2007). For the 2005 Council of Europe Convention, see Council of Europe, "Council of Europe Convention on Action against Trafficking in Human

Beings and Its Explanatory Report," Council of Europe Treaty Series no. 197 (2005), http://www.coe.int/T/E/human_rights/trafficking/PDF_Conv_197_Traffick ing_E.pdf (accessed 22 January 2007).

35. Commission of the European Communities, "Opinion of the Expert Group."

36. Commission of the European Communities, "Communication from the Commission to the European Parliament and the Council: Fighting Trafficking in Human Beings—An Integrated Approach and Proposals for an Action Plan," 52005DC0514, COM/2005/0514 final, Brussels, 18 October 2005, http://eur-lex .europa.eu/LexUriServ/LexUriServ.do?uri=CELEX:52005DC0514:EN:NOT (accessed 22 January 2007).

37. U.S. Department of State, *Trafficking in Persons Report,* 2006, http://www .state.gov/g/tip/rls/tiprpt/2006/ (accessed 20 January 2007).

38. For example, see U.S. Government Accountability Office (GAO), *Human Trafficking: Better Data, Strategy, and Reporting Needed to Enhance U.S. Antitrafficking Efforts Abroad,* GAO-06-825, July 2006, http://www.gao.gov/new.items/d06825.pdf (accessed 22 January 2007).

39. Commission of the European Communities, "Report from the Commission to the Council and the European Parliament Based on Article 10 of the Council Framework Decision of 19 July 2002 on Combating Trafficking in Human Beings," 52006DC0187, COM(2006) 0187 final, Brussels, 5 February 2006, http://eur-lex .europa.eu/LexUriServ/LexUriServ.do?uri=CELEX:52006DC0187:EN:NOT (accessed 22 January 2007); Commission of the European Communities, "Commission Staff Working Document: Annex to the Report from the Commission to the Council and the European Parliament Based on Article 10 of the Council Framework Decision of 19 July 2002 on Combating Trafficking in Human Beings," SEC (2006) 525, Brussels, 5 February 2006, http://ec.europa.eu/justice_home/doc_centre/crime/ trafficking/doc/sec_2006_525_en.pdf (accessed 22 January 2007).

40. Barbara Limanowska, *Trafficking in Human Beings in South Eastern Europe: 2004—A Focus on Prevention* (Warsaw and Sarajevo: UNICEF, UNOHCHR, OSCE/ ODIHR, 2005), 70–72, http://www.unicef.org/ceecis/Trafficking.Report.2005 .pdf (accessed 20 January 2007); "EU Pledges Increased Cooperation with Western Balkans in Justice and Home Affairs Issues," *International Herald Tribune,* 17 November 2006.

41. Barbara Limanowska, *Trafficking in Human Beings in South Eastern Europe: 2003 Update on Situation and Responses to Trafficking in Human Beings* (Warsaw and Sarajevo: UNICEF, UNOHCHR, OSCE/ODIHR, 2003), 11, http://www.ceecis.org/child_ protection/PDF/Traff2003.pdf (accessed 20 January 2007).

42. Limanowska, *Trafficking in Human Beings* (2005), 9.

43. Limanowska, *Trafficking in Human Beings* (2003), 13–14.

44. Limanowska, *Trafficking in Human Beings* (2005), 19, 21–23. U.S. international trafficking programs to countries in the region in Fiscal Year 2004 totaled approximately $6.9 million, of which $3.0 million was directed at prevention (primarily awareness/education), $2.3 million to protection, and $1.6 million to prosecution.

U.S. Department of State, Office to Monitor and Combat Trafficking in Persons, "The U.S. Government's International Anti-Trafficking Programs Fiscal Year 2004," 3 June 2005, http://www.state.gov/g/tip/rls/rpt/47383.htm#europe (accessed 20 January 2007).

45. Jane Gronow, *Trafficking in Human Beings in Southeastern Europe: An Inventory of the Current Situation and Responses to Trafficking in Human Beings in Albania, Bosnia and Herzegovina, Croatia, the Federal Republic of Yugoslavia, and the former Yugoslav Republic of Macedonia* (UNICEF Area Office for the Balkans, 2000), 2, http://www.unicef .org/evaldatabase/files/CEE_CIS_2000_Trafficking.pdf (accessed 20 January 2007).

46. Gillian Caldwell, Steven Galster, and Nadia Steinzor, *Crime and Servitude: An Expose of the Traffic in Women for Prostitution from the Newly Independent States* (Washington DC: Global Survival Network, 1997); United Nations Development Program, *Human Development Report* (New York: Oxford University Press, 1999), 5, http://hdr .undp.org/reports/global/1999/en/.

47. U.S. Department of State, "Introduction," *Trafficking in Persons Report*, 2006, http://www.state.gov/g/tip/rls/tiprpt/2006/65983.htm (accessed 20 January 2007).

48. For an example of this argument, see statements by Laura Lederer, cited in Allen D. Hertzke, *Freeing God's Children: The Unlikely Alliance for Global Human Rights* (Lanham: Rowman and Littlefield, 2004), 317.

49. Gronow, "Trafficking in Human Beings," 27–30, 94; Barbara Limanowska, *Trafficking in Human Beings in South Eastern Europe: Current Situation and Responses to Trafficking in Human Beings* (Belgrade, Warsaw, Sarajevo: UNICEF, UNO-HCHR, OSCE/ODIHR 2002), 108, 126, http://www.osce.org/documents/ odihr/2002/06/1649_en.pdf (accessed 24 January 2007).

50. See also Mendelson, *Barracks and Brothels*.

51. See also International Organization for Migration (IOM), Counter-Trafficking Service, *Changing Patterns and Trends of Trafficking in Persons in the Balkan Region* (Geneva: IOM, July 2004), http://www.iom.int/jahia/webdav/site/myjahiasite/ shared/shared/mainsite/published_docs/books/changing_patterns.pdf (accessed 20 January 2007).

52. U.S. Department of State, *Trafficking in Persons Report*, 2005, http://www .state.gov/g/tip/rls/tiprpt/2005 (accessed 20 January 2007).

53. For example, see Sally Stoecker and Louise Shelley, eds., *Human Traffic and Transnational Crime: Eurasian and American Perspectives* (Lanham: Rowman and Littlefield, 2005); Karen Beeks and Delila Amir, eds., *Trafficking and the Global Sex Industry* (Lanham: Lexington Books, 2006).

54. For example, see Andreas and Nadelmann, *Policing the Globe*; H. Richard Friman, *NarcoDiplomacy: Exporting the U.S. War on Drugs* (Ithaca: Cornell University Press, 1996).

55. Andreas and Nadelmann, *Policing the Globe*, 228.

56. Andreas and Nadelmann, *Policing the Globe*, 17–58, 228.

57. Paris, "Human Security," 87–102.

Bibliography

Agence-France Press. "Balkan Summit in Macedonia to Discuss Security, Border Controls," 23 May 2003. http://www.balkanpeace.org/index.php?index=article& articleid=11835 (accessed 22 January 2007).

Agustin, Laura. "Migrants in the Mistress's House: Other Voices in the 'Trafficking' Debate." *Social Politics* (Spring 2005): 96–117.

Albania. Council of Ministers. *The National Strategy for the Fight against Trafficking of Human Beings: Appendix*. Tirana: Council of Ministers, 2001.

———. Council of Ministers. Office of the Minister of State for Coordination. *Albanian National Strategy for Combating Trafficking in Human Beings: Strategic Framework and National Action Plan, 2005–2007*. http://www.caaht.com/ resources/NationalStrategy_2005-7_ENGLISH.pdf (accessed 5 June 2007).

———. Ministry of Interior. Anti-Trafficking Unit. *Report on the Implementation of Albanian National Strategy for Combating Trafficking in Human Beings, January–June 2006*. Tirana: Ministry of Interior, July 2006. http://www.osce.org/documents/ odihr/2006/10/20926_en.pdf (accessed 5 June 2007).

———. Ministry of Interior. Deputy Minister. "Short-Term Priorities for the Prevention and Fight against Trafficking in Human Beings and Some of the Main Achievements in 2006." Warsaw: OSCE Office for Democratic Institutions and Human Rights, 2007. Legislationline, posted 26 April 2007. http://www .legislationline.org/legislation.php?tid=178&lid=7415&less=false (accessed 5 June 2007).

———. Ministry of Justice. *Annual Statistics 2002*. Tirana: Ministry of Justice, 2003.

———. Ministry of Justice. *Annual Statistics 2003*. Tirana: Ministry of Justice, 2004.

———. Ministry of Justice. *Annual Statistics 2004*. Tirana: Ministry of Justice, 2005.

———. Ministry of Public Order. *Annual and Progress Report of Ministry of Public Order*. Tirana: Ministry of Public Order, 2005.

Albanian Center for Economic Research. "Common Country Assessment: Albania." June 2002. Prepared for the United Nations System in Albania. http://www.undp .org.al/download/cca2002.pdf (accessed 27 January 2007).

Albanian National Statistical Institute (INSTAT) and the International Labor
Organization—Program on the Elimination of Child Labor (ILO-IPEC). *Rapid
Assessment of Trafficking in Children for Labor and Sexual Exploitation in Albania.*
Tirana: INSTAT, ILO-IPEC, 2003.

Amnesty International. "'So Does It Mean that We Have the Rights?' Protecting
the Human Rights of Women and Girls Trafficked for Forced Prostitution in
Kosovo." AI Index: EUR 70/010/2004, 6 May 2004. http://web.amnesty
.org/library/Index/ENGEUR700102004?open&of=ENG-373 (accessed
20 January 2007).

Andreani, Alberto, and Tal Raviv. *Changing Patterns of Trends in Trafficking in Persons
in the Balkan Region.* Geneva: International Organization for Migration, 2004.

Andreas, Peter. "Clandestine Political Economy of War and Peace in Bosnia."
International Studies Quarterly 48, no. 1 (2004): 29–52.

———. "The Criminalized Legacies of War: The Clandestine Political Economy of
the Western Balkans." *Problems of Post-Communism* 51, no. 3 (May/June 2004):
3–9.

———. "Introduction: The Wall After the Wall." In Andreas and Snyder, *The Wall
Around the West,* 1–14.

Andreas, Peter, and Ethan Nadelmann. *Policing the Globe: Criminalization and Crime
Control in International Relations.* Oxford: Oxford University Press, 2006.

Andreas, Peter, and Timothy Snyder, eds. *The Wall around the West.* Lanham: Rowman and Littlefield, 2000.

Annan, Kofi. "Two Concepts of Sovereignty." *Economist,* 18 September 1999.

Army Times. "The Lessons Learned in Bosnia—and How They Apply to Iraq,"
December 2004. http://www.armytimes.com/print.php?f=1-292925-543796.php
(accessed 10 May 2005, link no longer active).

Bajpai, Kanti. "Human Security: Concept and Measurement." *Columbia International
Affairs Online (CIAO)* (August 2000). http://www.ciaonet.org/wps/baj01/ (accessed 20 January 2007; *CIAO* signup required).

Bales, Kevin. *Disposable People: New Slavery in the Global Economy.* Berkeley: University
of California Press, 1999.

"Balkan Human Trafficking Out of Control?" Radio Free Europe/Radio Liberty,
Balkan Report 7, no. 35 (17 October 2003). http://www.rferl.org/reports/
balkan-report/2003/10/35-171003.asp.

Barry, Kathleen. *The Prostitution of Sexuality.* New York: NYU Press, 1995.

BBC News. "Evidence of Sexual Abuse by UN Peacekeepers Uncovered," 30 November 2006. http://www.bbc.co.uk/pressoffice/pressreleases/stories/2006/11_
november/30/un.shtml (accessed 20 January 2007).

———. "Fortress Europe Raises the Drawbridge," 18 June 2002. http://news.bbc
.co.uk/1/hi/world/europe/2042779.stm (accessed 20 January 2007).

———. "Rice Signs US-Romania Bases Deal," 6 December 2005. http://news.bbc
.co.uk/2/hi/europe/4504682.stm (accessed 20 January 2007).

———. "'Zero Tolerance' for UN Sex Abuse," 5 December 2006. http://news.bbc
.co.uk/2/hi/americas/6208774.stm. (accessed 20 January 2007).

Beare, Margaret E. "Illegal Migration: Personal Tragedies, Social Problems, or National Security Threats?" In Williams, *Illegal Immigration and Commercial Sex*, 11–42.

Beeks, Karen, and Delila Amir, eds. *Trafficking and the Global Sex Industry*. Lanham: Lexington Books, 2006.

Bell, Ernest A. *War on the White Slave Trade*. Toronto: Coles, 1980.

Brady, Martha. "Laying the Foundation for Girls' Healthy Futures: Can Sports Play a Role?" *Studies in Family Planning* 29, no. 1 (1998): 79–82.

Brady, Martha, and Arjmand Banu Khan. *Letting Girls Play: The Mathare Youth Sports Association's Football Program for Girls*. New York: Population Council, 2002.

Bruch, Elizabeth. "Models Wanted: The Search for an Effective Response to Human Trafficking." *Stanford Journal of International Law* 40, no. 1 (Winter 2004): 1–45.

Bruinsma, Gerben J. N., and Guus Meershoek. "Organized Crime and Trafficking in Women for Eastern Europe in the Netherlands." In Williams, *Illegal Immigration and Commercial Sex*, 105–18.

Burrell, Ian. "From the Balkans to the Brothels in Soho." *Independent*, 21 January 2002.

Cabri, Ylli, et al. *Albanian Human Development Report 2000*. Tirana: United Nations Development Program, 2000. http://hdr.undp.org/docs/reports/national/ALB_Albania/Albania_2000_en.pdf (accessed 4 June 2007).

Caldwell, Gillian, Steve Galster, Jyothi Kanics, and Nadia Steinzor. "Capitalizing on Transition Economies: The Role of the Russian Mafiya in Trafficking Women for Forced Prostitution." In Williams, *Illegal Immigration and Commercial Sex*, 42–73.

Caldwell, Gillian, Steven Galster, and Nadia Steinzor. *Crime and Servitude: An Expose of the Traffic in Women for Prostitution from the Newly Independent States*. Washington DC: Global Survival Network, 1997.

Cardoso, Eliana, and Andre Portela Souza. "The Impact of Cash Transfers on Child Labor and School Attendance in Brazil." Working paper 04-W07, Department of Economics, Vanderbilt University, 2004. http://www.vanderbilt.edu/Econ/wparchive/workpaper/vu04-w07.pdf (accessed 20 January 2007).

Chauzy, Jean Philippe. "Geneva-Report on the Extent of Trafficking in Women and Children for Sexual Exploitation to, through and from the Balkan Region." *IOM Press Briefing Notes*, 8 January 2002. http://www.old.iom.int/en/archive/PBN080102.shtml (accessed 30 May 2007).

Chuang, Janie. "The United States as Global Sheriff: Using Unilateral Sanctions to Combat Human Trafficking." *Michigan Journal of International Law* 27, no. 2 (2006): 437–94.

Clark, Michele Anne. "Trafficking in Persons: An Issue of Human Security." *Journal of Human Development* 4, no. 2 (2003): 247–63.

Collins, Richelle Turner. "Suggestions of U.S. Pullout Grab Attention in Bosnia." *Stars & Stripes*, 14 January 2001.

Commission of the European Communities. "Commission Staff Working Document: Annex to the Report from the Commission to the Council and the European Parliament Based on Article 10 of the Council Framework Decision of 19

July 2002 on Combating Trafficking in Human Beings." SEC (2006) 525, Brussels, 5 February 2006. http://ec.europa.eu/justice_home/doc_centre/crime/trafficking/doc/sec_2006_525_en.pdf (accessed 22 January 2007).

———. "Communication from the Commission to the European Parliament and the Council: Fighting Trafficking in Human Beings—An Integrated Approach and Proposals for an Action Plan." 52005DC0514, COM/2005/0514 final, Brussels, 18 October 2005. http://eur-lex.europa.eu/LexUriServ/LexUriServ.do?uri=CELEX :52005DC0514:EN:NOT (accessed 22 January 2007).

———. "Council Directive 2004/81/EC of 29 April 2004 on the Residence Permit Issued to Third-Country Nationals Who are Victims of Trafficking in Human Beings or Who Have Been the Subject of an Action to Facilitate Illegal Immigration, Who Cooperate with the Competent Authorities." 32004L0081, Official Journal L 261 (8 June 2004): 19–23. http://eur-lex.europa.eu/LexUriServ/LexUriServ .do?uri=CELEX:32004L0081:EN:NOT (accessed 22 January 2007).

———. "Council Framework Decision of 19 July 2002 on Combating Trafficking in Human Beings." 32002F0629, Official Journal L 203 (1 August 2002): 1–4. http:// eur-lex.europa.eu/smartapi/cgi/sga_doc?smartapi!celexapi!prod!CELEXnumdoc &lg=EN&numdoc=32002F0629&model=guichett (accessed 22 January 2007).

———. "Opinion of the Experts Group in Connection with the Conference 'Tackling Human Trafficking: Policy and Best Practices in Europe' and Its Related Documents." Paper presented in connection with the conference "Tackling Human Trafficking: Policy and Best Practices in Europe," 11 October 2005. http:// ec.europa.eu/justice_home/doc_centre/crime/trafficking/doc/opinion_ expert_group_11_10_05_en.pdf (accessed 22 January 2007).

———. "Report from the Commission to the Council and the European Parliament Based on Article 10 of the Council Framework Decision of 19 July 2002 on Combating Trafficking in Human Beings." 52006DC0187, COM(2006) 0187 final, Brussels, 5 February 2006. http://eur-lex.europa.eu/LexUriServ/LexUriServ .do?uri=CELEX:52006DC0187:EN:NOT (accessed 22 January 2007).

———. *Research Based on Case Studies of Victims of Trafficking in Human Beings in 3 EU Member States, i.e. Belgium, Italy and the Netherlands.* Brussels: Commission of the European Communities, Payoke, On the Road, De Rode Draad, 2003. http:// www.ontheroadonlus.it/rootdown/RapIppocra.pdf (accessed 20 January 2007).

Coomaraswamy, Radhika. "Integration of the Human Rights of Women and the Gender Perspective: Violence against Women." Report of the Special Rapporteur on violence against women, its causes and consequences, United Nations Economic and Social Council, Commission on Human Rights, 56th session. E/ CN.4/2000/68. 29 February 2000. http://www.unhchr.ch/Huridocda/Huridoca .nsf/TestFrame/e29d45a105cd8143802568be0051fcfb?Opendocument (accessed 20 January 2007).

Council of Europe. "Council of Europe Convention on Action against Trafficking in Human Beings and its Explanatory Report." Council of Europe Treaty Series no. 197 (2005). http://www.coe.int/T/E/human_rights/trafficking/PDF_Conv_ 197_Trafficking_E.pdf (accessed 22 January 2007).

———. *Organized Crime in Europe: The Threat of Cybercrime, Situation Report 2004.* Strasbourg: Council of Europe, Octopus Program, 2005.

Council of the European Union. "Council Framework Decision on Combating Trafficking in Human Beings." 2002/629/JHA, Official Journal L 203 (1 August 2002). http://europa.eu/scadplus/leg/en/lvb/l33137.htm (accessed 22 January 2007).

Counter-Trafficking Regional Clearing Point. *First Annual Report on Victims of Trafficking in South Eastern Europe.* Vienna: International Organization for Migration, Stability Pact for South Eastern Europe, International Catholic Migration Commission, 2003. http://www.iom.hu/PDFs/First%20Annual%20Report%20on%20VoT%20in%20SEE.pdf (accessed 22 January 2007).

Darden, Major General James W. "Opening Remarks for Major General James W. Darden, USAR Deputy Director for Plans & Policy, United States European Command to the House Armed Services Committee Issue Forum 'Winning the Peace under the Dayton Peace Accords: Military Lessons Learned and Sustaining the Peace in Bosnia,'" 12 July 2004. http://armedservices.house.gov/comdocs/openingstatementsandpressreleases/108thcongress/04-07-12Darden.pdf (accessed 27 January 2007).

Demleitner, Nora V. "The Law at the Crossroads: The Construction of Migrant Women Trafficked into Prostitution." In *Global Human Smuggling: Comparative Perspectives,* edited by David Kyle and Rey Koslowski, 257–93. Baltimore: The Johns Hopkins University Press, 2001.

Dickson, Sandra. *Sex in the City: Mapping Commercial Sex across London.* London: The POPPY Project, Eaves Housing for Women, 2004.

Doezema, Jo. "Loose Women or Lost Women?" *Gender Issues* 18, no. 1 (Winter 2000): 23–50.

Drusko, Dzenana Karup. "White Slaves in House of Sex." *Dani* 86 (12 October 1998). http://www.bhdani.com/arhiva/86/tekst186.htm (accessed 22 January 2007).

Elezi, Ismet. *The Code of Laberia at a Comparative Plan.* Tirana: University Publishing House, 1994.

———. "On Criminology: Lectures for the Students of the Law Faculty Tirana University," unpublished manuscript, Tirana University, 1994.

Emigh, Rebecca Jean, and Iván Szelényi, eds. *Poverty, Ethnicity, and Gender in Eastern Europe during the Market Transition.* Westport, CT: Praeger, 2001.

EuropaWorld. "Women Increasingly Migrate for Economic Reasons; Trafficking Also Rising," 4 March 2005. http://www.europaworld.org/week214/women4305.htm (accessed 22 January 2007).

European Council. *European Security Strategy: A Secure Europe in a Better World.* Brussels: European Council, 12 December 2003. http://www.consilium.europa.eu/uedocs/cmsUpload/78367.pdf (accessed 30 May 2007).

———. "Presidency Conclusions." Special meeting of the European Council, Tampere, Finland, 15–16 October 1999. http://www.europarl.europa.eu/summits/tam_en.htm#a (accessed 20 January 2007).

European Union Force in Bosnia and Herzegovina. "EU Military Operation in Bosnia and Herzegovina." http://www.euforbih.org/sheets/fs050103a.htm (accessed 22 January 2007).

European Union Police Mission in Bosnia and Herzegovina. "Weekly Establishment of EUPM Personnel by Countries—Member States." European Union Police Mission. http://www.eupm.org/Documents/Weekly.pdf (accessed 17 April 2007).

Evans, Gareth, and Mohamed Sahnoun. *The Responsibility to Protect: Report of the International Commission on Intervention and State Sovereignty*. Ottawa: International Development Resource Centre, December 2001. http://www.iciss.ca/pdf/Commission-Report.pdf (accessed 29 January 2007).

Fondation Terre des Hommes. *Children Trafficking from Albania to Greece, Report*. Lausanne, Switzerland: Fondation Terre des Hommes, January 2003.

Friman, H. Richard. *NarcoDiplomacy: Exporting the U.S. War on Drugs*. Ithaca: Cornell University Press, 1996.

Fukuda-Parr, Sakiko. "New Threats to Human Security in the Era of Globalization." *Journal of Human Development* 4, no. 2 (July 2003): 167–79.

Geneva Global. "Sector Priorities: Human Liberty." http://www/genevaglobal.com/sector-priorities/human-liberty (accessed 4 June 2007).

Ghosh, Bimal. *Managing Migration: Time for a New International Regime*. Oxford: Oxford University Press, 2000.

Global Alliance against Traffic in Women (GAATW). *Human Rights and Trafficking in Persons: A Handbook*. Bangkok: GAATW, 2001. http://gaatw.net/books_pdf/Human%20Rights%20and%20Trafficking%20in%20Person.pdf (accessed 22 January 2007).

———. Foundation against Trafficking in Women, and International Human Rights Law Group. *Human Rights Standards for the Treatment of Trafficked Persons*. Bangkok: GAATW, 1999. http://gaatw.net/books_pdf/hrs_eng2.pdf.

Gronow, Jane. "Trafficking in Human Beings in Southeastern Europe: An Inventory of the Current Situation and Responses to Trafficking in Human Beings in Albania, Bosnia & Herzegovina, Croatia, the Federal Republic of Yugoslavia, and the Former Yugoslav Republic of Macedonia." Sarajevo: UNICEF Area Office for the Balkans, 2000. http://www.unicef.org/evaldatabase/files/CEE_CIS_2000_Trafficking.pdf (accessed 20 January 2007).

Guiraudon, Virginie, and Christian Joppke, eds. *Controlling a New Migration World*. New York: Routledge, 2001.

Hampson, Fen Osler, Jean Daudelin, John B. Hay, Holly Reid, and Todd Martin. *Madness in the Multitude: Human Security and World Disorder*. New York: Oxford University Press, 2001.

Haque, Md. Shahidul. "Ambiguities and Confusions in Migration-Trafficking Nexus: A Development Challenge." In *Trafficking and the Global Sex Industry*, edited by Karen Beeks and Delila Amir, 3–20. Lanham: Lexington Books, 2006.

Heba, Edison. "The Economic Organized Crime and Fight against It." Unpublished manuscript based on research carried out for GTZ (Deutsche Gesellschaft fuer Technische Zusammenarbiet, German Technical Cooperation), Tirana, 1997.

Helwig, Janice. "United States Mission to the OSCE: Statement on Trafficking in Human Beings." Paper delivered at the U.S. Helsinki Commission to the OSCE Human Dimension Implementation Meeting, Warsaw, 27 September 2005. http://osce.usmission.gov/archive/2005/09/HDIM_On_Trafficking_in_Human_Beings_09_27_05.pdf (accessed 22 January 2007).

Hertzke, Allen D. *Freeing God's Children: The Unlikely Alliance for Global Human Rights.* Lanham: Rowman and Littlefield, 2004.

HQ SFOR Public Information Office. "History of the NATO-led Stabilisation Force (SFOR) in Bosnia and Herzegovina." SFOR. http://www.nato.int/sfor/docu/d981116a.htm (accessed 20 January 2007).

Hughes, Donna. "The 'Natasha' Trade: The Transnational Shadow Market of Trafficking in Women." *Journal of International Affairs* 53, no. 2 (2000): 625–51.

Human Development Promotion Center (HDPC). *The Albanian Response to the Millennium Development Goals.* Tirana: HDPC, May 2002. http://intra.undp.org.al/ext/elib/download?id=444&name=Albanian%20Response%20MDG%202002%20%28English%29%2Epdf (accessed 27 January 2007).

———. *Human Development Report: Albania 2002*, prepared for the United Nations Human Development Programme. Tirana: HDPC, 2002. http://hdr.undp.org/docs/reports/national/ALB_Albania/Albania_2002_en.pdf (accessed 4 June 2007).

Human Rights Watch. "Anatomy of a Backlash: Movements and Moral Panics." In *World Report 2005.* New York: Human Rights Watch, 2005. http://www.hrw.org/wr2k5 (accessed 20 January 2007).

———. *Hopes Betrayed: Trafficking of Women and Girls to Post-Conflict Bosnia and Herzegovina for Forced Prostitution* 14, no. 9 (D), November 2002. http://www.hrw.org/reports/2002/bosnia/Bosnia1102.pdf (accessed 20 January 2007).

Human Security Centre. *The Human Security Report 2005: War and Peace in the 21st Century.* New York: Oxford University Press, 2005. http://www.humansecurityreport.info/HSR2005_HTML/Part2/index.htm (accessed 20 January 2007).

Hysi, Vasilika. "Organized Crime in Albania: the Ugly Side of Capitalism and Democracy." In *Organized Crime in Europe, Concepts, Patterns and Control Policies in the EU and Beyond*, edited by Cyrille Fijnaut and Letizia Paoli, 537–62. Dordrecht, The Netherlands: Springer, 2004.

Ilievska, Aleksandra. "Fighting Crime Together." *Transitions Online*, 9 June 2003. http://www.tol.cz/look/BRR/tolprint.tpl?IdLanguage=1&IdPublication=9&NrIssue=1&NrSection=1&NrArticle=9740 (accessed 22 January 2007).

"International Agreement for the Suppression of the 'White Slave Traffic.'" 18 May 1904. University of Minnesota Human Rights Library. http://www1.umn.edu/humanrts/instree/whiteslavetraffic1904.html (accessed 22 January 2007).

International Center for Migration Policy Development. "How to Halt Illegal Migration to, from, and through South East Europe?" Report on the activities of the Working Group on South East Europe of the Budapest Group, prepared by the Secretariat of the Budapest Group for the Meeting of the Working Group,

Skopje, 27–28 November 2000. http://unpan1.un.org/intradoc/groups/public/
documents/UNTC/UNPAN017488.pdf (accessed 20 January 2007).

"International Convention for the Suppression of the 'White Slave Traffic.'" 4 May
1910, University of Minnesota Human Rights Library. http://www1.umn
.edu/humanrts/instree/whiteslavetraffic1910.html.

International Council on Human Rights Policy. *Human Rights Crises: NGO Responses
to Military Interventions*. Versoix: International Council on Human Rights Policy,
2002. http://www.ichrp.org/paper_files/115_p_01.pdf (accessed 20 January
2007).

International Criminal Investigative Training Assistance Program (ICITAP). *Assistance to the Government of Albania*. Washington, DC: ICITAP, November 2004.

International Herald Tribune. "EU Pledges Increased Cooperation with Western
Balkans in Justice and Home Affairs Issues," 17 November 2006.

International Organization for Migration (IOM). *Applied Research and Data Collection
on Trafficking in Human Beings to, through and from the Balkan Region*. Geneva: IOM,
2001.

———. *Victims of Trafficking in the Balkans: A Study of Trafficking in Women and
Children for Sexual Exploitation to, through and from the Balkan Region*. Geneva: IOM,
2001. http://www.old.iom.int/documents/publication/en/balkan_trafficking
.pdf (accessed 30 May 2007).

———. "Ways to Curb the Growing Complexities of Irregular Migration." In *World
Migration Report 2003*, 58–70. Geneva: IOM, 2003.

International Organization for Migration Counter-Trafficking Service. *Changing Patterns and Trends of Trafficking in Persons in the Balkan Region*. Geneva: IOM, July
2004. http://www.iom.int/jahia/webdav/site/myjahiasite/shared/shared/main
site/published_docs/books/changing_patterns.pdf (accessed 20 January 2007).

International Organization for Migration (IOM)/Department for International Development (DFID). "A Report from the IOM and DFID Workshop on Trafficking
of Women in Albania." 1999. http://www.stranieriinitalia.it/briguglio/immi
grazione-e-asilo/1999/novembre/tratta-report.html (accessed 27 January 2007).

International Organization for Migration (IOM)/International Catholic Migration
Commission (ICMC). *III Research Report on Third Country National Trafficking
Victims in Albania*. Tirana: IOM/ICMC, 2002. http://iomtirana.org.al/en/
E-Library/Reports/3rd%20country%20Research%20Report%202002.pdf (accessed 27 January 2007);

———. *Research Report on Third Country National Trafficking Victims in Albania:
Inter-Agency Referral System (IARS) Project for Return and Reintegration Assistance to
Victims of Trafficking*. Tirana: IOM/ICMC, April 2001. http://iomtirana.org
.al/en/E-Library/Reports/3rd%20country%20Research%20Report%202001.pdf
(accessed 23 April 2007).

Ionas, Alexandrou. *SECI Regional Center for Combating Trans-border Crime: Key Notes*.
Bucharest: SECI, 2005. http://www.stabilitypact.org/rt/SECI%20Center%20
Key%20Notes%20_SP%20WT%20III%20Meeting%20Prague.pdf (accessed 20
January 2007).

Jansson, Eric. "Human Trafficking in Balkans Growing, UN, OSCE Say." *Financial Times,* 18 December 2003.

Jefferson, LaShawn R. "Letter to Colin Powell on the Trafficking in Persons Report 2003." Human Rights Watch. http://www.hrw.org/press/2003/06/us062703ltr .htm (accessed 20 January 2007).

Jones, Rochelle. "Prevention as the New Approach to Human Trafficking: AWID Interviews Barbara Limanowska." Association for Women in Development, 19 August 2005. http://www.awid.org/go.php?stid=1538 (accessed 22 January 2007).

Katro, Jeta, and Liri Shamani. *Prostitution and Trafficking of Women in Albania.* Tirana: Women in Development Association, 1999.

Keck, Margaret, and Katherine Sikkink. *Activists Beyond Borders.* Ithaca: Cornell University Press, 1998.

Kempadoo, Kemala, and Jo Doezema, eds. *Global Sex Workers: Rights, Resistance and Revolution.* New York and London: Routledge, 1998.

Koeppel, Thomas, and Agnes Szekely. "Transnational Organized Crime and Conflict in the Balkans." In *Transnational Organized Crime and International Security,* edited by Mats Berdal and Monica Serrano, 129–40. Boulder: Lynne Rienner, 2002.

Konrad, Helga. "Trafficking in Human Beings: The Ugly Face of Europe." *Helsinki Monitor* 3 (March 2002): 263.

Koslowski, Rey. "Economic Globalization, Human Smuggling, and Global Governance." In *Global Human Smuggling: Comparative Perspectives,* edited by David Kyle and Rey Koslowski, 337–38. Baltimore: The Johns Hopkins University Press, 2001.

———. "The Mobility Money Can Buy." In Andreas and Snyder, *The Wall Around the West,* 203–18.

Krastev, Ivan, et al. *Human Security in South-East Europe.* Skopje, Macedonia: United Nations Development Program,1999. http://www.ceu.hu/cps/bluebird/eve/ statebuilding/krastev_humansecurity.pdf (accessed 24 January 2007).

Laczko, Frank. "Human Trafficking: The Need for Better Data." *Migration Information Source* (November 2002). http://www.migrationinformation.org/feature/ display.cfm?ID=66 (accessed 20 January 2007).

Laczko, Frank, and Marco Gramegna. "Developing Better Indicators of Human Trafficking." *Brown Journal of World Affairs* 10 (Summer/Fall 2003): 179–94.

Lăzăroiu, Sebastian, and Monica Alexandru. *Who Is the Victim? Vulnerability of Young Romanian Women to Trafficking in Human Beings.* Bucharest: International Organization for Migration, 2003. http://www.old.iom.int/DOCUMENTS/PUBLICA-TION/EN/Romania_ct.pdf (accessed 20 January 2007).

Leigh, Carol. *Unrepentant Whore: Collected Works of Scarlot Harlot.* San Francisco: Last Gasp, 2004.

Lilja 4-Ever, DVD. Directed by Lukas Moodysson. 2002; Newmarket Films, 2003.

Limanowska, Barbara. *Trafficking in Human Beings in South Eastern Europe: 2003 Update on Situation and Responses to Trafficking in Human Beings.* Warsaw and Sarajevo:

UNICEF, UNOHCHR, OSCE/ODIHR, 2003. http://www.ceecis.org/child_protection/PDF/Traff2003.pdf (accessed 20 January 2007).

———. *Trafficking in Human Beings in South Eastern Europe: 2004—A Focus on Prevention*. Warsaw and Sarajevo: UNICEF, UNOHCHR, OSCE/ODIHR, 2005. http://www.unicef.org/ceecis/Trafficking.Report.2005.pdf (accessed 20 January 2007).

———. *Trafficking in Human Beings in South Eastern Europe: Current Situation and Responses to Trafficking in Human Beings*. Belgrade, Warsaw, Sarajevo: UNICEF, UNOHCHR, OSCE/ODIHR, 2002. http://www.osce.org/documents/odihr/2002/06/1649_en.pdf (accessed 24 January 2007).

Lindstrom, Nicole. "Regional Sex Trafficking in the Balkans: Transnational Networks in an Enlarged Europe." *Problems of Post-Communism* 51, no. 3 (May/June 2004): 45–52.

Long, Lynellyn. "Anthropological Perspectives on the Trafficking of Women for Sexual Exploitation." *International Migration* 42, no. 1 (2004): 5–31.

———. "EC Perspectives on the Albanian Readmission Agreement." In *Combating Irregular Migration in Albania and the Wider Region*, edited by International Organization for Migration (IOM). Geneva: IOM, forthcoming.

———. *From Handmaid to Entrepreneur*. Report summary for Women-to-Work. London, 2005.

———. "Trafficking in Women and Children as a Security Challenge in Southeast Europe." *Journal of Southeast European and Black Sea Studies* 2, no. 2 (May 2002): 53–68.

Luarasi, Aleks. *Family Relations*. Tirana: Luarasi, 2001.

Lynch, Colum. "UN Halted Probe of Officers' Alleged Role in Sex Trafficking." *Washington Post*, 27 December 2001. http://www.washingtonpost.com/ac2/wp-dyn?pagename=article&contentId=A28267-2001Dec26&notFound=true (accessed 20 January 2007).

Manohar, Sujata. "Trafficking in Women and Girls." Paper prepared for United Nations Expert Group Meeting, Glen Cove, New York, 2002. http://www.un.org/womenwatch/daw/egm/trafficking2002/reports/WP-SujataManohar.PDF (accessed 24 January 2007).

Mauss, Marcel. *The Gift, the Form and Reason for Exchange in Archaic Societies*. New York: W. W. Norton, 1990.

McBride Stetson, Dorothy. "The Invisible Issue: Prostitution and Trafficking of Women and Girls in the United States." In *The Politics of Prostitution: Women's Movements, Democratic States and the Globalization of Sex Commerce*, edited by Joyce Outshoorn, 245–64. Cambridge: Cambridge University Press, 2004.

Mendelson, Sarah. *Barracks and Brothels: Peacekeepers and Human Trafficking in the Balkans*. Washington DC: Center for Strategic and International Studies, 2005.

Miria, Silvana, and Valdet Sala. "Women—Victims of Many Abuses." In *An Overview of the Written Contribution of the Women's Movement in Albania (1990–1998)*, edited by Women's Center. Tirana: Women's Center, 1999.

Mojzes, Paul. *Yugoslavian Inferno: Ethnoreligious Warfare in the Balkans*. New York: Continuum Publishing Company, 1994.

Murray, Jennifer. "Who Will Police the Peace-Builders? The Failure to Establish Accountability for the Participation of United Nations Civilian Police in the Trafficking of Women in Post-Conflict Bosnia and Herzegovina." *Columbia Human Rights Law Review* 34 (Spring 2003): 475–527.

Nadelmann, Ethan. "Global Prohibition Regimes: The Evolution of Norms in International Society." *International Organization* 44, no. 4 (Autumn 1990): 479–526.

Naim, Moises. *Illicit: How Smugglers, Traffickers, and Copycats Are Hijacking the Global Economy*. New York: Doubleday, 2005.

NDI Regional Initiative for Central and Eastern Europe. *Delivering Democracy: Organizing Resources to Create Secure Societies National Democratic Institute Program for Women Political Leaders from Central and Eastern Europe*. Seminar, Warsaw, 1–4 March 2002. http://www.ndi.org/ndi/library/1383_cee_womenleaders_030102.txt (accessed 20 January 2007).

NGO Voice. "Recommendations on the Framework Decision on Combating Trafficking in Human Beings." COM (2000) 854 final/2, part 4, 14 September 2001. http://www.ngovoice.org/activities/page/projects/traffickLetter/page_1_print.html (accessed 20 January 2007).

O'Neill Richard, Amy. "International Trafficking in Women to the U.S.: A Contemporary Manifestation of Slavery and Organized Crime." Washington DC: Center for the Study of Intelligence, 1999.

Orenstein, Mitchell. "The New Pension Reform as Global Policy." *Global Social Policy* 5, no. 2 (2005): 175–202.

Organisation Mondiale contre la Torture, et al. "State Violence in Greece: An Alternative Report to the UN Committee against Torture." Report presented at the thirty-third session of the Committee against Torture, Athens, 27 October 2004. http://www.omct.org/pdf/procedures/2004/joint/s_violence_greece_10_2004.pdf (accessed 27 January 2007).

Organization for Security and Cooperation in Europe (OSCE). "Taking a Stand: Effective Assistance and Protection to Victims of Trafficking." Conference sponsored by the OSCE Special Representative on Combating Trafficking in Human Beings and the Anti-Trafficking Assistance Unit under the Aegis of the Alliance against Trafficking in Persons, Vienna, 2005.

Organization for Security and Cooperation in Europe/Office for Democratic Institutions and Human Rights. "Ensuring Human Rights Protection in Countries of Destination: Breaking the Cycle of Trafficking." Conference report, Helsinki, 23–24 September 2004. http://www.osce.org/odihr/item_11_15919.html (accessed 20 January 2007).

Outshoorn, Joyce. "The Political Debates on Prostitution and Trafficking of Women." *Social Politics* 12, no. 1 (Spring 2005): 141–55.

Owen, Taylor. "Human Security—Conflict, Critique and Consensus." *Security Dialogue* 35, no. 3 (September 2004): 345–87.

Paris, Roland. "Human Security: Paradigm Shift or Hot Air." *International Security* 26, no. 2 (2001): 87–102.

Poda, Zamir. *Organized Crime.* Tirana: SHBLU, 1998.

Radovanovic, Mara, and Angelika Kartusch. *Report on the Combat of Trafficking in Women for the Purpose of Forced Prostitution in Bosnia and Herzegovina.* Vienna: Ludwig Boltzmann Institute of Human Rights, 2001.

Reitner, Rayna R. "Introduction." In *Toward an Anthropology of Women,* edited by Rayna R. Reiter, 11–19. New York: Monthly Review Press, 1975.

Renton, Daniel. "Child Trafficking in Albania." Tirana: Save the Children in Albania, March 2001. http://www.savethechildren.it/2003/download/pubblicazioni/traffickingAlbania/traffickingAlbania.pdf (accessed 23 April 2007).

Rubin, Gayle. "The Traffic in Women: Notes on the 'Political Economy' of Sex." In *Toward an Anthropology of Women,* edited by Rayna R. Reiter, 157–210. New York: Monthly Review Press, 1975.

Sandoulet, Elizabeth, Frederico Finan, Alain de Janvoy, and Renos Vakis. "Can Conditional Cash Transfer Programs Improve Social Risk Management? Lessons for Education and Child Labor Outcomes." Social Protection Discussion Paper No. 0420, World Bank, December 2004.

Savona, Ernesto U., and Federica Curtol. *The Contribution of Data Exchange Systems to the Fight against Organized Crime in the SEE Countries.* Trento, Italy: Transcrime, 2004. http://transcrime.cs.unitn.it/tc/418.php (accessed 20 January 2007).

Scully, Eileen. "Pre-Cold War Traffic in Sexual Labor and Its Foes: Some Contemporary Lessons." In *Global Human Smuggling: Comparative Perspectives,* edited by David Kyle and Rey Koslowski, 74–106. Baltimore: The Johns Hopkins University Press, 2001.

Siegel, Richard Lewis. "The Right to Work: Core Minimum Obligations." In *Core Obligations: Building a Framework for Economic, Social, and Cultural Rights,* edited by Audrey Chapman and Sage Russell, 21–52. Antwerp: Intersentia, 2002.

Skrobanek, Siriporn, Chuitima Janthakeero, and Nattaya Boonpakdi. *The Traffic in Women: Human Realities of the International Sex Trade.* London: Zed Books, 1997.

Stability Pact for South Eastern Europe (SPTE). "Statement on Commitments, Legislation of the Status of Trafficked Persons." Statement presented at the Third Regional Ministerial Forum, Tirana, 2002.

———. Task Force on Trafficking in Human Beings. "Guidelines for National Plans of Action to Combat Trafficking in Human Beings and National Programmes to Combat Trafficking in Human Beings (National Plans of Action) Background Paper." Vienna: Stability Pact for South Eastern Europe, 2001.

———. "National Programmes to Combat Trafficking in Human Beings (National Plans of Action) Background Paper." Vienna: SPTE, 2001.

Stoecker, Sally. "Human Trafficking: A New Challenge for Russia and the United States." In *Human Traffic and Transnational Crime: Eurasian and American Perspectives,* edited by Sally Stoecker and Louise Shelley, 13–28. Lanham: Rowman and Littlefield, 2005.

Stoecker, Sally, and Louise Shelley, eds. *Human Traffic and Transnational Crime: Eurasian and American Perspectives.* Lanham: Rowman and Littlefield, 2005.

Surtees, Rebecca. *Second Annual Report on Victims of Trafficking in South-Eastern Europe.* Regional Clearing Point, International Organization for Migration (IOM). Geneva: IOM, 2005. http://www.iom.int/jahia/webdav/site/myjahiasite/ shared/shared/mainsite/published_docs/studies_and_reports/second_ annual05.pdf (accessed 20 January 2007).

Suter, Nicole. "Human Trafficking and Statistics: The State of the Art." Working Paper No. 15, submitted by the International Organization for Migration to the Statistical Commission and UN Economic Commission for Europe. Conference of European Statisticians, 2 November 2004.

"Task Force Mirage Regional Meetings." SECI Press Release, 9 October 2006. http:// www.secicenter.org/p180/_9th_of_October_2006 (accessed 20 January 2007).

Trafficking Policy Research Project. "Trafficking Policy Research Project: Examining the Effects of U.S. Trafficking Laws and Policies." www.bayswan.org./traffick/ trafficking.html (accessed 20 January 2007).

Turnbull, Penelope. "The Fusion of Immigration and Crime in the European Union: Problems of Cooperation and the Fight against the Trafficking in Women." In Williams, *Illegal Immigration and Commercial Sex,* 189–213.

United Nations. *Convention on the Privileges and Immunities of the United Nations.* Adopted by the General Assembly of the United Nations on 13 February 1946. http://www.unog.ch/80256EDD006B8954/(httpAssets)/ C8297DB1DE8566F2C1256F2600348A73/$file/Convention%20P%20&%20I%20 (1946)%20-%20E.pdf (accessed 4 June 2007).

———. *Protocol to Prevent, Suppress and Punish Trafficking in Persons, Especially Women and Children, Supplementing the United Nations Convention against Transnational Organized Crime.* Geneva: United Nations, 2000.

———. "United Nations Millennium Development Goals." UN Web Services Section, Department of Public Information. http://www.un.org/millenniumgoals/ (accessed 20 January 2007).

United Nations Children's Fund (UNICEF). *Rights of Women and Children in Albania.* Tirana: UNICEF, 1998.

United Nations Department of Peacekeeping Operations, Best Practices Unit. *Human Trafficking Resource Package.* New York: United Nations, December 2004. http://www.peacekeepingbestpractices.unlb.org/pbpu/view/viewdocument .aspx?id=2&docid=601&menukey=_7_23.

United Nations Development Program (UNDP). *Albanian Human Development Report.* Tirana: UNDP, 1998.

———. *Human Development Report.* New York: Oxford University Press, 1994. http://hdr.undp.org/reports/global/1994/en/.

———. *Human Development Report.* New York: Oxford University Press, 1999. http://hdr.undp.org/reports/global/1999/en/.

United Nations Division for the Advancement of Women. "Convention on the Elimination of All Forms of Discrimination against Women, States Parties."

http://www.un.org/womenwatch/daw/cedaw/states.htm (accessed 29 January 2007).

United Nations General Assembly. "Crime Prevention and Criminal Justice: Report of the Ad Hoc Committee on the Elaboration of a Convention against Transnational Organized Crime on the Work of Its First to Eleventh Sessions, Addendum, Interpretive Notes for the Official Records (*travaux preparatoires*) of the Negotiation of the United Nations Convention against Transnational Organized Crime and the Protocols Thereto." UN Document A/55/383/Add.1, 3 November 2000. http://www.uncjin.org/Documents/Conventions/dcatoc/final_documents/383a1e.pdf (accessed 29 January 2007).

———. "Letter Dated 24 March 2005 from the Secretary General to the President of the General Assembly." UN Document A/59/710, 24 March 2005. http://daccessdds.un.org/doc/UNDOC/GEN/N05/247/90/PDF/N0524790.pdf?OpenElement (accessed 20 January 2007; link no longer active).

———. "Note by the Secretary General, Ensuring the Accountability of United Nations Staff and Experts on Mission with Respect to Criminal Acts Committed in Peacekeeping Operations." UN Document A/60/980, 16 August 2006. http://daccessdds.un.org/doc/UNDOC/GEN/N06/471/41/PDF/N0647141.pdf?OpenElement (accessed 20 January 2007; link no longer active).

United Nations Global Programme against Trafficking in Human Beings. *Toolkit to Combat Trafficking in Persons*. New York: United Nations Office on Drugs and Crime, October 2006. http://www.unodc.org/pdf/Trafficking_toolkit_Oct06.pdf (accessed 20 January 2007).

United Nations Mission in Bosnia and Herzegovina. "Bosnia and Herzegovina: UNMIBH Background." http://www.un.org/Depts/dpko/missions/unmibh/background.html (accessed 22 January 2007).

United Nations Mission in Bosnia and Herzegovina/International Police Task Force. "Operating Procedures for Trafficking Victims." Guidance No. 9-A (revised), para. 4.2, 22 September 2000.

United Nations Mission in Bosnia and Herzegovina/United Nations Office of the High Commissioner for Human Rights (UNMIBH/OHCHR). "Report on Joint Trafficking Project of UNMIBH/OHCHR." May 2000.

United Nations Office on Drugs and Crime. "Signatories—Protocol to Prevent, Suppress and Punish Trafficking in Persons, Especially Women and Children, Supplementing the United Nations Convention against Transnational Organized Crime." http://www.unodc.org/unodc/crime_cicp_signatures_trafficking.html#U (accessed 29 January 2007).

———. "Signatories—United Nations Convention against Transnational Organized Crime." http://www.unodc.org/unodc/en/crime_cicp_signatures_convention.html#U (29 January 2007).

———. *Trafficking in Persons: Global Patterns*. Vienna: UNODC, April 2006. http://www.unodc.org/unodc/en/trafficking_persons_report_2006-04.html (accessed 26 January 2007).

———. "UN Global Programme against Trafficking in Human Beings." www.unodc .org/unodc/en/trafficking_human_ beings.html (accessed 20 January 2007);

United Nations Treaty Collection. "Convention for the Suppression of the Traffic in Persons and the Exploitation of the Prostitution of Others." http://www.unhchr .ch/html/menu3/b/treaty11a.htm (accessed 29 January 2007).

United States. Division A—*Trafficking Victims Protection Act of 2000* (TVPA), *Victims of Trafficking and Violence Protection Act of 2000*. Public Law 106-386, 106th Cong., 28 October 2000. http://www.state.gov/documents/organization/10492.pdf.

U.S. Agency for International Development (USAID). *The CAAHT Baseline Survey: A Summary*. Tirana: USAID, February 2005. http://www.caaht.com/resources/ CAAHTBaselineSurveyReports/Baseline.pdf (accessed 27 January 2007).

———. Albania. "Albania and Greece Sign First Bilateral Agreement on Trafficking." 27 February 2006. http://www.usaidalbania.org/(z32chp551f3llz550iaurk55)/en/ Story.aspx?id=87 (accessed 5 June 2007).

U.S. Congress. *Trafficking Victims Protection Reauthorization Act of 2003*. HR 2620, 108th Cong., 1st sess., 7 January 2003. http://www.state.gov/g/tip/rls/61130 .htm (verified 20 January 2007).

———. *Trafficking Victims Protection Reauthorization Act of 2005*. HR 972, 109th Cong., 1st sess., 4 January 2005. http://www.state.gov/g/tip/rls/61106.htm (verified 20 January 2007).

U.S. Department of Defense, Office of the Inspector General. "Assessment of DOD Efforts to Combat Trafficking in Persons." 2003. http://www.hrw.org/reports/ 2002/bosnia/ig.pdf (accessed 27 January 2007).

U.S. Department of State. "Fact Sheet on the U.S. Government's International Anti-Trafficking in Persons Initiatives." 12 July 2001. http://www.state.gov/g/tip/rls/ fs/2001/4051.htm. (accessed 20 January 2007).

———. "Introduction." In *Trafficking in Persons Report*, 2006. http://www.state.gov/ g/tip/rls/tiprpt/2006/65983.htm. (accessed 20 January 2007).

———. "Pathbreaking Strategies in the Global Fight against Sex Trafficking." Conference recommendations, 23 February–26 February 2003. http://www.state .gov/g/tip/rls/rpt/20834.htm (verified 20 January 2007).

———. *Trafficking in Persons Report*, 2004. http://www.state.gov/g/tip/rls/tiprpt/ 2004/ (accessed 20 January 2007).

———. *Trafficking in Persons Report*, 2005. http://www.state.gov/g/tip/rls/tiprpt/ 2005/ (accessed 20 January 2007).

———. *Trafficking in Persons Report*, 2006. http://www.state.gov/g/tip/rls/tiprpt/ 2006/ (accessed 20 January 2007).

U.S. Department of State. Office to Monitor and Combat Trafficking in Persons. "The U.S. Government's International Anti-Trafficking Programs Fiscal Year 2004." 3 June 2005. http://www.state.gov/g/tip/rls/rpt/47383.htm#europe (accessed 20 January 2007).

U.S. Government Accountability Office (GAO). *Human Trafficking: Better Data, Strategy, and Reporting Needed to Enhance U.S. Antitrafficking Efforts Abroad*. GAO-06-

825, July 2006. http://www.gao.gov/new.items/d06825.pdf (accessed 22 January 2007).

Vachudova, Milada Anna. "Eastern Europe as Gatekeeper: The Immigration and Asylum Polities of an Enlarging EU." In Andreas and Snyder, *The Wall Around the West*, 153–73.

Van Meurs, Wim. "Stabilizing the Balkans—US and EU Policies." Workshop lecture, American Institute for Contemporary German Studies Workshop, Washington DC, 26 September 2000.

Vatra Center. *The Girls and the Trafficking*. Tirana: Vatra Center, 2005.

Williams, Phil. "Human Commodity Trafficking: An Overview." In Williams, *Illegal Immigration and Commercial Sex*, 1–10.

———, ed. *Illegal Immigration and Commercial Sex: The New Slave Trade*. London: Frank Cass, 1999.

———. "Trafficking in Women and Children: A Market Perspective." In Williams, *Illegal Immigration and Commercial Sex*, 145–70.

Wolfensohn, Galit. *Responding to Child Trafficking—An Introductory Handbook to Child Rights-Based Interventions Drawn from Save the Children's Experiences in Southeast Europe*. Tirana: Save the Children, May 2004. http://www.childcentre.info/projects/traffickin/dbaFile11301.pdf (accessed 27 January 2007).

Wong, Diana. "The Rumor of Trafficking: Border Controls, Illegal Migration, and the Sovereignty of the Nation-State." In *Illicit Flows and Criminal Things: States Borders, and the Other Side of Globalization*, edited by Willem van Schendel and Itty Abraham, 69–100. Bloomington: Indiana University Press, 2005.

Zonta International Foundation. "International Service Projects, 2002–2004, STAR Network of World Learning: The Bosnia-Herzegovina Anti-Trafficking Community Mobilization Project." http://www.zonta.org/site/DocServer?docID=4025 (accessed 20 January 2007).

Contributors

Andrea Bertone is director of www.HumanTrafficking.org at the Academy for Educational Development in Washington, DC. She has served as associate director of Project Hope International and as associate director of College Park Scholars International Studies, University of Maryland.

H. Richard Friman is professor of political science, Eliot Fitch Chair for International Studies, and director of the Institute for Transnational Justice at Marquette University. He is the author of five books and numerous book chapters and articles on transnational justice issues tied to the illicit global economy.

Vasilika Hysi is professor and former dean of the faculty of law at the University of Tirana, Albania, and has served as executive director of the Albanian Helsinki Committee and as coordinator of the UNDP Action Plan.

Gabriela Konevska is a member of the government of the Republic of Macedonia, vice president for European integration; former president of the nongovernmental organization Transparency Macedonia; former personal political advisor to Dr. Erhard Busek, SECI Coordinator and Special Coordinator for the Stability Pact South-Eastern Europe; former head of the Stability Pact Secretariat at the Initiative to Fight Organized Crime; and former director of the Regional Center for Combating Trans-Border Crime, SECI Initiative, Romania.

Nicole Lindstrom is assistant professor in the departments of international relations and European studies and political science at the Central European University and is a former research fellow at the New School for Social Research.

Lynellyn D. Long is independent consultant and former chief of mission for the International Organization for Migration, Bosnia-Herzegovina. She has also served as the Population Council's representative in Vietnam and as an adjunct faculty member at The Johns Hopkins University School of Public Health. She has written extensively on issues of human trafficking, refugees, and women.

Julie Mertus is associate professor and codirector of the Master of Arts in Ethics, Peace, and Global Affairs at American University. She has worked extensively in Central and Eastern Europe and is the author of eight books and multiple articles and chapters on issues of human rights.

Simon Reich is professor at the Graduate School of Public and International Affairs and director of the Ford Institute for Human Security at the University of Pittsburgh, and former director of research and analysis at the Royal Institute for International Affairs at Chatham House in England. He is the author of four books and numerous articles and book chapters.

Martina E. Vandenberg is an associate in the Washington DC offices of Jenner & Block and formerly served as Europe Researcher Women's Rights Division for Human Rights Watch. She also is the author of the 2002 Human Rights Watch Report *Hopes Betrayed: Trafficking in Women and Girls to Post-Conflict Bosnia and Herzegovina for Forced Prostitution.*

Index

Albania: child trafficking in, 102–5, 112, 113–14; Criminal Code, 17, 98, 106–7, 112; criminal groups and trafficking in, 96, 98, 101, 104, 107, 118, 149; democratic transition in, 17, 96, 99, 101, 102; as destination country for trafficking, 17, 96, 177n1; under dictatorship, 96, 99, 101; human trafficking in, 49, 96, 97–98, 99–101; institutional reform in, 97, 108–10; and international anti-trafficking measures, 17, 106, 110–12, 180n39; Kanun (the Code), 97, 177n2; legal reform in, 97, 106–8, 112, 117; National Strategy to Combat Trafficking in Human Beings, 102–3, 105, 109; organized crime and government response, 17, 100, 105, 107–9, 117; as origin country for trafficking, 96, 98; prostitution in, 97–98, 102, 107, 112, 177n5; public awareness of anti-trafficking measures in, 97, 105, 106, 113, 114, 116; regional agreements by, 110–11, 115; as source country for trafficking, 2, 17, 41, 101; Strategy for the Fight against Trafficking in Children and the Protection of Child Victims of Trafficking, 105, 109; as transit country for trafficking, 2, 17, 96, 98, 100, 101

Amnesty International, 2, 47

Annan, Kofi, 82, 140, 172n5

anti-trafficking policy: conceptual approaches to, 11–12, 15, 63; economic approach to, 67–68, 75, 78, 148; human rights approach to, 65–67, 75, 148; law enforcement approach to, 64–65, 68, 75, 77–78, 79; migration approach to, 63–64, 68, 75, 77, 78, 79; top-down approach to, 15, 16, 61–62, 69, 79; unintended consequences of, 16, 62, 75, 147, 150. *See also* counter-trafficking efforts; human trafficking

Arizona Market, 84, 173n12

Belgium, 102, 104, 115

Bosnia and Herzegovin: ad hoc approach to trafficking policy, 16, 86–88, 90, 94; anti-trafficking efforts, 17, 34–35, 47, 57, 59; contractors in, 83–84, 86, 90, 92, 173n11, 173n20; as destination country for trafficking, 2, 41, 91; European Union Force in (EUFOR), 95; human trafficking in, 17, 29, 30, 49, 50, 151; international peacekeepers in, 16, 82–83, 84–85, 94–95;

Unit (TPIU), 46–47; unemployment in, 167n28. *See also* Serbia; UN Mission in Kosovo (UNMIK)

UN Convention against Transnational Organized Crime: as anti-trafficking tool, 121, 129, 142; described, 7, 21, 62, 120, 142, 161n3; South Eastern European Cooperative Initiative (SECI) role in, 133; victim protection provisions of, 181n3, 182n7; in Western Balkan countries, 69, 110. *See also* UN Protocol to Prevent, Suppress and Punish Trafficking in Persons, Especially Women and Children (Trafficking Protocol)

UN Convention for the Suppression of the Traffic in Persons and the Exploitation of the Prostitution of Others, 6, 161n2

UNICEF, 71, 81

United Nations: Children's Fund, 130, 165n13; crimes by personnel of, 17, 82, 95, 150, 171n5; Department of Peacekeeping Operations (DPKO), 82, 90, 92; Development Fund for Women (UNIFEM), 41, 130; human security approach of, 139–40; and human trafficking, 2, 15, 48, 133, 147; in Kosovo, 41–42; Millennium Development Goals, 137, 140; peacekeepers, 2, 83, 84; unpopularity in United States, 141. *See also* Annan, Kofi; Convention on the Privileges and Immunities of the United Nations; International Police Task Force (IPTF); Klein, Jacques Paul; UN Administered Province of Kosovo; UN Convention against Transnational Organized Crime; UN Convention for the Suppression of the Traffic in Persons and the Exploitation of the Prostitution of Others; UN Mission in Bosnia and Herzegovina (UNMIBH); UN Mission in Kosovo (UNMIK); UN

Office of the High Commissioner for Human Rights (UNOHCHR); UN Office on Drugs and Crime; UN Protocol to Prevent, Suppress and Punish Trafficking in Persons, Especially Women and Children (Trafficking Protocol)

United States: anti-trafficking efforts, 10, 15, 111; Department of Defense, 83, 86; Department of State, 69, 89, 90, 91, 136, 165n13; Federal Bureau of Investigation, 131, 149; funding of counter-trafficking efforts, 7, 22, 23, 146, 186n44; and the global prohibition regime, 143, 152–53, 159n34; human security agenda, 12, 140–41; Joint Commission Observers (JCOs), 85, 172n8; Romanian military bases, 95; and the UN Protocol to Prevent, Suppress and Punish Trafficking in Persons, Especially Women and Children (Trafficking Protocol), 9, 143. *See also* South Eastern European Cooperative Initiative (SECI); *Trafficking in Persons (TIP) Report*; Trafficking Victims Protection Act (TVPA); U.S. Agency for International Development (USAID)

UN Mission in Bosnia and Herzegovina (UNMIBH), 87, 88, 89, 91, 92, 94, 172n9

UN Mission in Kosovo (UNMIK): and human trafficking, 47, 48, 53, 57, 176n56; Operation Mirage, 65; and prostitution, 41–42, 46

UN Office of the High Commissioner for Human Rights (UNOHCHR): anti-trafficking efforts of, 10, 71–72, 86, 87, 93, 130; human rights approach of, 66; reports on trafficking, 81, 165n13; and South Eastern European Cooperative Initiative (SECI) Regional Center for Combating Trans-Border Crime, 133. *See also* Rees, Madeleine